Book of Famous Scots
who changed the world

By Bill Fletcher

LANG SYNE PUBLISHERS LTD
GLASGOW

Baxters Book of Famous Scots was published by Lang Syne Publishers Ltd., Clydeway Centre, 45 Finnieston Street, Glasgow G3 8JU in 1995.

I.S.B.N. 1 85217 014X
©Bill Fletcher 1995

Pictures are from the author's own collection, the National Galleries of Scotland, Kirkcaldy Museum and Art Gallery, Glasgow Museums, University of Cambridge, Reuters Ltd, Woodman Sterne and Alasdair MacFarlane.

Origination by Newtext Composition Ltd., Glasgow
and (Colour) QBF Edinburgh.
Printed by Dave Barr Print.

CONTENTS

To Libbi
for everything

"Out of a mixture of this extraordinary array of people that we have looked at - Stone-Agers, Druids, Picts, Celts, Britons, Irish, Scots, Gaels, Danes, Norwegians, Angles, Saxons, Jutes, Romans, English, Normans, Flemish, French, Spaniards, Jews - emerged the Scottish nation. Out of a melting pot of pirates and prelates, bishops and buffoons, parsons and princes, murderers and maniacs, kings and conquerors, queens and questioners, plunderers and patriots, Calvinists and Catholics, episcopalians and evangelists, plotters and propagandists, torturers and traitors, in a maelstrom of rape, pillage, murder, treachery, witch-hunting, dictatorship, persecution, civil war, plagues, riots, and smuggling, emerged a golden age of philosophers and poets, scientists and sceptics, adventurers and admirals, capitalists and chemists, explorers and economists, inventors and innovators, doctors and druggists, biographers and botanists, novelists and narrators - Scots whose activities changed the world".*

Bill Fletcher.

Glossary of Scots Words

biggin	–	house
carking	–	anxious
cauld blast	–	cold wind
cutty sark	–	short shirt
dochter	–	daughter
ilka	–	every
lea	–	untilled land
plaidie	–	piece of cloth wrapped round shoulders
shaw	–	wood
twa	–	two

Introduction
by Gordon Baxter
O.B.E., D.L., LL.D., D.B.A.

Years ago, my father passed me a newspaper cutting – it quoted from a speech reported to have been made in Dundee in the 1920's by Winston S. Churchill, later to become the greatest Englishman of his generation – it said.

'Of all the small nations of this earth, perhaps only the ancient Greeks surpass the Scots in their contribution to mankind.'

I quote it often – particularly at Scottish gatherings during my overseas missions selling my firm's Scottish products!

This book will appeal to people of goodwill towards our small, proud nation and to Scots folk everywhere who are interested in their roots and in the labours of their forebears who did so much to fashion their contemporary world.

I am glad that Bill Fletcher has recorded the story of Scotland's sons in his racy, readable way and that my family firm has been able to sponsor its presentation to a wide audience at home and abroad.

Gordon Baxter
President
W. A. Baxter & Sons Ltd.

PREFACE

For more than a quarter of a century I have lectured, on behalf of the Continuing Education Department, on 'Great Scots' to American Elderhostel visitors who came to Strathclyde University. This was always a most enjoyable activity for there is nothing more rewarding than lecturing to Americans - particularly mature Americans. They have always been most generous in their appreciation and thought-provoking in their questions. I made many friends and I learned much from them as they kept in touch and generously sent information to me. I am grateful to that great army of people who came on holiday to learn. I trust that they took back to the U.S.A. some knowledge of the sons of our small country and the part that they played in creating and spreading civilization. This book is an extended form of these lectures. All of these Scots, by their activities, have changed how the people of the world think, act, and have their being. Even with these strict criteria how many more could have been included, but all books must be limited in size. Some readers may criticise my choice of Scots. It has not been possible to include all of them and I am well aware that the omission of John Napier (mathematician and inventor) James Hutton (geologist), John Anderson (educator), Joseph Black (chemist), James Bruce (explorer), Thomas Campbell (poet), David Douglas, Robert Fortune and George Forrest (plant-hunters), Thomas Graham (chemist), Lord Kelvin (physicist – born in Ireland), John Muir (conservationist), Patrick Manson and Ronald Ross (malaria), Robert Watson Watt (radar), and Alexander Bain (fax machine) and others will offend some. But a choice had to be made.

I trust that visitors to Scotland from many countries will find this book interesting and instructive and will take home with them a knowledge and love of this small country. Our image is not wholly of tartan and whisky – though these are important!

It is my sincere hope too that these essays will inspire young Scots and make them realize what a magnificent heritage they share. Perhaps they will be encouraged to add to that heritage for the benefit of future generations.

Through the years, as I have visited the many places where these 'Great Scots' were born or where they have operated, I have been treated with the utmost courtesy and I trust that those responsible will take this as my thanks.

My especial thanks are due to The Mitchell Library, Glasgow; Glasgow University Library and Strathclyde University Library. The staff of all these institutions have been most helpful at all times. Also to my friend Sir Samuel Curran FRS, himself a Great Scot, for his continued support in this project.

A special word for my wife Libbi who has constantly encouraged me and who has read and re-read the scripts, correcting errors and transposing many parts into better English. If, however, any errors of fact, or English, are still to be found they are my sole responsibility.

A final thanks to Ken Laird of Lang Syne Publishers Ltd. who has worked like a slave to ensure that this book sees the light of day, and to Dr. and Mrs. Gordon Baxter, of Baxters of Speyside Ltd. who by their financial support, have tried to ensure that its production reaches the same high quality as their food products.

Bill Fletcher

WHO ARE THE SCOTS?

"From scenes like these old Scotia's grandeur springs".

The Scots are a mongrel race. This is their strength, and the blending together of many nationalities in the past is one of the reasons for this small nation producing so many talented people; people whose activities altered the way that mankind lives and thinks.

The essay that follows is in no sense a Scottish history. Rather it is a look at the various peoples who contributed their genetic material to the Scottish pool. We shall also look at the evolution of the environment (physical, social, cultural, political and theological) which needed to be right before these genes could operate to produce so many outstanding people in this small country; people who changed the world.

In the beginning

With the ending of the Glacial period 10,000 years ago, the land that we now call Scotland emerged from a 1000 metres-deep ice-sheet under which it had lain frozen for thousands of years. Any plants, animals, or humans, that had existed before the great glaciation had been frozen out of existence or had retreated south to warmer climes. Now as the temperature rose they slowly started to make their way back. On the barren tundra the mosses and lichens paved the way for the birches, pines, oaks, and their associated plants, and animals - bears, wolves, elk, beaver, boar. The land was green again and the waters were alive. Once more humans could venture north.

The Hunters and Gatherers

And so, 8,500 years ago, they came, with their stone spear-heads attached to sticks, hunting animals, catching fish and living in skin tents and caves. These nomadic Mesolithic hunters and food-gatherers were our first post-glacial people though the land which we would later know as Scotland was still attached to Europe by the great North Plain.

The Farmers

Some 3000 years later, by which time Britain had separated from Europe as the waters from the melting glaciers created the English Channel, and the great North Plain was transformed into the vast North Sea, there came a second wave of humans with more advanced ideas. They were our first farmers and they brought with them cereals, sheep, cattle, and pigs. With their polished stone tools they built houses, cut down forests, cultivated the land, sowed seeds and gathered harvests.

The Bronze Age People
But taller people with rounded heads were on the horizon and they took over some 4000 years ago because their tools and weapons, made of bronze, were better. The great standing stones or megaliths, that are to be found in various parts of Scotland, indicate that this may well have been a Druid, priest-dominated society. The Bronze Age lasted until 600 B.C.

The Picts
Bronze was in turn superseded by a superior metal, iron, brought by one of the fierce warlike peoples of Europe, the Celtic-speaking Picts, the 'painted people', who first invaded south Britain and then spread northwards. They were good farmers, and they dominated the country from their hill forts.

The Romans held sway in England, then called Britannia, for more than 400 years from 55 B.C. to 356 A.D. They made three major forays into Scotland which was then known as Caledonia and although they reached as far north as Montrose, the resistance of the Picts was so fierce that they were eventually content to build walls, Hadrian's and Antonine's, to keep the 'barbarians' at bay.

The Britons
When the Romans left Britain in 356, the Angles, Saxons, and Jutes from what is now Denmark and north Germany, invaded in force occupying most of the country, and drove the Britons south into Cornwall, across the Channel into what is now Brittany and, pertinent to our story, east and north to form the Celtic-speaking Welsh Kingdom which stretched northwards from what is now Cardiff, deep into what is now West Scotland. Later, in the 7th century, the Anglo-Saxons drove a wedge through this kingdom thus eventually giving rise to Wales in the south and the new Kingdom of Strathclyde in the north-west, with its capital at Dumbarton.

The Angles
Meantime, around 550 A.D. the Angles moved from eastern England up the coast and penetrated south of the Forth where they established the Kingdom of Lothian. Their language was 'Inglis' and it formed the basis of the Lowland Scottish language that was later to spread through the country.

The Scots
For long the west coast had been ravaged by Irish marauders, the 'Scotti', meaning pirates in Latin, and in time this was corrupted to 'Scots'. These Gaelic speakers settled on the mainland around 575 and established the Kingdom of Dalriada in the area of the Firth of Clyde and Argyll.

Four joined in one
In time the four kingdoms were to be united. Under Kenneth MacAlpin, Dalriada and Pictland became 'Alba' in 843. One of his successors, Malcolm 11, defeated the Angles in battle in 1018 and incorporated Lothian into his kingdom. His grandson Duncan inherited the throne of Strathclyde and thus in 1034 became the first king of Scotland.

Viking raiders from Denmark and Norway who had long ravaged the Western Isles began to settle there in the 9th century and married local women. Their offspring, known as 'Gall-Gaels', later gave rise to the great clans ('clann' is the Gaelic for children) - the MacDonalds, the MacDougalls, and the Campbells and many others.

Duncan's son, Malcolm Canmore succeeded him in 1058 but the country that he ruled was a bleak place. More than half was barren mountains and of the remainder most was made up of bogs and forests of coniferous trees. The total human population was thought to be about 250,000 dwelling in turf/stone houses and living off the land.

The Normans
In 1066 William of Normandy with his knights invaded England and in the wake of the Conquest many old Anglo-Saxon families moved to Scotland. The scene was set for the many wars with Norman England. Then there was a change of policy. When David 1, who had spent 40 years at the Norman English court, succeeded to the Scottish throne he invited many Norman barons and knights to come with him, gave them estates and towns, and encouraged them to build castles. All brought followers

with them, setting up a feudal system very similar to that which they had established in England.

David also reorganized the Church along similar lines, dividing the country into 11 'sees' with a Bishop at the head of each. By the year 1200 abbeys had been built at Kelso, Dryborough and Melrose in the Borders, Newbattle and Holyrood in the east, and Paisley in the west.

At this time the establishment of burghs - small cohesive units where business could be developed both internally and externally - was also very important. It led to the emergence of the craftsman, the merchant, and the trading classes.

Thus technology, trading, learning, and patriotism, were formalised and encouraged in the Lowlands and by the late 14th century Scotland was a large wool and leather exporter to Europe. This trade, and its expansion over the centuries, entailed the coming of people from Europe to settle and add their genes to the Scottish pool.

From early times, Jews have come to Scotland to escape the pogroms and persecutions of Europe. They have continued to do so into the present century and they have added enormously to the business, cultural and scientific life to this country.

The Stewart dynasty

The first of the Stewart kings came with the accession, in 1371, of Robert Stewart, the son of the eldest daughter of Robert the Bruce, to initiate a dynasty that was to result in the Union of the Crowns in 1603. What Scotland needed was a long period of peace, stability, and learning. And there was hope. The University of St. Andrews was established in 1412 and thirty-nine years later the University of Glasgow was founded. These seats of scholarship became powerful forces in developing and spreading, clear learning in the land.

James III married Margaret of Denmark in 1496 and she brought Orkney and Shetland Islands, to be added to the Scottish crown, as her dowry.

James IV promoted a great influx of continental art and artists; architecture and music were encouraged and a school of Scottish literature was established. He passed an act in 1496 making it compulsory for the Scottish gentry and freeholders to send their eldest sons and heirs to school - the earliest example of compulsory elementary education in Europe. It was a golden age of learning and culture, but it was a delicate flower and it was blasted when James and 12,000 of the elite of Scotland, died at the hands of the English on Flodden Field in 1513. This was a blow from which Scotland took a long time to recover.

His son James V married Mary of Guise who after his death became Regent and their daughter, Mary, married the Dauphin of France. Both events led to a powerful French influence being exerted over Scotland, with Catholicism seeming to be firmly entrenched. But changes were on the way.

After Martin Luther in Germany proclaimed 'Protestantism' in 1517, a Frenchman, John Calvin, went further, establishing an academy in Geneva in 1559, which accepted the God of the Old Testament, complete rejection of any form of ceremonial, including music, and a belief in predestination - that salvation is for those chosen by God only. John Knox, a graduate priest of St. Andrews, was converted to Protestantism after visiting Calvin's school in Geneva. Returning to Scotland he found that the French were routed and expelled from Scotland by Elizabeth of England, so that he was now free to expound his beliefs. Calvinist Presbyterianism took firm root.

The dogma of thrift, education, and hard work, cornerstones of the Calvinist religion, was driven home in all Scottish families. It was the staple diet of the home for many generations to come and must have been yet another potent factor in the emergence of our 'Great Scots'.

Education

In the aftermath of the involuntary abdication of Mary, who had succeeded her father, her son James VI, following a series of Regents, became king at the age of 11 and proceeded to build a brilliant court of lawyers, artists, doctors, geographers and astronomers, around him. He also encouraged the development of printing presses.

The first Act issued by a government invoking the need for a school in every parish came from the Scottish parliament during James's reign in 1616 although there were many schools in Scotland before that. And Scotland now had five universities.

The Spanish come to Scotland

The Spanish Armada of 130 ships and a force of 30,000 men was at England's gate, but thanks to Sir Francis Drake and the weather, it was scattered. The Spanish Admiral decided that the remains of his fleet should head towards the friendlier waters of Scotland. But the weather wasn't friendly! Buffeted by rough seas the ships ran for home via the north of Scotland and en route, struck by a hurricane, a number of ships sank. Survivors made their way ashore to be made welcome by the natives. And so still more genes were added to the Scottish pool.

The Union of the Crowns

When Elizabeth died in 1603 James VI of Scotland succeeded to the throne of England as James 1. But on moving to London, James took little interest in Scotland other than to try to knock the warring clans into order and to Anglicise them. He set out to control the Highland clans, passing an Education Act of 1616 which declared Gaelic should be abolished. Chiefs were ordered to send their sons to Lowlands schools.

Translation of the Bible

Another of James's educational actions that had a very profound effect in anglicising the Scots was translating the Bible into English. It was published in 1611 and not only was it a major influence in spreading the gospel, but it also spread the use of the English language in Scotland.

But James's successors, Charles I, Charles II and James II, as they attempted to establish Episcopalianism in Scotland, became deeply involved in religious battles with the Covenanters. These were the 'killing times' and once more Scotland suffered.

When he took a Catholic wife and had a Catholic son and heir, James II was deposed as king of Britain and he fled to France. Thus the light of the Stewarts dimmed though their flame was to flicker a few times before finally dying at Culloden Moor in 1746.

The Darien Disaster

The Scots, flexing their trade muscles, attempted in 1698 to establish a colony at Darien in the isthmus where North and South America meet. It was a major disaster. Darien was in the heart of the tropical jungle and fever and hunger took a dreadful toll. The expedition was abandoned and only one of the original six ships made it back to Britain. Of the expeditionary force of more than 1,200, many the elite of the land, only 300 people survived.

The Union of Parliaments

The Darien disaster must have been a major factor in making some Scots realise that the only way to get overseas markets was to join the English. The Scottish Parliament voted to terminate itself on 25th March 1707, and power passed to the London parliament under the Act of Union. There was rioting throughout the country; many Scots who thought that the Union was a traitorous act said so in no uncertain manner - but in vain.

A flowering of talent

As the Scots lost their independence, with king and parliament in faraway London, with their country linked to a more populous and more powerful neighbour, one might have imagined that nationalism in Scotland would have subsided and that the people would have sunk into lethargy. Quite the opposite! As they moved towards the middle of the 18th century, the Scots flaunted their identity and for the next 200 years there was a flowering of talent the like of which had not been seen before in the country.

Education

Many of these Scots who were to lead the world in so many spheres came from poor circumstances, some were university trained, many were not, but they were all well-versed in the three R's - reading, writing, and arithmetic. Unfortunately efforts were entirely concentrated on the education of male children. That's a sadness and it means that there are no women in our lists. But it does not mean that the women were not interested in education; quite the contrary. Denied it themselves they were even more determined that their sons and brothers should have every opportunity and we will find many examples in the essays that follow. I do not think that the women would have been jealous of the success of their menfolk. Indeed they revelled in it. This must have been a potent factor in this small nation producing so many distinguished men. Our 'Great Scots' believed in education in all its forms and they grabbed it voraciously when and where they could; and they all had an infinite capacity for hard work.

Opportunity

In addition to learning and ability there must be the opportunity to develop and apply. And opportunity came with what many Scots feared most - the Act of Union with England in 1707. Before the Union, Scotland was an exhausted country torn apart by hundreds of years of internal and external strife. It has been described as being "in dire poverty - a famishing people, a stagnant trade, rude manufactures, and profitless industry." As a result of the Union the colonies were now open to the Scots. Traders and merchants took full advantage and the standard of living in Scotland rose. The river Clyde, widened in 1773, became an international waterway. Glasgow became heavily involved in the tobacco trade with Virginia and the commercial spin-off was enormous. Edinburgh began to emerge as an important financial centre. Paisley's woollen mills and Dundee's jute mills became centres of world trade. Not only the colonies were opened up for trade; so too was England itself, and the road south became a very busy highway indeed.

It was within this fertile environment that the Scottish energies and abilities, which had always threatened to shine through in the architecture of the Druids, the ornament fashioning of the Celts, the ballad making of the Angles, the romanticism of the Gaels, the adventurous spirit of the Vikings and the technology of the Normans, now flowered. There was no lack of wars, but now they were left in the main to the professionals. Gifted people at all levels of society were free to develop their talents. Poverty was no hindrance; indeed it was often a spur, as noted in the influx of Irish following in the tragedy of the potato famine in the 1840's. Ultimately it was a combination of environment and genes, and of the latter some Scots were lucky enough to get the right mixture.

The middle of last century saw great numbers of Irish coming to Scotland as a result of the potato famine. Many of their descendants have enriched our lives.

This century has seen an influx of Italians, Poles, Indians, Pakistanis, Africans, West Indians, Greeks, Chinese, and others, into Scotland. In time, these new Scots will have an enormously beneficial impact as their genes are added to the pool. This is the lesson of history.

The full beneficial impact of equal opportunities for women has yet to be felt. Only 50% of our population has been tapped in the past. There will be a very different pattern of input by the sexes in any book of 'Great Scots' written 100 years from now.

DAVID HUME (1711-1776)

Philosopher

"We must learn to live with probabilities rather than certainties"

Perhaps it is not surprising that David Hume, destined to become one of the world's greatest philosophers, and perhaps the greatest to write in the English language, having surveyed the history of Scotland, and Europe, declared himself an atheist. The surprise was that his study hadn't also turned him away from monarchy. The story of the Church and the Crown in Scotland, and elsewhere, was certainly a sorry tale of bloodshed and bigotry. But his atheism was based on more than history.

It is very doubtful if he would have got away with his views a century before. He would have gone to the stake. Hume's proclaimed atheism was a signal, not only that the power of the Church, Catholic and Protestant, was waning, but also that its views were moderating and becoming less extreme, though it still had a very long way to go. There was a climate in which views, however anti-establishment, could be freely expressed without fear of death, though they could still gravely affect one's livelihood, future, and place in the community.

Early life

David Hume was born in Edinburgh in 1711, son of a fairly well-to-do lawyer and country gentleman, who died aged 33, leaving a widow of 30, with three young children of whom David, aged two, was the youngest. Mrs Hume moved with the children to the family estate of 'Ninewells' near Berwick, on the Scottish borders. There David fished, shot, rode, and read, and was brought up a Calvinist Presbyterian Whig, a strong supporter of the Union of 1707, and of the accession of the House of Hanover. He did not attend school in Berwick, but he had a succession of tutors.

At the age of 11, in 1722, with his elder brother John, David became a student at Edinburgh University, living in the family house in the town with his mother. He spent three years on 'an ordinary Course of Education' which included classes in Greek, Logic, Metaphysics and Natural Philosophy. The Professors were paid £100 a year, the money being raised by putting two pennies Scots on each pint of ale brewed and sold within the City!

It was assumed that Hume would follow in his father's footsteps, and for three years he did study Law; but he never found it to his taste though it did influence his future thinking. He turned instead to the private study of Philosophy where his great classical hero was Cicero, and his great modern hero was Newton. He was studying French too and soon mastered the language. It is thought that it was at this time that Hume, as a result of his reading, rather reluctantly also lost his religious beliefs. It is said that he 'reasoned himself out of religion'. He was determined to be a scholar and a philosopher.

He was working hard – too hard – and his health, both physical and mental, broke down. During the next four years (1729 – 1734) he was ill, but he took up a more active life; he was also reading voraciously.

Bristol

In time however he did have to earn a living and at the age of 23, he was was on his way, with a letter of Introduction, to take a post as a clerk in the thriving port of Bristol. But his health was not the only thing that made him leave home; scandal was brewing at Ninewells. A serving girl, Agnes Galbraith, confessed to the minister, the Rev. George Hume, not only that she was pregnant, but that his nephew, David Hume was responsible. She was rebuked by the Kirk Session for her 'Sin and Scandal' and ordered to appear in sackcloth before the congregation of the Kirk on three successive Sundays. The Session did not believe that Hume was the father; anyhow he was in Bristol and nothing more was heard of the case.

His job there didn't last long. He got the sack for unwisely attempting to correct his boss's grammar! By mid-summer he was in France.

A productive period

Hume moved to France with lots of letters of Introduction, for a short stay in Paris which he enjoyed very much, but found expensive; on to a year in Rheims; then to La Fleche on the Loire, where during his three-year stay he completed his first book, 'A Treatise on Human Nature' in 1737.

He returned to London that same year and sought a publisher, but he was concerned lest his book should land him in trouble with the authorities, and with this in mind he cut out the section on his criticism of miracles. He was convinced that his book would have a momentous impact on the public, but it was to be two years before he found a publisher and when it did appear, anonymously, in 1739, it was a bit of a flop. To help things along, and to make his thoughts more widely known, Hume published an anonymous 'Abstract' a year later, giving a summary of the views expressed in his book. When the reviews started to come in they were pretty damning. New ideas are seldom, welcomed by the establishment. And his ideas were revolutionary.

This was the 'Age of Reason', but Hume was proposing that our knowledge was not gained by reason at all but by experience. It is experience that teaches us that when 'cause' happens, then we can expect 'effect'. In his brilliant analysis of Hume's thoughts , Peter Jones (see further reading) explains:

"Here is a billiard ball lying on the table and another ball moving towards it with rapidity. They strike and the ball which was formerly at rest now acquires a motion. But we only know that the second ball will move through experience of the event. What would Adam, innocent but alert, have been entitled to infer as he watched the moving ball approach the first motionless ball? Nothing. He could have guessed with equal propriety that the balls became fish on contact, that the two balls become one, or that they disappear, or indeed anything at all. Only when he has witnessed several collisions will he make the proper inference – only experience established matters of fact".

We conduct our lives on the basis of probabilities. We are determined by custom alone to suppose that the future will be comparable to the past.

This was a very productive period for Hume and in 1741/42 he published 'Essays, Moral, Political, and Literary' in two volumes. He had learned his lesson. This experiment in essay writing, couched in the style of Addison, was very successful in dealing with a range of subjects – 'Of Love and Marriage', 'Of Impudence and Modesty', 'Of Moral Prejudices' – some 27 essays in all.

The Edinburgh Chair

On the basis of his writings, which revealed an extraordinarily acute mind, he was proposed for the Chair of Moral Philosophy in Edinburgh University. The Principal (who it was thought had an eye on the Chair himself) took exception to Hume's critical views of religion and the Church which he had expressed in his books and papers, and opposed his appointment to the extent of making his allegation of the applicant's irreligious attitude widely known. Hume felt that he must defend himself and did so in an anonymous pamphlet 'A Letter from a Gentleman to his Friend in Edinburgh'. To no avail; he did not get the professorship. The members of the Edinburgh Town Council may not have read his ' Treatise on Human Nature' in which among other things there was an attack on religion, but they were made aware of it.   They appointed a 'safer' candidate.

What Hume did get was a tutorship to the Marquess of Annandale, at St. Albans, but since the Marquess was insane, the job did not last long, and was remarkably unrewarding.

Hume was now 35 and keen to travel and widen his experience and knowledge.

With the Army in France

He jumped at the chànce to be Judge Advocate to a military expedition, led by a distant relative, General James St. Clair, that was being sent to Canada to oppose the French. In the event the expedition didn't go to Canada because the weather was too bad for sailing; instead new orders were given to the General – "Land anywhere you like in France". The orders were vague, and so was the General. He had no maps and he proceeded to wander with his lost troops, around the French countryside. From the beginning to end the sortie was like something from a Gilbert and Sullivan opera. Happening, more by luck than design, upon the town of L'Orient, the General laid siege to it, but such was the ineptitude that cannon-balls were bouncing off the walls of the town and inflicting casualties on the British force. Nevertheless the inhabitants were scared stiff and decided to surrender. But their 'intelligence' wasn't all that good; they were too late! The General's troops had withdrawn long before, and were on their way back to England. Whether any medals were struck for the little foray we do not know, but Hume, who had a wonderful sense of humour, and who recorded the whole affair, must have been highly amused.

Despite his experiences in France, Hume accepted an invitation from the General to accompany him on a secret mission to Vienna and Turin in 1748 to stir up more activity on the part of Britain's allies in the War of the Austrian Succession. Travelling in Holland, Germany, Austria, the Alps, and northern Italy was much to his taste.

Back to Scotland

On his return to Ninewells in Scotland, he found that his good friend,

Archibald Stewart, the Provost of Edinburgh, was being indicted for his behaviour and lack of leadership, during the occupation of the city by the Jacobite troops in 1745. Hume immediately wrote a pamphlet in his defence, 'A True Account of the Behaviour and Conduct of Archibald Stewart, Esq: late Lord Provost of Edinburgh, in a Letter to a Friend' Stewart had earlier been acquitted; but the gesture was appreciated.

In 1748 he also re-wrote Volume 1 An Enquiry concerning Human Understanding followed in 1754 by Volume 3 An Enquiry concerning the Principles of Morals of his 'Treatise on Human Nature'. Between times in 1752, he published his 'Political Discourses' consisting of a series of essays on political and economic issues. For the first time he used his own name and acknowledged that he was the author of his previous books. In 1749 he had published his 'Philosophical Essays' which included his inflammatory essay 'Of Miracles'. He was taking notes for his proposed 'History of England'; and he was exercising his very considerable wit and humour to attack religion.

When his brother married and brought his wife to Ninewells, the now very obese, witty, philosopher, aged 40, took up residence with his unmarried sister in Edinburgh.

The Edinburgh of 1751, into which he moved was intellectually stimulating but environmentally depressing. "And in a Morning, about seven o'clock, before the Excrements are swept away fron the Doors, it stinks intolerably, for which, I believe, it exceeds all parts of the World. For after 10 o'clock in the evening, it is Fortune favours you if a Chamberpot, with Excrements etc. is not thrown on your Head, if you are walking in the Streets; it is then not a little Diversion to a Stranger, to hear all Passers-by, cry out with a loud Voice, sufficient to reach the Tops of the Houses (which are generally six or seven Stories high, in the Front of the High-Street), 'Hoad yare Hoand' i.e. hold your hand, and means do not throw till I am past". (Mossner -see further reading).

Although there was an unwritten agreement that the warning 'Gardez-loo' (look out for the water) should be issued before decanting, it was not always observed and even if it was, those passers-by who were not nimble of foot, or who were hard of hearing, were liable to have the deluge descend upon them. Little wonder that as he approached Edinburgh, the renowned Dr. Johnson remarked to Boswell "Sir, this City has a strange effluvium". And yet Edinburgh, and Scotland, spearheaded by Hume, was on the verge of the 'Great Enlightenment'.

Despite his experience with Edinburgh University, Hume applied for the

Chair of Logic in Glasgow University in 1752, but again he was unsuccessful. His questioning the existence of God was still dogging him. Presumably the Universities, being essentially theological insitutions, did not like logic when it led them into uncomfortable paths like questioning the existence of God.

Perhaps things turned out for the best. Within a few days he was appointed Keeper of the Advocates Library in Edinburgh, and with this wonderful 30,000 collection of books at his disposal, he was able to prepare his monumental six-volume 'History of England'. Such a source was necessary, for even in London there were no public libraries until the opening of the British Museum in 1759.

Soon after being appointed, however, he was under great pressure to resign his post for having purchased three French classics which the Curators considered to be pornographic – a charge that future historians were to dismiss as ludicrous. He forestalled his opponents by making a Bond of Annuity so that his salary was paid over to the blind poet, Thomas Blacklock. Thus Hume retained the right to his post and the use of the Library without pay. But the situation did not last long. Within a year he resigned. He had held the post for five years.

In 1752 Hume published his 'Political Discourses' consisting of a series of essays, seven of which were in the field of economics, though that term had not yet been coined. He was now being widely acclaimed for his writings, and 'the Atheist' was the darling of Edinburgh dinner-parties. He became Secretary of the Philosophical Society and had many friends including Adam Smith who visited him often from Glasgow, and whose thinking was much influenced by Hume, Allan Ramsay, the artist who painted two portraits of Hume, and many liberal-minded clergymen.

But he had powerful enemies too, particularly among the clergy who were much incensed by his questioning of the moral qualities of the supposed Deity. Hume decided to "leave the public to judge between my adversaries and me". Not so the Assembly of the Church of Scotland before whom was placed a motion that David Hume and his cousin, the Rev. John Hume – who had dared to write a play 'Douglas' for public performance – should both be excommunicated. Fortunately for David and John, though excommunication in practice would have meant little, the moderates won the day.

The Toast of Paris

Hume had a great love for, and attachment to, France where in turn his work was much admired. Not surprisingly then, in 1763, with the war over, he accepted an invitation from the British Ambassador in Paris, Lord Hertford, to become Secretary, and later Charge d'Affairs, to the Embassy. This was an appointment that found much favour with the French. The aristocracy of both sexes, the statesmen, the philosophers, the writers, the historians, lionised him and the salons of Paris were open to this obese ungainly Scot whom they named 'le bon David'. He charmed them all, particularly the ladies.

Returning to London after his three-year spell of duty in France, he was appointed an Under Secretary of State being, among other duties, responsible for Scottish affairs, including, to Hume's amusement, the Scottish Church!

In 1769 he returned to Edinburgh to meet up again with old friends, male and female. He enjoyed the company of lively and vivacious women, to whom he was apparently very attractive; considered belated marriage but decided against it. When Benjamin Franklin, an old friend, visited Edinburgh, Hume entertained him in his elegant home of which he was justly proud; no doubt they discussed American Independence which Hume supported strongly. It is said that both James Madison and Alexander Hamilton studied, and were influenced by, Hume's writings before helping to draw up the American Constitution.

David Hume died in Edinburgh on 25th August, 1776 of intestinal cancer, saddened that he "had not yet finished the great work of delivering his countrymen from the Christian superstition". He was buried in a tomb designed by his friend Robert Adam, in Old Calton Burying Ground, Edinburgh.

His attitude, and philosophy, may be gauged from a remarkable letter that he sent dated 20th August 1776. to an old friend and admirer, the Countess de Bouffleur, mistress to the Prince de Conti:

> *"Tho I am certainly within a few weeks, dear Madam,*
> *and perhaps within a few days, of my own death,*
> *I could not forbear being struck with the death*
> *of the Prince of Conti - so great a loss in*
> *every particular. My reflection carried me*
> *immediately to your situation in this melancholy*
> *incident. What a difference to you in your whole*
> *plan of life! Pray write me some particulars;*
> *but in such terms that you need not care, in case*

of decease, into whose hands your letter may fall.

*My distemper is a diarrhoea, or disorder in my
bowels, which has been gradually undermining me
these last two years; but, within these six months,
has been visibly hastening me to my end. I see
death approach gradually, without any anxiety or
regret. I salute you, with great affection and
regard, for the last time.*
David Hume"

REFERENCES AND FURTHER READING

'David Hume'. J.Y.T. Greig. Cape, 1931.
'David Hume'. A.H. Basson. Harmsworth, 1958.
'The Life of David Hume'. E.C. Mossner. Clarendon Press, Oxford, 2nd. edition, 1980.
'David Hume'. Peter Jones in 'A Hotbed of Genius' (The Scottish Enlightenment, 1730 -
1790), editors David Daiches, Peter Jones, and Jean Jones, Edinburgh University Press,
1986.

ADAM SMITH (1723 - 1790)

Economist

"No, we will stand till you are first seated, for we are all your scholars".
(William Pitt, Prime Minister, 1787)

In the first week of July 1990 the city of Edinburgh was awash with exhibitions and conferences attracting a world array of statesmen who attended and participated in innumerable seminars and lectures on economics. Two weeks later the Royal Bank of Scotland brought 200 delegates to be addressed by 11 Nobel Laureates in economics. The Royal Scottish Museum mounted a major exhibition. The reason for all this activity? It was to mark the 200th anniversary of the death of the man who, according to the 19th century historian H.T. Buckle, "had written probably the most important book that has ever been written". Not everyone would agree with these sentiments, and there would be lively supporters for the Bible, the Koran, and 'The Origin of Species', but it is certain that "An Inquiry into the Nature and Causes of the Wealth of Nations" (commonly abbreviated to "The Wealth of Nations") by Adam Smith has had a profound influence on the lives of practically all people on Earth, from the frantic dealers on Wall Street, New York, to the dignified Masai warriors of Kenya.

Kirkcaldy

Adam Smith was born, on 5th June 1723, in Kirkcaldy, some six months after his father's death. Young Adam was weakly, and to make matters worse he was stolen by a band of gypsies when just three years old. Although he was retrieved after a few hours by his uncle, this must have been a traumatic experience for the boy and his mother. It is small wonder, in view of the circumstances of his birth, his frailty, and his kidnapping, that the bond between mother and child was strong; and it was to grow ever stronger. Indeed until her death, in her 90th year, mother and son were seldom apart, and lived much of their lives together. No doubt that is why he did not marry.

Glasgow University

Young Adam attended the local school where, as a bright child, he was given a good grounding in Latin, Greek, and mathematics, before, at the age of fourteen, setting off for Glasgow University. By modern-day standards he was young to be embarking on a University course; but not by the standards of those days. Indeed he was a few years older than most of his fellow students. It may be that his mother held on to him as long as possible. It seems rather surprising that he went to Glasgow rather than Edinburgh University which was much more convenient. Whatever the reason it was certainly Glasgow's gain; and perhaps Smith's too.

He spent three years at Glasgow studying particularly Greek, mathematics, Natural Philosophy, and the subject which appealed to him most of all - Moral Philosophy. The Professor was Francis Hutcheson whose teaching on moral and economic subjects entranced the young boy and had a profound influence on him, as it had also had on David Hume who was later to become Smith's lifelong and closest friend.

Oxford years

He must have been very bright in that he won a Snell Exhibition for advanced study at Balliol College, Oxford. Under its original terms such students would then be required to take orders in the Episcopal Church but, fortunately for Smith, as he did not find the ecclesiastical profession to his taste, this requirement had been rescinded after the Union. Studying at Oxford seemed like a wonderful opportunity, but in the event, compared with Glasgow, Smith was bitterly disappointed in the level of teaching and tuition. In addition he made few friends as the 'Scotch' were not well liked in England at this time.

There was however one major compensation. The library facilities were excellent and Smith read avidly including a wide range of Greek, Latin, and French literature. He was also reading philosophy, though he was severely rebuked for including Hume's 'Treatise on Human Nature' in his list. But it must have been a very lonely life for the young man and after six years of 'exile' he returned home in 1746.

A successful return to Scotland

Back in Kirkcaldy he was among friends, and one of them, Lord Kames the famous Scottish judge, persuaded him to give two series of lectures on rhetoric, literature, and economics to students of Law and Theology in Edinburgh, during which he made it clear that he was strongly opposed to any form of Government interference in business or industrial affairs. The lectures were very successful and well-received and he repeated them in a further two successive winter sessions.

Partly as a result of these lectures, but also because of his scholarship and growing reputation, he was appointed, towards the end of 1750, to the Chair of Logic at his old alma mater, the University of Glasgow. He had no sooner settled in, and had not yet given any lectures, when the chair of Moral Philosophy fell vacant. This was much more to Smith's taste and he transferred ere a year was out.

He was keen that David Hume, who had become a close friend and whose work he admired enormously, should fill the Chair of Logic but the powers that be would have none of it. Hume was an atheist!

Smith now had a house in the University into which he moved his mother and his cousin Jane Douglas. He had a stipend plus student fees and since there were some 80-90 attending his Moral Philosophy classes, out of a total student population of 300 in the University, he was reasonably comfortable. Not so the students who lived in cramped uncomfortable quarters and had to be in the classroom, ready to receive instruction at 7.30 a.m. on freezing cold winter mornings! And this was followed by an 'examination' at 11a.m.

Since Smith's method of determining whether he was gaining the attention of the class was to fasten his gaze on a number of students, he must have encountered many a rheumy, if not closed, eye. Nevertheless his fame as a lecturer grew and students were flocking in from all parts of the civilized world.

His subject matter covered natural theology, ethics, and what was termed jurisprudence which included the principles of law and government. In addition to his lecturing he was writing and out of his ethics lectures grew his first book 'The Theory of Moral Sentiments' which was published in 1759. This marked him out as a front-ranking Moral Philosopher but it was to be overshadowed by another book that was beginning to take shape in his mind.

In sharp contast to his Oxford years he had a wide circle of friends including the famous chemist James Black, David Hume the philosopher and the geologist James Hutton. Smith was no 'ivory tower' professor. He had many friends among the Glasgow merchants and met them socially to dicuss, among other topics, economics and free trade. He was a member of a number of clubs and societies including the 'Anderston Club', to which he introduced James Watt, and the Literary Society of Glasgow. In Edinburgh, through the good offices of David Hume, he was elected a member of the Philosophical Society, which later became the Royal Society of Edinburgh. He was an original member of the 'Poker Club' of which the avowed aim was to stir up action for a Scottish militia. He reviewed Johnson's Dictionary, not wholly in a complimentary fashion, in the first edition of the 'Edinburgh Review', a journal that had but a short life because of the suspicion that Hume was associated with it, and later met the great man himself in London during which it is said they had "many altercations". Johnson thought Smith "a dull dog". For his part Smith declared that Johnson's roughness "was due to a certain degree of insanity".

Smith took an active part in business, conducting a number of legal affairs; he was 'quaestor' or treasurer of the University (1758 - 1764), Dean of Faculties (1760 - 1763) and was appointed Vice-Rector in 1762. He helped to set up James Watt as a mathematical instrument maker and supported and provided rooms for Robert Foulis in setting up his 'Academy for Painting, Engraving. Moulding, Modelling, and Drawing' – both in the University.

His post as Vice-Rector was no sinecure since he had to preside over all University affairs – professors are not the easiest people in the world to deal with - but he later proclaimed his thirteen years at Glasgow "by far the happiest and most honourable period of my life".

France

But they were coming to an end. In 1763 the stepfather of the 3rd Duke of Buccleuch offered Smith the post of travelling tutor to the young Duke who was just about to leave Eton. Wisely, Smith accepted, though he left Glasgow with very real regrets. His salary was to be £500 per year and a pension for life of £300. It is a measure of the quality of the man that at the last meeting with his students he insisted that he should refund to each one the remainder of the fees paid to him as the academic session was not yet complete. This was strongly resisted by the students who insisted that the instruction that they had received far outweighed any monetary considerations. After much to-ing and fro-ing Smith called them up one by one and stuffed the money in their pockets.

And so Smith and the young Duke left London for France in February 1764, meeting Hume and Voltaire, the novelist, poet and atheist whom Smith admired almost above all others. In the salons of Paris he discoursed learnedly with philosophers, one of whom was later to translate his 'Wealth of Nations', and with the physiocrats (economists). Women fell in love with him though their love was not reciprocated.

But this idyllic edifice crashed about his ears when the Duke's younger brother, Hew Campbell Scott, who had joined their entourage, died suddenly. Some authorities said it was an illness, others that he had been murdered in the streets of Paris. Smith was devastated and with the Duke returned to Britain with the remains of the young boy in 1766. They had been two and a half years abroad.

The Wealth of Nations

Smith returned to live with his mother and Jane Douglas in Kirkcaldy and immersed himself in the writing of the 'Wealth of Nations'. But his health was deteriorating and, despite being elected a Fellow of the Royal Society of London, he was cutting himself off from all social and intellectual contact. On top of that, progress with the book was slow. It was his close friend Hume who shook him out of his lethargy, visiting him often and persuading him to make visits to London. There he met Benjamin Franklin, the United States scientist, author and statesman and discussed aspects of his proposed book with him.

At last, on 9th March 1776, " An Inquiry into the Nature and Causes of the Wealth of Nations" was published. It was an enormous success, the first edition being sold out in six months, and it was recognised by politicians, economists, and indeed by some members of the general public, as being a fundamental book. Not only did it establish political economy as a science in its own right, but it was, and still is, widely quoted and extensively used by governments down to the present day. Pitt studied it carefully and used it when introducing his budget in 1792. Mrs. Thatcher claimed Smith as an ally when introducing her new agenda for the Tory party. Would this have offended Smith? There are many who would claim that his disciples (e.g. Milton Friedman and the Chicago School) apply his pronouncements on the free market and non-government interference more rigorously than he himself would; that his ideas have been hijacked by the right. Be that as it may, there is no doubt that his book has had an extraordinary impact on political thinking and it seems to be just as relevant today as it was 220 years ago. In it he dealt with a variety of subjects relating to wealth - market forces, free trade, taxation, division of labour, the role of government - and he particularly emphasised that 'wealth' did not mean money; the real wealth of a nation consists of commodities, things that can be used and enjoyed.

For a technical treatise it is a remarkably easy book to read; it is worthy of study by the layman; Smith was a very good writer.

Following publication of the book, he was much in demand for consultation by statesmen and economists. There was one great sadness. His close friend Hume was in failing health and near to death. He asked Smith to guarantee publication of his 'Dialogues concerning Natural Religion'. Smith demurred, fearing that the views expressed in it would harm his own reputation, and other arrangements were made. But when Hume died later in the year he edited his biography and wrote in the strongest terms of his virtues and of his courage in the face of death. For this he was scurrilously attacked by George Horne (afterwards Bishop of Norwich).

In December 1777, Smith was appointed Commissioner of Customs (possibly due to the influence of the Duke of Buccleuch who remained a lifelong friend) with a stipend of £600 a year. He carried out his duties well despite being extraordinarily absent-minded. Characteristically, when he got the post Smith immediately offered to forego the pension that he held from the Duke, but the Duke would have none of it. Thus Smith, with £900 a year, was quite a wealthy man. He bought Panmure House in the Canongate, Edinburgh, and moved there with his mother and Jane Douglas; he also brought along David, the son of another cousin. Life was good; he had an extensive library which he enjoyed, and he dined weekly at the 'Oyster Club' with his friends Joseph Black and James Hutton. Edmund Burke, the statesman, philosopher, and writer, visited him and he accompanied Burke through to Glasgow for the latter's Honorary Degree. Smith himself was elected Lord Rector of Glasgow University by the students in 1778. It was an honour that he treasured, but his health was not quite up to his giving the traditional oration. He visited London earlier in the year and dined with the Prime Minister, William Pitt, at the home of Henry Dundas M.P. It was on this occasion that Pitt refused to sit down at table until Smith was seated, making the remark "No, we will stand till you are first seated, for we are all your scholars".

Seven years later Smith's beloved mother died in her 90th year. He was devastated; and his own health was declining despite a visit to London to consult John Hunter the famous Scottish surgeon. Time was running out for him so he sent for Hutton and Black and asked them to burn 16 volumes of his manuscripts. This they did much to his relief.

Adam Smith died on 17th. July 1790 and was buried in the Canongate churchyard, Edinburgh. His grave is marked by a simple monument.

REFERENCES AND FURTHER READING

'The Wealth of Nations'. Adam Smith. 1776. Innumerable editions (including Everyman's Library), in many languages.
'Life of Adam Smith'. John Rae. London 1895. Reprinted with additional material by Jacob Viner, N.Y. 1965.
'The House of Adam Smith'. E. Ginsberg, 1930.
'Adam Smith as Student and Professor'. W.R.Scott, 1937.
'Adam Smith: the Man and his Works'. E.G.West. New York, 1969.
'Adam Smith'. R.H. Campbell and A.S. Skinner. London ,1982.
'Adam Smith'. D.D.Raphael. Past Masters Series. Oxford University Press, 1985.
'Adam Smith' D.D.Raphael. In 'A Hotbed of Genius - The Scottish Enlightenment 1730 - 1790'. Ed. David Daiches, Peter Jones, Jean Jones. Edinburgh University Press, 1986.

PLACES TO VISIT

Kirkcaldy Museum and Art Gallery - small display of Adam Smith's personal possessions and other items from his life.
The site of his now demolished house is marked with a plaque at High Street, Kirkcaldy.
A large monument marks his last resting place in the Canongate, Churchyard, Royal Mile, Edinburgh.

ROBERT ADAM (1728 - 1792)
Architect

"Rome —the most glorious place in the universal world".

Early Influences

William Adam, born in Kirkcaldy was a very successful architect in Edinburgh. As well as his private practice, he also held the very lucrative post of Master Mason to the Board of Ordnance in North Britain, with responsibility for the construction of the forts that were being built to subdue the Highlanders and he also had many commercial interests including coalfields and a brewery producing strong ale. He married 17-year-old Mary Robertson, sister of the minister of Old Greyfriars Kirk, Edinburgh, and together they had a family of four sons of whom Robert, born on 3rd. July 1728, was the second, and three daughters. With the money that he made from his various enterprises he bought a 4,000 acre estate, Blair Adam, in Fife. The family grew up in a cultured, influential and wealthy environment. The children's cousin, William Robertson, who spent his childhood with them, was destined to be an eminent historian and Principal of Edinburgh University, and their father was a close friend of Allan Ramsay the poet.

Schooling

Soon after Robert was born, the Adam family moved to Edinburgh and it was here, after early schooling in Kirkcaldy, that young Robert, at the age of six, attended the High School. For six hours a day, six days a week, for five years, he was exposed to Latin, and only Latin. Nothing else was taught. The pupils had to pick up for themselves any other subjects that interested them. Indeed it is said that some senior boys were assigned the task of reporting to the Masters any boys who spoke Scots during the lessons or afterwards in the schoolyard. Such boys risked a public whipping.

University

At the age of 15 he moved on to Edinburgh University to fill in the gaps such as English, Ethics, Logic, Greek, History, Mathematics and Natural

Skara Brae, Orkney - the Stone Age Village uncovered by a storm in 1850.

The Crown Jewels of Scotland on display at Edinburgh Castle.

The Callanish Standing Stones, about 12 miles west of Stornoway, Isle of Lewis, which date to about 3000 B C.

A tattooed Pictish warrior

A mural depicting the Norman invasion which set the scene for many wars with England

A Broch, or defensive tower, at Shetland which dates from around 100BC - 100AD

Melrose Abbey in the Borders, subjected to many English attacks

The Battle of Culloden in 1746 where the Stewarts' flickering flame finally dimmed.
From a painting by the Scottish artist Graeme Baxter

Edinburgh where David Hume was born in 1711

Kirkcaldy where Adam Smith was born in 1723

A bust of the great economist

The College, High Street, Glasgow, in Smith's day

*Robert Adam at the height of his fame as the
most successful architect in the land*

The magnificent Culzean Castle on the Ayrshire coast – one of his finest creations

This oval staircase at Culzean, surrounded by columns, leads to the beautifully decorated rooms and galleries

Above and below - Mellerstain House in the Borders is a classic Adam design

Portrait of James Watt

An early model of his steam engine

Portrait of William Murdoch who pioneered gaslight

Murdoch's house at Redruth

Memorial stone tablet

Portrait of James Boswell

Boswell and his family

*On their travels Johnson and Boswell visited Glasgow where they saw the Trongate (above)
and the Clyde (below)*

Philosophy, that had been left by his narrow school curriculum , but he did not graduate. His studies were interrupted after two years when Bonnie Prince Charlie raised his standard at Glenfinnan and led his army south. When things settled down again, Robert did not return to University.

Early assays

He had ambitions to be a painter, but when his father died, the estate and the family business passed to the eldest son John (already in the business) who took Robert into partnership. John also took over the post of Master Mason from his father and found that a new outpost, Fort George, had to be built on a promontory on the Moray Firth. He took Robert north with him. Here the young man drew, developed his taste for architecture, and learned practical skills. He and his brother completed their father's work at Hopetoun House adding a few ideas of their own, for their father followed the strictly classical (Palladian) architecture that was prevalent at that time; they were responsible for the decoration of the Red Drawing Room and the Yellow Drawing Room, showing a lightness of touch that their father lacked. Other commissions completed were Dumfries House including the decoration and furnishings, Sir John Maxwell's splendid House in Pollok Estate on the outskirts of Glasgow, and Marchmont House, Berwickshire, all of which had been designed by their father.

Then in 1754 came the news that Robert had been waiting and hoping for. Charles Hope, the younger brother of the Earl of Hopetoun was going on a Grand Tour. Would Robert care to go with him? Robert was paying his own way, so they went as equals. Hope could give him an entree to everyone who mattered in Europe, both British residents there and members of the European aristocracy.

The Grand Tour

Robert set out on 3rd October 1754, not only to further his architectural knowledge, but also 'to meet the right people' for he knew that this was important in furthering his career. In London, on his way to join Hope on the continent, he had 'done the sights' visiting Westminster Abbey, St. Pauls, the Mansion House, and made a trip to Windsor to view the castle. But cultural pursuits played a minor role when he reached Brussels. Charles Hope had many friends in high places in Europe, and although Robert was more than willing to go along and be invited to social evenings and dinner parties, he found that the card and gaming-parties that inevitably followed were boring in the extreme.

From Brussels they went on to Tournai to meet princes, earls, dukes and duchesses, to dine and to play cards; the pattern was repeated when they reached Paris and here Robert resolved to play the part; he had himself fitted out in the finest velvet, lace and silk costumes and for the three-week stay he was a 'dandy'. Although the welcome was not as warm as it had been in Brussels and Tournai, this had its advantages. There was more time for sightseeing, but although they visited many fine art-galleries, Robert spoke disparagingly of the architecture of the city.

Now they were off to Italy via Nice, where they had a very warm welcome from a fellow Scot, James Paterson, a general in the Piedmontese army, who commanded the province. They were feted all the way on their journey and, perhaps more to Robert's taste, visited many Roman remains in the south of France.

From Nice, Hope and Adam crossed to Genoa where they were entertained by many influential Scots before moving on to Florence. The Carnival was at its height. Under the guidance of yet another Scot, a Colonel Milne who owned mines nearby, they were introduced to the titled and wealthy of the city and they passed their days and nights in a whirl of gaiety, dancing and laughter. More importantly, however, Adam made the acquaintance of Charles-Louis Clerisseau, a man in whom "there is the utmost knowledge of architecture , of perspective, and of designing and colouring I ever saw". He became part of Adam's entourage and accompanied him wherever he went. From now on social activities were to take a second place. With Clerisseau, Adam studied Florentine architecture; he purchased three volumes on the design of their houses, though he thought the style "a little heavy".

Rome

When he entered the city it is said that Robert did little but walk and stare in astonishment at "the most glorious place in the universal world" His Latin studies, though they had been in considerable depth, had not prepared him for the wonders that he saw as he stood on Campus Martius (the 'Field of War'), on the banks of the Tiber, saw St. Peters in the distance, strolled through the Forum, stood on the Capitol, and viewed the Pantheon with awe.

He was taken under the wing of Abbe Peter Grant the Scottish Catholic Agent in Rome (a close friend of the Pope) who introduced him to the Scottish painter Allan Ramsay (eldest son of the poet of the same name) and to all the influential people in Rome including the Old Pretender's physician, Dr. Irvine, with whom he dined. "Now nearly eighty, he drinks four or five bottles of wine every day and does not look sixty."

Around this time, after they had been together for about three months Adam parted from Hope and he established Clerisseau in his own apartment where together they lived and talked architecture. With the Abbe Grant they set off for Naples visiting Nero's villa, and drove to see the wonders of the ancient city of Herculaneum which had been excavated in recent times after having been enveloped by lava from erupting Vesuvius in A.D.70.

Back in Rome there was an intensive period of training, with Clerisseau guiding him in the intricacies of perspective, a painter teaching him design, and another teaching him landscape painting. All of this was expensive and the cost of a retinue of servants had to be added to it. But Adam had budgeted for this outlay which was in the region of £ 900 per year. He was spending his mornings drawing, his afternoons visiting and sketching places of architectural interest. The drawings that he made of the Forum, the Colosseum, and many other buildings reveal a very talented pupil and he was now building up a massive portfolio of his own work. He was "determined to probe the roots of the classical style - to measure and record afresh every example of Roman architecture."

He was also mixing with some of the most influential figures in the Roman art world - Cardinal Albani (a nephew of Pope Clement X1) owner of the famous Villa in which was displayed his world-famous collection of sculptures; the painter, Giovanni Battista Piranesi, who became one of his instructors; and Allan Ramsay. All had very powerful influences on him. He now liked to designate himself 'Bob the Roman'. He was not however neglecting his social contacts - among them the Duke of Bridgewater, Lord Huntingdon, Lord Villiers (son of the Earl of Jersey), Sir William Stanhope (brother of the Earl of Chesterfield), Lord Rosebery, and Lord Elgin, who were all, at different times, touring Italy. Adam had a liking for titled people and besides they were, in his eyes, potential future clients! His confidence was growing apace. In the wake of the destruction of Lisbon by an earthquake, Adam hoped that he might be chosen to plan its rebuilding. He made many preliminary sketches and he enlisted the aid of many of his influential friends to help attain his goal; but it was not to be. Adam was over-ambitious and the commission went to another.

The Grand Tour was almost over. After taking farewell of his many friends, with his great collection of marbles, antique vases, friezes, Old Masters, bulging portfolios of his own drawings, and with diplomas from

Rome, Florence and Bologna, he left Rome in May 1757 and set out for home. He went via Florence, Bologna, Padua, and Venice, being acclaimed wherever he went. He made a six-day sea journey to the Dalmatian coast, where he viewed the classical sights and spent five weeks surveying and drawing the ruins of Emperor Diocletian's Palace at Spalatro. Moving north he crossed the snow-covered Alps into Austria, and so to Antwerp, reaching Harwich in January 1758.

London

Back in London, Robert was elected a Member of the Royal Society of Arts. He set up in business and was later joined by his brother James, when he returned from his own Grand Tour. He took up residence in Lower Grosvenor St.(with the help of a loan from brother John in Scotland) and his two sisters accompanied by young brother William, who was later to join the firm, came from Edinburgh to keep house for him. Within a short time the elite of London were flocking to his house to see the wonderful collection of marbles and paintings that he had brought home with him. His book 'Ruins of Emperor Diocletian's Palace at Spalatro' was published in 1766 and he presented a specially bound copy to King George 111.

Robert was ready to put into practice the ideas that he had picked up in Italy. One of his first commissions was to erect a screen in front of the Admiralty in Whitehall but most of his early work involved the reconstruction of large country houses that had been built at an earlier period. This he did with taste and style and soon he was being recognised as one of the outstanding architects in the land, translating his ideas from Imperial Rome to the English countryside; the triumphal arch of Rome became the south front of Kedleston Hall in Derbyshire; and the Portico of Octavia became the Portico at Osterley House. In 1761 he was appointed 'Architect of the King's Works', though no commissions were to come his way from that direction.

Although the great days of building massive country houses were all but over before Adam came on the scene, the period of building elegant mansions in London was very much to the fore. In the early 1770's he erected one at 20 St. James Square for Sir Watkins Williams Wynne, a second at 20 Portman Square for the Countess of Home, and a third at 26 Grosvenor Square for the Earl of Derby.

The brothers had expanded their interests into owning timber firms, brickworks, stone and paving businesses, and Aberdeen granite-quarries. At the height of their power they were employing 3000 craftsmen -

bricklayers, masons, plasterers, joiners, coppersmiths, locksmiths, and plumbers.

The Adelphi Development

Robert Adam was at the height of his power. In addition to being the most successful architect in the land, he was now sitting in the House of Commons as Tory Member for Kinross-shire. But he was about to over-reach himself. The three-acre Durham Yard area of Thames-side, just south of the Strand, became available and in the most massive project ever undertaken by the firm, the four Adam brothers moved into speculative building. In 1768 they gained the lease of the Yard for 99 years at £1,200 per annum and on a series of brick arches rising from the river level, built a terrace of high-quality prestigious houses. Beneath the arches they constructed a line of vaults with access from the three adjoining wharves to the river. These vaults, it was proposed, would be let to the Government Ordnance Department.

The development did not meet with overwhelming approval in London:

> 'Four Scotchmen by the name of Adams
> Who keep their coaches and their Madams,
> Quoth John in sullen mood, to Thomas,
> Have stole the very river from us.'

This may not have been good poetry, or even good English, but it does indicate the rising opposition to the Adam brothers - and perhaps also to 'Scotchmen' in general, who (perhaps because of their abilities and their entrepreneurial ways) were not the most popular race in London at this time.

Even before the houses were completed the Adam brothers had spent £120,000 (an enormous sum in those days) and unable to meet their creditors, and their workmen's wages, work on the Adelphi was suspended. An additional factor was that the Board of Ordnance declined to rent the vaults.

In order to meet their debts and satisfy their creditors, a five-day sale of Robert's and James's collection of Italian paintings, drawings and Roman antiquities, was held in Christies. But even this was not enough, and Robert hit upon the idea of running a lottery which would at one stroke meet the debt and at the same time sell the houses. Although there was some opposition in the House of Commons to the idea, particularly by

Robert Walpole, Robert made an impassioned speech and permission was granted. The lottery raised over £200,000 and the brothers were again solvent. Robert himself moved into No. 4, Royal Terrace, the Adelphi.

Back to Scotland

But business in England was declining and Robert, who had already opened an office in Edinburgh in 1772, was finding more and more work in his home country where he had always been very highly regarded and where he had many major commissions completed and on-going, even at the peak of his London success. He made many journeys north by post-chaise to inspect them and on arriving there, there was always a queue of new customers asking for his services.

Among his commissions were, an addition to the County Court House at Kinross, the reconstruction of Auchincruive House, Ayrshire, (now the property of the Scottish Agricultural College), the building of Seton Castle, East Lothian, and more importantly, the building of the Register House in Edinburgh. This magnificent building with its domed central hall within a rectangular block of working offices, is said to be based on the Pantheon in Rome. He saw the whole project through from its planning in 1772, the laying of the foundation stone in 1774 to its completion in 1792.

During one of his visits to Glasgow he met a committee "who agreed to give me sole direction and surveying (of the Trades Hall, Glassford St.) and paid on account thereof £52. 10s". He was building many town-houses in Edinburgh including what is now 8 Queen St. and occupied by the Royal College of Physicians.

Culzean Castle

Although Adam had done some castle-building in England and in Scotland, it was with Culzean Castle that it reached full fruition. The Earl of Cassilis, Member of Parliament at the same time as Adam, and a descendant of the Kennedys who had been such a powerful force in south Scotland through the ages, invited him to create a castle at Culzean, Ayrshire, his ancient family seat overlooking the Firth of Clyde.

It was an enormous challenge, for the site was on a steep-cliffed outcrop overlooking the Firth of Clyde and the only landward approach was across a deep ravine; it was immediately obvious why this had been a Kennedy stronghold. Adam rose to the challenge, bridging the ravine and creating a triumphal archway as a dramatic approach to the castle. Inside, a magnificent oval staircase surrounded by columns, leads to the beautifully decorated rooms and galleries. The castle's great round tower, enclosing the salon, broods over the sea.

Unfinished Business

He was asked to prepare plans for a new building for Edinburgh University to replace the existing straggle of buildings and in 1789 the foundation stone was laid. Unfortunately not all of his scheme came to fruition and only the north-west corner and the magnificent triumphal-arch entrance from South Bridge St. leading to the tall domed space, are his. The remainder of the building was completed at the beginning of the 19th century by another architect.

A similar fate was to await his other major undertaking in Edinburgh. This was Charlotte Square which was built at the west end of George Street, to 'balance' George Square at the east end. Sadly, only the north side was completed before death intervened.

On March 2nd, 1792, a few months after returning to London from Edinburgh, Robert suffered a severe and unexpected stomach haemorrhage and he died the next day. On 10th March he was buried privately in the south transept of Westminster Abbey.

He left behind, Volumes 1 and 2 of 'Works of Architecture of Robert and James Adam' published in 1773 and 1779 respectively. Volume 3 was published posthumously in 1822. In the years to come his influence was to spread far beyond England and Scotland and his style which has been termed 'neo- classical'can be seen in the design and decoration of buildings in many countries including the U.S.A., France, Sweden and Russia.

REFERENCES AND FURTHER READING

'The Age of Adam' James Lees-Milne. B.T.Batsford Ltd. 1947.
'Robert Adam and his Circle'. John Fleming. John Murray, 1962.
'The Decorative Work of Robert Adam' Damie Stillman. Academy Editions, 1973.
'The Work of Robert Adam' Geoffrey Beard. John Bartholomew and Son, 1978.
'Robert Adam' Colin MacLean. History of Medicine and Science Unit. University of Edinburgh, 1982.
'Robert Adam in Scotland' Margaret H.B. Sanderson. H.M.S.O. Edinburgh, 1992.
'Adam Style' Steven Parissien. Phaiden Press 1992

PLACES TO VISIT

Many of Adam's houses and buildings are to be seen throughout Scotland and England; the cities of Edinburgh and London are particularly rich in this respect. Among the outstanding buildings are:

Scotland
Hopetoun House, West Lothian.
Register House, Edinburgh.
The Old College, South Bridge St. University of Edinburgh.
Charlotte Square, Edinburgh
The Royal College of Physicians, 8 Queen St. Edinburgh.
Trades Hall, Glassford St. Glasgow. Still occupied by the Trades House of Glasgow
Culzean Castle, Ayrshire. One of the National Trust for Scotland's most popular properties.

England
Kedleston Hall, Derbyshire.
Syon House, Middlesex.
Osterley Park, Middlesex.
Harwood House, Yorkshire.
Wynne House, 20 St. James's Square, London.
Hume House, 20 Portman Square, London.
Sir John Soane Museum, Lincoln Inn Fields, London.
Robert Adam's brother William, who survived him, inherited his collection of 53 volumes of 9000 architectural drawings. William went bankrupt in 1822 and the family collection of paintings, books, and antiquities was sold off. However he retained the drawings which were offered by his neice to the British Museum who refused them. They were later sold for £200 to Sir John Soane and are today to be seen with other works of art in the museum which was formerly Sir John's home.

JAMES WATT (1736 - 1819)

The Steam Engine

"I had entered Glasgow Green — the idea came to my mind".

At the beginning of the 18th century Greenock was a tiny isolated fishing village of a single row of thatched cottages looking out on to a sandy beach on the River Clyde. Vast changes were, however, on the way.

With the union of the Scottish and English parliaments in 1707, the Clyde scene altered dramatically. The great trading empires of North America and the West Indies, with their vast riches of tobacco, cotton, and sugar, were opened up to the Scots. Whereas formerly the east coast Firth of Forth ports such as Leith, Dundee and Aberdeen, trading with Europe, had been of paramount importance, now the focus of attention moved to the west, to the Firth of Clyde, which became alive with ships. Greenock, strategically placed to take advantage of the new situation, expanded rapidly, and traded vigorously across the Atlantic.

Early days

This was the Greenock into which James Watt was born on 19th January, 1736. His father (also named James) revelling in the new-found prosperity, was a shipwright, carpenter, coffin-maker, and general merchant, a man of considerable standing in the town, being successively town treasurer, bailie, and chief magistrate. His wife Agnes Muirhead, a woman of ability, bore her husband five children; three died in infancy, a son died aboard his father's ship in the Atlantic, and James junior (hereafter referred to as James) was thus the sole survivor. He was a sickly child often suffering from headaches that were, particularly in times of stress, to plague him for much of the remainder of his life. Perhaps it is not surprising that his parents cosseted and indulged him.

In his early years James was educated at home, particularly by his mother, who taught him the 'three R's'; his father showed him how to use tools. When later, he did go to school, he was unprepared for the rough and tumble of the playground and he was subjected to much bullying. He was thought to be rather dull academically, but there was one subject - mathematics - in which he excelled. At home he was happy reading science books, drawing, and using the tools that were always around him.

His father had planned that James should come into his business, but it hit a bad spell, so that when the boy was 18 he was sent off to Glasgow to be apprenticed as an instrument maker. Glasgow was also booming in the new prosperity, having built the town of Port Glasgow downstream as a port for its goods, which were then ferried up and down in small ships. Although Glasgow had not itself yet realized its full potential as a port, this was to come with the deepening and widening of the Clyde in 1769 by a Chester engineer, John Golborne, thus making it possible for merchant ships to sail right into the heart of the city . James worked in Glasgow for a short time with an optician, but learned little and, after consulting his father, he was on his way, on horseback with two guineas in his pocket, to seek an apprenticeship in London. He bought the horse in Greenock and sold it at the end of his journey.

London

The journey took twelve days and when he got there he lived in constant fear of being 'pressed'. Many pressgangs roamed the streets at night seizing all able-bodied men that they could get their hands on. It was very dangerous to get drunk in London; you were liable to wake from your stupor and find yourself aboard a man o' war en route for the firing line. The pressgangs were known to 'enlist' as many as 1000 citizens on a 'good night', and turn them over to His Majesty's Navy.

The 'press' was occasioned by the Seven Years War (1755 - 1762) with France and, as always, Britain was ill-prepared and desperately in need of people to man her ships. In addition to the pressgangs there were kidnappers acting on behalf of the East India Company who needed recruits for their army. When the demand for soldiers was slack, any spare people could always be turned over to the colonists in North America who were sorely in need of labour for their tobacco and cotton fields.

James found employment with a Mr. John Morgan, an instrument maker but it cost him £20, supplied by his father, and the products of his labour. He worked long hours - till 9pm - and it is little wonder that his health, never very good, deteriorated. He returned to Greenock after only one year of the seven-year apprenticeship to live with his father, his mother having died when James was but a boy.

University days

The thin, stooped, delicate frame hid a strong will. Ere long he was off to Glasgow again, this time in an attempt to set up in business as an instrument maker, but he was frustrated in this by the powerful Incorporation of Hammermen of the Trades House of Glasgow. The Trades House had its beginnings in 1605 and the purpose of its 14 Incorporations was to maintain standards and to determine who should, and who should not, be allowed to ply their trades in Glasgow. They decided that James Watt came into the latter category because he was neither the son of a burgess, nor had he been trained in Glasgow.

Fortunately James had friends within the University. A kinsman of his mother, George Muirhead, Professor of Humanity (Greek) had introduced him, on his previous visit to Glasgow, to Professor Robert Dick of the Natural Philosophy Department, and Dick now invited him to set up a workshop within the University grounds where he would be instrument maker to the University, and beyond the jurisdiction of the Trades House. He would also have a little shop where he could sell such instruments as he might make.

These were happy times for Watt. He enjoyed the company of the professors and for their part, they held the very talented young man in high esteem. But business was poor and the university didn't have many scientific instruments to repair. In his spare time he made fiddles, flutes, and guitars, and a barrel organ for his good friend, Dr. Joseph Black, Professor of Chemistry, who said of him that he was "a young man possessing most uncommon talents for mechanical knowledge and practice , with an originality, readiness and copiousness of invention".

A shop in the Sautmercate

Later in 1759, by which time he was 23, the Hammermen relented and he was allowed to set up shop in the Saltmarket, Glasgow. Then he moved along the street. "James Watt has removed his shop from the Sautmercate to Mr. Buchanan's land in the Trongate, where he sets up all sorts of mathematical and musical instruments with varieties of toys and other goods" states an advertisement in the 'Glasgow Herald' of 1st December, 1763.

Watt married his cousin, Margaret Miller, in 1764 and he might have have remained for the rest of his life in his little shop had he not been given for repair, by Professor John Anderson, a model of a Newcomen steam engine, which Anderson had recently procured from London. This engine, invented by Thomas Newcomen of Dartmouth in 1712, was widely used for pumping flood water from the coal mines, and from the tin mines of Cornwall. In the course of repairing the model, Watt realized that the design was bad, that the original must be very inefficient, consuming large amounts of coal (sometimes thirteen tons in a day, he found on enquiry) to raise a head of steam. It could surely be improved. But how?

The Newcomen engine worked on the principle that steam lifted a piston fitting closely inside a cylinder; the steam was then cooled by an injection of cold water, creating a vacuum and the piston fell back to its original position; the water was reheated raising the piston again. And so on. Watt felt this to be terribly wasteful of heat. He came to the conclusion that in order to make an efficient steam engine, the cylinder should not be cooled; it should always remain as hot as the steam that entered it. But how could this be achieved if it was necessary to cool the steam?

A Walk in the Park

The solution came to him one Sunday in the Spring of 1765. "I had gone to take a walk on a fine Sabbath afternoon. I had entered the (Glasgow) Green by the gate at the foot of Charlotte Street —- the idea came to my mind that as steam is an elastic body it would rush into a vacuum, and if a communication were made between the cylinder and an exhaust vessel, it would rush into it and might be condensed there without cooling the cylinder". He had hit upon the idea of a separate condenser for the steam. There is now a simple memorial boulder in Glasgow Green where Watt walked, though it is overshadowed by the enormous obelisk raised in 1807 to mark Lord Nelson's victory at Trafalgar - the first monument to Nelson to be erected in Britain.

Watt returned to his workshop, tried out the idea, and even improved on it by putting a hot water jacket round the cylinder to conserve more heat. He confided his thoughts to his university friends - John Robison who was later to become Professor of Natural History at Edinburgh, Black, and Anderson. They were enthusiastic and urged him to pursue the idea.

Black introduced him to Dr. John Roebuck, of the Carron Iron Works at Falkirk. Roebuck had coal-mines nearby to fuel his furnaces and was experiencing great difficulty due to flooding. He found the Newcomen engine of little use, and after studying Watt's design he undertook to pay off his debts (£1000 to Black - a very considerable sum), to secure a patent, and to provide the means for carrying out further experiments. In return, Roebuck was to have a two thirds share in the engine.

In the meantime, in order to make a living, for the engine was still far from being a practical proposition, Watt turned to surveying and in 1796 he planned and supervised the Monkland Canal which was used to transport coal from the mines of Lanarkshire to the furnaces of Glasgow. In the middle of all this his wife died and left him with two young children, the elder of whom was only six. Roebuck went bankrupt. Watt was at his lowest ebb. But the tide was turning.

Boulton and Soho

Matthew Boulton was probably the most successful manufacturing business man of his time in England. For a number of years he had been interested in Watt's engine, having been told of it by his friend Roebuck. He invited Watt to visit him at his works in Soho, Birmingham, where, using water-power, Boulton manufactured steel-gilt buttons, watch-chains and sword-hilts, steel buckles, and medals. He saw the potential of Watt's invention and he took Roebuck's share in the engine patent in lieu of debts of £1200. Watt sent his engine to Soho and followed it there in May 1774. He was now 39 and was about to enter the most successful period of his life.

The two men, so different in temperament, struck up an immediate rapport. Watt suffered from chronic ill-health, headaches, and bouts of depression. "My headache keeps its weekaversary today – I am plagued with the blues; my head is too confused to do any brainwork". Always there was Boulton, who was genuinely fond of him, to cajole and encourage. In the middle of it all, Watt was offered an appointment by the Russian Government at the then enormous salary of £1000 per year. Much to Boulton's relief, he turned it down. In 1775 he set up house in Birmingham with his two children.

The first engine made at Soho was ordered by John Wilkinson, to blow the bellows of his iron works. It was a great success. The fame of Boulton and Watt was spreading; new buildings were erected at Soho. Business was booming. It was while visiting Glasgow for orders for his engine that Watt proposed marriage to a Miss Anne MacGregor, the daughter of a successful dyer. Before agreeing to the marriage, Miss MacGregor's father demanded to see the partnership agreement that was drawn up between Watt and Boulton. There was none, such was the trust that these two men had for each other, and during the long years of their partnership and friendship that lay ahead, none appears ever to have been drawn up. Father MacGregor was fobbed off by some excuse by Boulton, which he must have accepted, for Watt married his daughter.

In the Cornwall tin mines the Watt engine was rapidly replacing the Newcomen, but Watt went through agonies trying to make the mine-captains pay their royalties. "These disputes are so very disagreeable to me that I am very sorry that I ever bestowed so great a part of my time and money on the steam engine – I have been molested with headaches all this week". he recorded. It was a considerable relief to him when William Murdoch took over that part of the business.

It was Murdoch who invented the 'sun and planet' modification to the Watt engine that opened up all sorts of new possibilities. "It goes round twice for each stroke of the engine" said Watt. Patented in 1782, the problem of rotary motion by steam power was solved and the opportunities for employing the engine were boundless. Orders were flowing in from all parts of the country, and beyond - from breweries, paper mills, whisky distilleries, cotton mills, sugar mills in America and the West Indies. Orders for pumping engines were coming in from France, Spain, Italy - from all over Europe. Wherever power was needed Watt's engine was to be found. And Boulton, as well as manufacturing it, was also using it in his own factories. The steam engine not only revolutionized existing industries; it made possible the creation of new ones. They were now freed from the restrictions of water- power and could move close to the source of steampower, the coal fields. Britain roared into the Industrial Revolution in a cloud of steam generated by coal, powered by Watt's engine, and became the richest nation on Earth.

By 1786, at the age of 50, James Watt's financial difficulties were over and he was now on his way to becoming a very rich man. Boulton was still ploughing his money into new enterprises, but Watt was enjoying life as he had never done in his youth, although still taking an active interest in the business. His health taking a dramatic turn for the better, he lost his dread of smallpox that had haunted him all his life and he began to travel widely through France and Germany, to reap the fruits of his success. He enjoyed his visits to Scotland, particularly Edinburgh, where he and Walter Scott became close friends. It is said that he never lost his dry sense of humour nor his pleasant Scottish accent.

The Lunar Society

Watt had been introduced by Boulton to the prestigious Lunar Society which was founded by the Scottish doctor, William Small (sometime influential tutor to Thomas Jefferson), Boulton, and Erasmus Darwin (grandfather of Charles; it was he who had introduced Boulton to Roebuck). The Society was so-called because it held its meetings on the Monday nearest to the full moon, so that members could see their way home. Inevitably they were called 'Lunatics'. This was exciting company. Benjamin Franklin was a corresponding member, and in addition to those mentioned, Josiah Wedgwood, the founder of the pottery firm, Joseph Priestley the discoverer of oxygen, William Withering, who introduced digitalis for the treatment of heart disease, and William Murdoch, the inventor of gas-lighting, were also numbered among its 14 members. It was a stimulating, influential, and radical group, supporting both the American and the French Revolutions. Many writers believe that the Lunar society was the kernel of the Industrial Revolution. Watt enjoyed the dinners and the talk.

Succession and Honours

In time Boulton's son Matthew, and Watt's son James, much to their fathers' pleasure took over the business.

Boulton's health began to decline; he died on 17th August 1809, aged 81 and was buried in the Church graveyard at Handsworth. Watt outlived him by ten years dying in his 84th year at his home in Heathfield, and being buried near to his old friend who had made all things possible. A statue, made possible by public subscription, was erected in Westminster Abbey in 1824.

During his life-time many honours came his way. He was elected a Fellow of the Royal Society of Edinburgh (1784), a Fellow of the Royal Society of London at the same time as Boulton (1785), Foreign Associate of the Institute of France (1814). The University of Glasgow conferred on him the Honorary Degree of Doctor of Laws (1806). He was offered a baronetcy by Lord Liverpool, the Prime Minister, but gracefully declined. To mark his contribution to learning, the British Association for the Advancement of Science adopted the 'Watt' as a unit of power measurement.

But Watt had his 'blind spots' in dealing with Murdoch over locomotion and gas-lighting, and with Miller over steam-ships, as we see in other chapters.

REFERENCES AND FURTHER READING

"Memorials of James Watt". George Williamson. Thomas Constable 1856.

"Lives of Boulton and Watt". Samuel Smiles. John Murray, 1865.

"James Watt". H.W. Dickenson. Cambridge Universty Press, 1936.

"Six Great Inventors". J.G. Crowther. Hamish Hamilton, 1954.

"The Lunar Society of Birmingham". Ritchie Calder. Scientific American.

PLACES TO VISIT

Scotland

Statue of James Watt in George Square, Glasgow, and in foyer of Royal College Building, University of Strathclyde.

McLean Museum and Art Gallery, Greenock - special exhibits.

Glasgow University Hunterian Museum. Permanent exhibits relating to Watt.

Royal Scottish Museum, Chambers Street, Edinburgh. Exhibits include models of early steam engines; model of Murdoch's steam carriage; Watt engines.

England

Birmingham Museum of Science and Industry. James Watt Building has exhibits relating to him, and to Boulton and Murdoch, including the world's oldest working steam engine: Murdoch's original steam carriage and many of Watt's inventions.

Avery Historical museum, Smethwick, Warley, has several exhibits of Boulton and Watt.

WILLIAM MURDOCH (1754 - 1839)

Gaslight

"I never did pretend to the discovery of the inflammable principle of the gas from coal"

In the middle of the 18th century Scotland provided little opportunity for young men of ability to develop their talents in industry, so, William Murdoch, aged 24, set out from the little village of Billo Miln (now Bello Mill) in the Parish of Auchinleck, Ayrshire, where he was born, to walk over 400 kilometres (250 miles) to Birmingham where he hoped to find employment with Boulton and Watt at their now famous Soho works.

Father and Son

William was the third of six children born to John Murdoch and his wife Anna Bruce, and was baptised by the Reverend John Dun who had been James Boswell's private tutor. For generations the Murdochs had been prosperous millers at Bello Corn Mill and tenant farmers on the Boswell estates. The house in which they lived has a plaque on the door testifying to that fact.

John, like his father before him, had served as a gunner in the Royal Artillery (from 1744 - 1752) seeing active service in Flanders and probably taking part with the Government forces in the Battle of Culloden (1746).

William had a good education at one of the local schools, at a cost of 30 shillings a year, and he spent much of his boyhood and youth manufacturing and experimenting under his father's guidance - woodworking, engineering, stone-masonry, and mill-wrighting, all provided outlets for his high mechanical and inventive ability; and he gave portent of things to come when he lit up a little cave beside the mill, with gas obtained by heating cannel coal in an old pot borrowed from his mother.

Off to Soho

Most accounts say that Murdoch went to Soho 'on spec', but it would seem unlikely that the great Boulton would himself interview a wandering worker. Since William's father knew Roebuck, and indeed they were business acquaintances, and since the latter was also friendly with Boulton and had introduced Watt to him, it is a fair assumption that it was he who provided John's son William with an introduction to the great man.

The interview took place when Watt was off in Cornwall. In view of the latter's marked aversion at that time to the employment of Scots mechanics it does look as if the interview was arranged by Boulton for this obviously highly-skilled young man at a time when Watt would not be there. The interview itself has gone down in engineering folk-lore. Murdoch carried a circular stove-pipe hat which, in his nervousness, he dropped. Boulton was struck by the peculiar sound as it hit the floor and on enquiry was told by Murdoch that he had turned it on his own lathe. That clinched it. He was employed on the spot at 15 shillings (75p) a week.

Cornwall

It was not long before Boulton (and Watt) realized that they had on their hands a man of outstanding ability. In a short time he became their most trusted worker and adviser in all their mechanical undertakings. When he was promoted senior engine- erector his wages went up by 6 shillings to 21 shillings (105 p) and he was sent to the Cornwall tin mines at Redruth, much to Watt's relief, to take over from him.

This was no easy assignment for the 'mine-captains' were tough - "the rudest men that I ever met in my whole life" said Watt. Many of them, if they possibly could, sought to evade paying the royalties that were due on the use of the pumping engines; they also resented the intrusion of these Scotsmen. Murdoch decided that there was only one way to settle it. He peeled off his jacket, rolled up his sleeves, and picking out the biggest and toughest of them 'engaged him in fisticuffs'. The contest was soon over for Murdoch, unlike Watt, was a tall powerful fellow and soon laid his opponent low with a few well-aimed blows. It is pleasing to report that the contest ended with handshakes all round. The Cornishmen were tough but fair, and good sports. Murdoch had earned their respect. He made one concession; they had difficulty in pronouncing his name so he changed it to 'Murdock'. He was to remain in Cornwall for 19 years.

It was not only in fighting that Murdock earned their respect. As Boulton and Watt had done, they recognised that they had among them a man whose mechanical ability amounted almost to genius. Time after time, when the pumping engines broke down and flooding was imminent, it was Murdock who went in there and repaired them. And when he married a Cornish lass, Ann Paynter, and took house among them, he could do no wrong. Unfortunately they had only five years of happy married life together. Ann died in childbirth leaving two sons, John and William. Both were sent to their grandfather's home at Bello Mill, where they went to school at Ayr Academy, later returning to live in Birmingham with their father.

Murdock in the meantime 'flew from mine to mine' putting the engines right. Feeling that he was perhaps worth more than his 21 shillings a week, he asked Boulton for a rise to £2:2/-, but although his employer thought very highly of him Boulton was not prepared to go that far!. He fobbed him off with a present of ten guineas from the owners of United Mines to "the most obliging and industrious workman that we have ever known". Boulton himself added another ten guineas. There is evidence that Watt not only agreed that Murdock should not have a rise (on the grounds that other workers would want similar treatment) but that it was actually he who persuaded Boulton not to accede. It was at this time that some of the mine-owners made moves to entice Murdock away from Boulton and Watt, but Murdock would have none of that despite the fact that Watt may have been jealous of his popularity with the mineowners.

A mechanical horse

In his spare time Murdock was busy building a locomotive powered by one of Watt's steam engines. When his model, rather like a tricycle, 48 cms long and 35 cms high, was finished in the summer of 1784 (it is now in Birmingham Museum) he tried it out on the long avenue leading to the parsonage and in doing so "nearly frightened out of his wits the village pastor who encounted the hissing fiery little machine, while enjoying his evening walk". The pastor, his thoughts no doubt on higher things, must have thought that it was 'Auld Nick', the devil himself, descending upon him. There is a plaque commemorating the event on the house in Redruth in which Murdock once lived:

WILLIAM MURDOCK
lived in this house
1782 - 1798
MADE THE FIRST LOCOMOTIVE HERE
and tested it in 1784

He built a steam carriage which he drove from mine to mine and he divulged his plans to Boulton and Watt.

Although Watt had included a plan of a locomotive engine in his patent of 1784 he took no steps to put it into execution and indeed when he heard of Murdock's experiments he did all that he could to persuade Boulton to dissuade him from the project stating that, although he had no objection in principle he did not want Murdock distracted from the work that he was there to do. "William should do as we do and apply himself to the business in hand". Also, more revealingly "I did not like that a scheme of mine which I had revolved in my mind for years and hoped at some favourable time to bring to perfection - should be wrested from me —- or I should be impelled to go into it as a secondary person - but I have now made the latter objection give way - as to the first, I think that it will take place at any rate, so we must make the best of it."

Boulton, ever the business man, advanced Murdock £100 to help with his experiments. But he and Watt set impossible conditions which were that if, within one year, Murdock succeeded in making an engine capable of drawing a postchaise carrying two persons and the driver, with 200 lb. of luggage, fuel for four hours, and water for two hours, going at the rate of four miles an hour, then a partnership would be entered into in which Boulton and Watt were to find the capital and Murdock was to conduct the business and take his share of the profits. A tall order and it was not to be. Murdock had so many urgent matters to attend to that he could not possibly meet the conditions and in 1786 reluctantly gave up the idea. A pity for otherwise Murdock and not Trevithick (some 16 years later) would have invented the first practical steam carriage in Britain. It is interesting to note that Trevithick was born in Cornwall and spent his early life there.

A feast of ideas

However Murdock's inventive mind was in full swing. As well as the many improvements that he made in Watt's engine contriving alterations for casting, boring, turning, fitting, he also invented the oscillating engine, the double D slide valve (which saved steam and ensured greater simplicity in the manufacturing and working of the engine), a rotary engine, cast-iron cement, a steam-gun, and many other items. He constructed a lift worked by compressed air, and used the same kind of power to ring bells in his own house. Sir Walter Scott, with whom he was friendly, later had the same device fitted to his house at Abbotsford. Another of his ingenious schemes was the method of transmitting letters and packages through a tube exhausted by an air-pump.

Gaslight

Murdock never claimed to have discovered the use of gas for lighting purposes. What he did was to make it a practical proposition. In 1791 in Cornwall he began experiments in the evening when his work was done, which were really extensions of the experiments in gas lighting that he had carried out as a boy in the cave at Bello Mill. He filled domestic kettles with wood or coal or peat, dry- heated them, fitting a perforated thimble to the spout and igniting the gas that issued forth. Finding that coal was the best source of gas, he examined samples from various parts of the country, setting up pilot plants in his garden to wash and collect the gas as it was produced.

He lit up his own house and offices at Redruth in 1792, sending the gas some 20 metres along pipes. This was the first practical application recorded of coal- gas lighting. He also constructed a lantern with a jet attached to a bladder of gas and managed to light himself across the moors when returning from work. It is said that "many a drunk Cornish miner believed that he had seen a pixie" when crossing the moors.

In 1794 on a visit to Soho, he told Watt about his successful experiments, suggesting that a patent should be taken out. Watt was not encouraging and was so concerned about his own steam-engine patent which was under threat, that he was unwilling to enter into any new developments. When Murdock returned permanently to Soho from Cornwall in 1798, with a much more appropriate salary of £1000 per annum, he lit up some of the works offices, and again attempted, unsuccessfully, to persuade Boulton and Watt to take out a patent. In celebration of the short-lived Peace of Amiens in 1802 he lit up the front of the Soho works in brilliant fashion and from that date the works-lighting was extended. Other firms followed suit, and not only in Birmingham.

Watt was changing tack. Reporting on a visit to Glasgow in 1805 "the new lights are much in vogue — and I hear that a cotton-mill in the neighourhood is lighted up with gas", he proposed that machinery and plant should be erected at Soho under Murdock's direction, at a cost of £5000 for the purpose of manufacturing gas apparatus. But it was too late for Murdock to make money from it. His hope of a patent had gone. Other competitors were in the field and the 'London and Westminster Chartered Gas-light and Coke Company', ironically under the management of a man trained by Murdock at Soho, were authorized to light up London.

The failure of the public to understand the nature of gas-lighting is amusing now but understandable then. It was popularly believed that the gas which was carried along the pipes was alight and that the pipes would be very hot. When the House of Commons was fitted out, members were seen to be feeling the pipes with their gloved hands and expressing their surprise when they found them to be cool.

Although Murdock made no money from his invention he had the minor consolation that he was awarded the Rumford Gold Medal by the Royal Society in 1808. Neither the Royal Society of London nor the Royal Society of Edinburgh made him a Fellow though Boulton and Watt were Fellows of the former, Watt of the latter, and Murdock's portrait hangs on its walls. Maybe Watt didn't push very hard.

Boulton died in 1809, Watt in 1819. Murdock continued with the Company until 1830 when he retired at the age of 76. Practically until his death in 1839 (although in his later years his faculties were failing) he retained his interest in the firm that he had served so faithfully and so well - some might say, perhaps too well. Young Boulton and young Watt, who took over the running of the firm from their fathers, held him high in their affection and gave him the standing that was long his due. He was buried beside Matthew Boulton and James Watt in the Parish Church, Handsworth.

REFERENCES AND FURTHER READING

'Lives of Boulton and Watt'". S.Smiles. John Murray, 1865.
'Light without a Wick'. Alexander Murdoch. Robert Maclehose, 1892.
'The Chemical Revolution' A. and N. Clow. 1952.
' Man of Little Showing'. James. A. McCash. College Courant (Journal of the Glasgow University Graduates Association) Nos. 36 and 37 (1966) and No. 39 (1967).
'The Third Man: The Life and Times of William Murdock, Inventor of Gaslight'. John Giffiths. Andrew Deutch, 1992.

PLACES TO VISIT

Scotland

Bello Mill, near Cumnock, is now a ruin. Nearby is the cave where he carried out his early experiments in gas-lighting, and his home (plaque on the wall though the house is occupied).
Painting of Willam Murdoch in rooms of Royal Society of Edinburgh.

England

In Redruth there is a plaque on the house in which Murdoch lived but, disappointingly, little else to indicate his association with Cornwall. In the district there are many tin mines some of which are tourist attractions but no mention of Murdoch.
Murdoch's steam-carriage is in Birmingham Museum.

JAMES BOSWELL (1740 - 1795)

Biographer

"I do indeed come from Scotland but I cannot help that."

James Boswell's father, having inherited the estate of Auchinleck, Ayrshire, which had been granted to an ancestor by James 1V, and becoming a Judge in the Scottish Court of Session, adopted the honorary title, Lord Auchinleck.

After a period of private tuition, first by the minister of the local church and then at a private school in Edinburgh, James moved to the High School in that city. He quickly showed how adaptable he could be when, professing himself to be a Jacobite, he quickly changed tack when his uncle offered him a shilling if he would pray for King George 11.

Edinburgh and Glasgow

He entered Edinburgh University, destined for the law, showing considerable ability in precise note-taking; a useful skill for a student, for a future lawyer, and equally so for a future biographer. He was also attracted to the arts, writing short poems for the 'Scots Magazine', being very fond of drama and associating with the players, and he also developed a considerable liking for wine.

At the age of 19 he moved to Glasgow University to further his studies in Civil Law and he attended lectures in Moral Philosophy and Rhetoric, given by Adam Smith. In spite of having an affair with an actress, he decided, much to the distress of his parents, that his future lay in turning Catholic and becoming a priest. He was only dissuaded from doing so by extracting a promise from his father that he would be allowed to join the army.

A Taste of London

He spent two months in London, trying to obtain a commission in the Guards. The Duke of Argyll when asked by Lord Auchinleck to use his influence is reported to have replied, "I like your son; that boy must not be shot at for three and six pence a day". We have only James's word for that, but it was clear that he agreed with the Duke; he didn't want to be shot at either! What he liked about the Army was the uniform and more particularly the social life of an officer. He was said to enjoy the pleasures of the 'beau monde' and the company of intellectuals. No doubt he would have found the former in the Army, but less likely the latter! He consoled himself by visiting the theatre and enjoying the company of the young ladies who strolled around Covent Garden. One of his pleasures was attending public hangings. (There must have been plenty of these to choose from as, very much later, when Boswell was an advocate, it is reported that one of his clients was hanged for stealing a sheep).

A Spell in Edinburgh

Returning to Edinburgh to continue his legal studies was not quite to Boswell's taste but he made the best of it. He mixed with any willing ladies; with the intelligentsia of the town and numbered David Hume among his friends; with members of the acting profession, including David Ross who opened the first theatre there in December 1767, for the opening programme of which Boswell contributed a prologue; and with army officers including Captain Andrew Erskine, son of the Earl of Kellie, with whom he carried on a long correspondence in prose and verse. Erskine and he edited 'A Collection of Original Verse' to which Boswell contributed 28 poems. It was not a success. He was however pleased to be admitted to the 'Select Society' - which, among other things, was an association for curing gentlemen of the Scotch accent! Boswell could certainly not be described as a modest man, saying of himself that "there is no better fellow alive".

A meeting with Johnson

But always he longed for London and he persuaded his father to let him return there in 1762. He sampled the pleasures of the Town but more importantly, through the good offices of an actor, Tom Davies, who now kept a bookshop, he met Samuel 'Dictionary' Johnson on 16th May, 1763. He stood rather in awe of the great man who had rather an aversion to Scots, and in response to his question, replied "I do indeed come from Scotland, but I cannot help that". Johnson's riposte, "That Sir I find is what a very great many of your countrymen cannot help" was not calculated to restore his confidence. Nevertheless Johnson did take rather a liking to the young man who was so willing to listen to him, and they subsequently had many meetings, suppers, and long conversations together. Johnson, no doubt with an eye on his own immortality, persuaded

Boswell to keep a journal of their discussions, which were perhaps more likely to be in the nature of monologues. Boswell was in fact already taking notes and he amassed a collection of Johnson's sayings. The Sage promised him that he would later accompany him on a trip to the Hebrides.

A European adventure

One man who was not happy about Boswell's sojourn in London was his father Lord Auchinleck who threated to disinherit him. This brought Boswell up with a jerk and he promptly accepted a £200 per year allowance from his father to study study civil law at the University of Utrecht and with many letters of introduction he set off. Johnson bade him farewell at Harwich.

He had intended staying two years in Utrecht but ere long he was in Berlin and writing to his father asking him to support him in a journey to Italy. At first giving a downright refusal, the long-suffering Lord Auchinleck relented. James however had some visiting to do before that. At Motiers, Switzerland, he called on the revolutionary French philosopher Jean-Jacques Rousseau whose writings strongly influenced French revolutionary thought and who introduced the slogan 'Liberté, Equalité, Fraternité'. Boswell was elated and he later wrote down in both English and French, an account of the dialogues that he had with him.

His second trip was to visit the poet and dramatist Voltaire, the embodiment of the 18th century enlightenment, at Ferney, near Geneva. The two had long brilliant animated discussions on religion in which Boswell more than held his own. Boswell was exhilarated.

He was nine months in Italy visiting all the important cities, enjoying the Italian life and the company of the Italian ladies.

When Boswell reached Rome he wrote to Rousseau reminding him that he had promised to give him a letter of introduction to the great General Pasquale Paoli, who was leading the Corsicans in their battle for independence against the Genoese.

Armed with this letter, Boswell crossed to Corsica, made himself known to Paoli, was given a very warm welcome and talked for hours with the great man. He also "played some of our old Scotch airs including 'Corn rigs are bonny' (on a German flute) and sang 'Hearts of Oak' to the Corsicans, with whom he was a great favourite.

In favour of the Corsicans

On reaching Scotland, Boswell was admitted advocate and some work came his way from time to time. But his thoughts were now constantly wandering to Corsica. In 1768 he published an account of his travels there prefaced by a short history of the country, 'The Journal of a Tour to Corsica', and followed this up by editing a volume of 'Essays in favour of the brave Corsicans'. Both were enormously successful.

Dressed in a Corsican costume he called upon William Pitt, Earl of Chatham, (nominally Secretary of State but virtually Prime Minister) and pleaded their cause to such good effect that he later had a three-page letter from Pitt praising his presentation. "I am really the great man now" he said as he enjoyed dinner parties with the famous, drank to excess, gambled and fell into debt. But he was not a great man with Johnson who was cool towards the Corsican cause - probably because he could not discourse on it with the same authority as Boswell. The Doctor was not keen on competition. Nevertheless Boswell continued to push the cause and by August 1768 he had raised £700 by private subscription in Scotland and used it to send guns to Paoli. In vain. The Genoese had sold the island to the French who over-ran the Corsicans; Paoli escaped to England.

A man led by a bear

Boswell, whose appetite for the ladies seemed to be insatiable, plunged into innumerable affairs, before marrying his cousin, Margaret Montgomerie, in Scotland, on 25th November 1769. For three years he stayed there but the pull of London was strong and he made a trip in 1772 principally to meet Johnson and to remind him of his promise to travel with him to the Hebrides. The following year found Boswell in very high spirits. Not only, due to Johnson's influence, had he been elected a member of the prestigious Literary Club in London, but he was now off on a memorable tour with him. His wife and his father however were less than happy about the tour, Margaret remarking that though she had seen "many a bear led by a man, she had never before seen a man led by a bear". His father was equally condemnatory, saying, "He is going over Scotland with a brute - he is clean gyte (mad) for pinning himself to the tail of an auld dominie". Nevertheless off they went.

A Trip to the Hebrides

Johnson made his eight day journey to Edinburgh by post-chaise, a method of transport which he much enjoyed, where he lodged with Boswell, whose wife gallantly gave up her bed for the great man.

On 19 August Johnson aged 64 and Boswell aged 33, set out together on their journey, crossing the Forth at Leith and making their way to St.

Andrews where they supped with the Principal of the University. Johnson almost wept when he saw the ruins of the cathedral and on Boswell wondering where Knox was buried, he replied, "I hope in the highway. I have been looking at his reformations".

They moved up the north-east coast to Aberdeen where Johnson, spreading aphorisms as he went, was introduced to the delights of Scotch broth. He had several platefuls. "You have never eaten it before Sir?" asked Boswell. "No and I don't care how soon I eat it again", replied Johnson. They visited King's and Marischal Colleges with the Principals and professors and Johnson was granted the Freedom of the City "which he received very politely".

Their journey continued round the Moray Firth, breakfasting on haddocks at Cullen and dining in Elgin where they viewed the ruins of the cathedral. At Nairn they walked to view the remains of the residence of the Thane of Cawdor. Boswell was very much at home at Fort George, where they were welcomed by Major Brewse of the Engineers.

At Inverness they changed from post-chaises to horses as the going was rough and they rode along the shores of Loch Ness, through the Great Glen towards Fort Augustus. As they travelled they noticed a little dwelling made of earth which caught their interest. To let in the light there was a hole which could be stopped with a piece of turf and in the middle of the floor was a peat fire with the smoke escaping through a hole in the roof. There was a partition beyond which "we saw a good many kids" and indeed on the fire there was a pot with goat's meat. Mrs. Fraser, who spoke only Gaelic, lived here with her husband, who was eighty years of age, and their five children the eldest of whom was thirteen! She gave them a dram of whisky. They gave her a shilling - though she would have preferred snuff.

They reached Fort Augustus and passed through Glen Shiel where they were surrounded by men women and children, some black and wild in their appearance, all Macraes, who spoke only Gaelic. "'Twas the same as being with a tribe of Indians", said Boswell. He distributed snuff and tobacco to the adults while Johnson lined up the children and gave them a penny each.

They had to have two horses for Johnson "as he was a great weight and the guides agreed that he should ride the horses alternately". They were met by a Captain MacLeod who escorted them over to Skye.

Over the Sea to Skye

During their stay the weather was poor (and remained so during most of their journey). But "we were shown the land of Moidart where Prince Charles first landed. That stirred my soul", and they met a Mrs Mackinnon in whose house the Prince had lodged during his flight. More was to come. Malcolm MacLeod, now 62, had rowed the Prince from the island of Raasay, to Portree in Skye, and now he was taking them to Raasay singing Highland lilts as they went. Johnson's spurs were lost overboard but that was of little moment. "This is now the Atlantic" said Johnson, "If I should tell at a tea-table in London that I have crossed the Atlantic in an open boat, how they'd shudder and what a fool they'd think me to expose myself to such danger".

In Raasay they were warmly welcomed by Raasay himself, by various lairds, and by Sandie MacLeod who was aide-de- camp to the Prince in 1745, and who spent 18 years in exile as a consequence. Malcolm MacLeod kept them enthralled by his memories of the consequences of the Stewart rising. He himself afer the '45 had been imprisoned in London for a number of years and when Flora Macdonald had been asked to choose a companion to accompany her home from London she chose Malcolm, "I went to London to be hanged, and came down in a chaise with Miss Flora Macdonald".

When Boswell and Johnson returned to Skye, after three days on Raasay, they met the redoubtable lady herself. Flora Macdonald was now a Mrs Kingsburgh and she and her husband welcomed the travellers to their home. She told them stories of her adventures with the Prince and that night Johnson had the honour of sleeping in the bed that had once been occupied by the Prince. A visit to Dunvegan Castle to be entertained by Lady MacLeod rounded off their visit to Skye.

A Stormy Passage

They set off for Mull on 3rd. October on a vessel of 12 tons, skippered by Hugh Macdonald who was assisted by a one-eyed mate. The weather was very rough and as they passed the islands of Eigg and Muck, Johnson proceeded to be very sea-sick, followed closely behind by Boswell who was oversure of his sea-legs and had eaten too well. Near Ardnamurchan the storm got worse and the skipper spoke of heading for Coll - "Let's run for it in God's name". One of the sailors held a glowing peat to warn those on the shore that they were near. Its sparks, flying in all directions, threatened to fire the ship, especially as there was gunpowder aboard. The sails were in danger of being torn to pieces and the shouting in Gaelic alarmed Boswell. "A man is always suspicious of what is said in an unknown tongue". He said his prayers in English. Johnson on the other hand, when he had recovered from his seasickness took it all philosophically.

Mull

They decided that it would be safer to make the last leg of their journey to Mull aboard a Campbeltown ship that had called in to take aboard nine tons of kelp. Through storms and high winds they reached the port of Tobermory. Although Johnson enjoyed most of the Highland food that was provided, steadfastly throughout the Scottish tour, much to Boswell's disappointment, he refused to drink whisky. Boswell more than made up for him.

They made a boat-trip to the small island of Icolmkill (Iona), where Columba (Boswell persists in calling him Columbus) had brought Christianity to Scotland, and where many Scottish, Irish, Danish and one king of France are buried. On seeing that their memorials were mere gravestones flat on the earth with no inscriptions, Boswell remarked that he had read of Icolmkill but it did not quite come up to his expectations. Johnson, on the other hand, replied that it came up to his because he had taken his impression from an account in Sacheverell's 'History of the Isle of Man' where it was stated that there is not much to be seen! They drank from St. Columba's well, slept in a barn and viewed the ruins of the Cathedral.

Later Johnson was to write: "The man is little envied, whose patriotism would not gain force upon the plain of Marathon, or whose piety would not grow warmer among the ruins of Iona".

On the Mainland

Leaving Mull they crossed the Firth of Lorne to Oban on the mainland, staying overnight at an inn before riding, on sheltie ponies, south-east through the rain to an inn at Inveraray where a soaked Johnson was persuaded to take a glass of whisky. "Come" he said "let me know what it is that makes a Scotsman happy". They called on the Duke of Argyll who dined them well and gave Johnson a stately steed from his own stables to replace his sheltie. They moved on to Tarbet and rode down Loch Lomondside to stay with Sir James and Lady Colquhoun at their seat, 'Rossdhu'. Here again they were well treated, being furnished with a boat to explore the islands of the loch.

Boswell ordered a post-chaise from Glasgow and it took them, exploring Dumbarton Castle en route, to that city. They stayed at the Saracen's

Head Inn and played host to three professors of the university. Later Johnson expressed the view that he "cared not much of any of them". He toured the sights. "Mr. Anderson (one of the professors with whom he had supped at his home), accompanied us while Dr. Johnson viewed that beautiful city". Johnson told Boswell that when Dr. Adam Smith had boasted of it in London he had replied "Pray, Sir, have you seen Brentford?". They set out into Ayrshire sending a messenger ahead to the Earl of Louden that they would dine with him. On receiving the message it is said that the Earl "jumped for joy". Now they were approaching Auchinleck and Boswell warned Johnson to keep off Whiggism and Presbyterianism as they were very touchy subjects with his father. They spent seven days there, the first two of which went smoothly; then the collision occurred over these very subjects with "things becoming exceedingly warm and violent". This caused Boswell much distress but the next day the two men, if not friends, were talking reasonably together again, though Johnson refused to attend the Parish church with them. Lord Auchinleck named Johnson "Ursa Major".

They arrived back in Edinburgh, after an absence of 83 days, staying at Boswell's house and once more doing a round of dining with the intelligentsia. They visited Edinburgh Castle which Johnson observed "would make a good prison in England". On 22nd November 1773, Boswell, perhaps with a sigh of relief, bade farewell as the Sage journeyed to England. The Tour was over.

The Later Years

Over the next few years Boswell made annual visits to London, mainly to talk with Johnson, but also to enjoy the pleasures of the city. He was in financial difficulties but these were somewhat relieved when his father died on 30th.August 1782 leaving him an estate of £1600 a year. He adopted the country life for a time, settling down to being the Laird of Auchinleck. But always the pull of London was strong.

His last meeting with Johnson took place at a dinner party given by Sir Joshua Reynolds in London. Johnson was in very poor health and he died soon thereafter on 13th December 1784.

In the Spring of 1786, Boswell published an account of their trip, 'Journal of the Tour of the Hebrides'. It was an immediate success and ran to three editions in the first year. He was also preparing his 'Life of Johnson'.

His wife's health was giving cause for concern and she died of tuberculosis in 1789 leaving him with five children, the eldest being 16. He arranged schooling and boarding for them. He had almost completed his 'Life of Johnson', but only by borrowing money did he retain the copyright. It appeared in two volumes costing two guineas, on 16th May 1791 and was to become the most famous biography in the English language. Probably as a result of the quality of this book, he was elected to the prestigious position of Secretary of Foreign Correspondence at the British Academy. He was however drinking heavily, his health was deteriorating, and he died at his home in Great Portland St., aged 54, on 19th May 1795 and was buried, according to his wish, at Auchinleck.

REFERENCES AND FURTHER READING

'The Life of James Boswell' 2 vols. Percy Fitzgerald. Chatto and Windus, 1891.
'James Boswell' C.E. Vulliamy. Geoffrey Bles, 1932.
'Boswell's Journal of a Tour to the Hebrides with Samuel Johnson LL.D. 1773' Frederick. A. Pottle and Charles H. Bennet. William Heinemann Ltd. 1963.
'Boswell the Biographer' George Mallory. Smith, Elder and Co. 1912.
'James Boswell' Philip Collins. Longman Green, 1956.
'Boswell's London Journal 1762 - 1763'. Frederick A. Pottle. William Heinemann Ltd. 1950.
'Pride and Negligence - the History of the Boswell Papers' Frederick A. Pottle. McGraw Hill, 1982.
'The Moth and the Candle - a Life of James Boswell' Iain Finlayson. Contable, 1984.
'Boswell: The Great Biographer 1789 - 1795'. ed Marlies K. Danziger and Frank Brady. McGraw Hill, 1989.
'New Light on Boswell' ed. Greg Clingham. Cambridge University Press, 1991.
'James Boswell (1740 - 1795) - The Scottish Perspective' Roger Craik. H.M.S.O. 1994.

PLACES TO VISIT

Scotland
Boswell Museum - Barony Church, Auchinleck, Ayrshire.

JOHN PAUL JONES (1747-1792)

Founder of the American Navy

"I have not yet begun to fight"

When John Paul was a boy there was nothing that he liked better than sailing on the Solway Firth near to the little village of Arbigland in Kirkcudbrightshire, where he was born. His father was partly farmer, partly gardener to the local squire, and partly fisherman.

A life on the ocean wave

When he was only 12 years of age John was offered the chance of becoming an apprentice on a ship that was making a voyage from nearby Whitehaven to Virginia, the West Indies, and home again. He persuaded his father to let him accept and a few days later he was westward bound.

Thus began the seafaring career of the man whom some would liken to Nelson and who was to found the American Navy. He was a natural seaman. Voyage followed voyage and on one of these both the Master of the ship and the Mate died of fever. John Paul took over command and brought her safely home. The owners were so delighted that they made him Master. At the age of 21 he was on the way to becoming a very wealthy young man, some of the wealth accruing from the slave trade. But all was not plain sailing. On one of his voyages he had his carpenter flogged. The man died later and when John Paul arrived back in Kirkcudbright he was clapped in jail and charged with murder. He was cleared, but the stigma hung over him. On occasions he faced mutiny and in Tobago he ran his sword through the leader of the mutineers. Fearing that he would face a second charge of murder he changed his name and 'disappeared'. In effect he inherited his brother's estate in Virginia and John Paul Jones settled down to the life of an affluent tobacco planter.

A request from Washington

The sea however was still in his blood and on the outbreak of the American War of Independence (1775 - 1783) he was in no doubt as to where his loyalties lay. He was American and by now had added Jones to his name. He was invited to draw up plans for what was in effect the

John Paul Jones, founder of the American Navy

U.S. Naval Academy today

The Academy's memorial to Jones

McAdam's house at Sauchrie

The Memorial to the
roadbuilder at Ayr

The char-a-banc was a popular form of
transport

McAdam gravestone at Moffat

Thomas Telford (inset) and the Caledonian Canal, linking the North Sea with the Atlantic Ocean, which was one of his biggest projects in Scotland

The cottage at Alloway, Ayrshire, where Robert Burns was born. Painted in 1876 by Samuel Bough

Tarbolton where Burns was inducted as a freemason in July, 1781

Dumfries the town where the Bard spent his final days

Burns from a portrait by Alexander Nasmyth

Henry Bell's Comet launched in 1812

Wheel from the 'Comet' at Helensburgh Public Park

Bell's Anvil

William Symington

A painting by John Knox which commemorates the maiden voyage of Henry Bell's Comet in 1812.

Charles McIntosh, top, and the famous coat he invented

The author and a friend, the late Murdoch MacPherson who was a BBC producer, at Park's house during preparation of a programme

The Yarrow at Fouldshields, a popular spot for Park

Mungo Park

Sir Walter Scott and family at Abbotsford from a painting by Sir David Wilkie

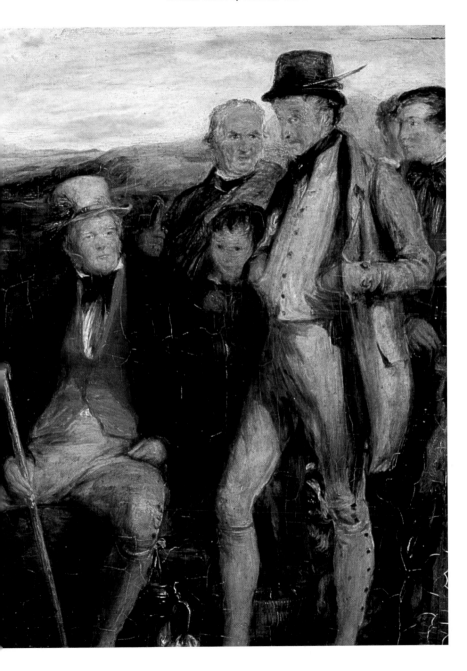

Portrait of Sir Walter, one of the most prolific writers Scotland has produced

The magnificent Abbotsford

*Scott Monument in Princes
Street Gardens, Edinburgh*

Interior of Abbotsford

*Statue in George Square,
Glasgow*

Oil pioneer James Young

Drygate, Glasgow, where he was born

The Addiewell works at West Calder

Mining the raw materials

Brickworks at Pumpherston

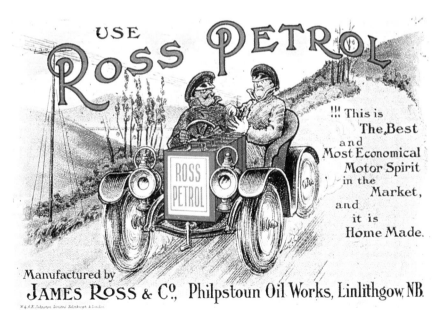

An early advertisement for Ross Petrol

founding of the American Navy. He was asked to advise on the proper qualifications of naval officers and "the kind or kinds of armed vessels most desirable for the service of the United Colonies keeping in view the limited resources of the Congress".

His recommendations were read by George Washington, the American Commander-in-Chief, who immediately accepted saying: "Mr. Jones is clearly not only a master mariner but he also holds a strong and profound sense of the political and military weight of command at sea". New ships were ordered according to his specifications.

To France

Yet strangely, when appointments were being made to the new navy Jones was given the rank of lieutenant (though he did lose seniority by refusing the first two commands that he was offered). But he took it all in his stride and a year later he was a Captain, carrying the war into British waters. Taking command of 'Ranger', a sloop of war being fitted at Portsmouth, New Hampshire, he put up recruiting posters " One of the best Cruizers (sic) in America" and asking for "Gentlemen volunteers who have a Mind to take an agreeable Voyage in the pleasant Season of the year". It also stated that "they would make their fortunes". Gentlemen volunteers were, however, in for a few unpleasant surprises! The 'Ranger' sailed for France where after a short love affair with the wife of a wealthy merchant in Paris, Jones returned aboard to face rather a rebellious crew. The prize money which was supposed to come from capturing other ships, had not yet materialized and Jones had news for them which was not very popular. Interpreting rather widely his remit to "proceed in the manner you shall best judge for distressing the Enemies of the United States by sea or otherwise" he proposed a shore raid.

The Solway Firth

The target was Whitehaven on the Solway Firth, the port from which he had sailed as a boy those many years ago. A shore raid was dangerous and not likely to yield much booty. Many of the sailors pleaded fatigue, but Jones assembled 40 'volunteers', went ashore, scaled the walls of the harbour, set fire to a little colliery ship, and retreated back to his ship in the face of opposition from the townsfolk.

Now he sailed across the Firth where he had cruised as a boy. He planned to capture the Earl of Selkirk on St. Mary's Isle and hold him to ransom. Unfortunately when the raiding party went ashore under the command of a Lieutenant Wallingford, the Earl wasn't at home so instead the Lieutenant took the family silver. Some of the local people fired cannons at them and it is reported that the Countess complained to a Mr. Craik that "your late gardener's son, born in your grounds, has returned as a buccaneer and that the great villain has taken the family silver."

Jones was rather ashamed of this action and later sent the silver back to its rightful owners.

He was promoted Commodore, Commander-in-Chief of the American Squadron in Europe, and 'dressed in his American Uniform with a Scotch bonnet edged with gold' he took his ship back to Brest, handed 'Ranger' over, and waited for a new command.

In the waters of Leith

To his disappointment he got an elderly East Indiaman, 'Le Duc de Duras', 146 ft. in length and carrying 40 guns. He re-equipped her with more effective guns and renamed her 'Le Bonhomme Richard'. Enlisting several seamen released by the British in exchange for their own, he set sail with his squadron for Scotland, which always seemed to attract him like a magnet. His destination this time was the Firth of Forth and his target Leith, the port of Edinburgh, planning to hold it to ransom for £200,000. He threw the good folks on shore into considerable panic and confusion as they speculated as to where he would land.

In the event he didn't land anywhere. The Reverend Mr. Shirra moved to the water's edge and implored the Lord "to blow the scoundrel out of our gate". Whether because of Mr. Shirra or not, a severe storm blew up and Jones, losing one or two of his ships, was forced to withdraw from the Firth into the open sea. Mr. Shirra, and the Lord, got the credit!

The battle of Flamborough Head

Now Commodore Jones was to face the biggest battle of his career. A British supply convoy appeared near Flamborough Head off the Yorkshire coast, escorted by two warships, the 'Countess of Scarborough' and the newly-commissioned 'Serapis'. The latter took up a defensive position to allow the supply ships to escape. Jones gave the order to attack, but the other ships of his convoy drifted away. It was a head-on battle between 'Serapis' and 'Le Bonhomme Richard' which was watched by crowds of onlookers gathered on the shore as the guns on each side roared and flashed. Two of Jones's 18 pounders blew up, killing their crews.

As the two ships approached each other they were linked together by grappling irons. Great holes were blown in 'Richard's' side and the situation wasn't helped by one of Jones's support ships appearing and by mistake raking 'Richard' with broadfire. All seemed lost, and it was at this point that the captain of the 'Serapis', Richard Pearson, demanded Jones's surrender and got the famous reply "I have not yet begun to fight." Things were, however, pretty desperate for Jones when the day was saved by one of his seamen clambering aboard the British ship and lobbing a couple of grenades down an open hatchway and thus blowing up a keg of gunpowder.

Twenty British sailors were killed in the explosion. This was more than enough. Pearson stepped on to 'Richard's' deck and offered Jones his sword as a token of surrender.

Jones accepted the surrender, but not the sword and took Pearson to his cabin for a 'quick one'. It must have been a very quick one for 'Richard' was sinking. The two captains moved to 'Serapis' as 'Richard' disappeared below the waves. The 'Serapis' headed for Holland where Jones was given a hero's welcome. He had become a legend in his lifetime and when he visited Paris he was feted by the French who poured honours on him. He said that his six weeks stay there was the happiest period of his life.

Kontra Admiral Jones

His return to America was equally triumphant and there was talk that he would be promoted to the rank of Rear Admiral. But he had enemies among the politicians and there were many jealous captains who were senior to him; his appointment was blocked.

With the war over Jones sailed for Paris in 1783 to meet again many of his old friends and for five years he enjoyed life there. But still he hankered for active service at sea and he returned to New York to again take up the question of his promotion. But again he was unsuccessful; instead Congress voted him a gold medal. Then very interesting news was brought to him by the President of the United States. The Russian Ambassador wanted to know if Jones would be interested in a commission in the Imperial Russian Navy. Kontra Admiral Pavel Ivanovich Jones, as he came to be known, was very interested.

Catherine II, Empress of Russia, wanted to take complete control of the Black Sea and to annex Constantinople. She thought that Jones was the man to do both for her and while welcoming him with open arms she promoted him Rear Admiral of the Black Sea Fleet. He was now a Rear Admiral, not of the American, but of the Russian Navy. But there were already three Rear Admirals in the Black Sea Fleet. Jones mistakenly thought that he was the senior and that meant trouble. The three admirals did not take kindly to a fourth, particularly as the fourth was a foreigner. Jones in fact commanded only a squadron consisting of his flagship, eight frigates, and four other armed vessels. As might be expected there was complete confusion, although the Turkish fleet was scattered by the Russians, largely it is said on Jones's advice and tactics.

Paris

Jones, however, got little credit for it and when the decorations and awards were handed out few came his way. In 1789 he left Russia a deeply disappointed man. He never commanded a ship again though he was just 42 years of age. He thought of returning to America, but he never saw it again. Instead, after touring Europe in failing health, he returned to Paris in 1790 and died, aged 45, on 18th July, 1792. He was buried in the Protestant cemetery there.

A last trip to America

More than 100 years later, in 1906, President Theodore Roosevelt of the United States sent four cruisers of the Fleet, which were joined at sea by several battleships, to bring his body home. It was eventually, in 1913, after a temporary resting place of some seven years, buried in a marble sarcophagus modelled on the tomb of Napoleon, in the chapel of the Naval Academy, Annapolis, Maryland.

At last John Paul Jones had got the recognition that he craved.

REFERENCES AND FURTHER READING

'Paul Jones - Founder of the American Navy'. Augustus. C. Buell. 2 vls. Charles Scribners, 1902.

'John Paul Jones'. Samuel Eliot Morrison. Little, Brown and Co. 1959.

'John Paul Jones Bicentennial Salute'. James Urquart. Sangspiel Publishers, 1976.

PLACES TO VISIT

Paul Jones Cottage, Arbigland Estate, Solway Firth. Now a museum with its interior more or less as it was in the early 18th century. Open April till October.

Bust in *Kirkcudbright museum*.

U.S.A.

Magnificent Marble Tomb in the crypt of *U.S. Naval Academy*, Annapolis, Maryland

Bronze statue in *Potomac Park*, Washington, D.C.

Miniature portrait painted in 1780. In National Portrait Gallery, *Smithsonian Institute*, Washington, D.C.

JOHN LOUDON McADAM (1756-1836)

Roadmaker

"McADAM, hail!
Hail Roadian! hail Colossus! who dost stand
Striding ten thousand turnpikes on the land!
O universal Leveller! all hail.
(From 'Odes and Addresses to Great People'
(Thomas Hood, 1825)

The Romans had taught the Britons how to make roads; every Roman legionary was trained in the art and carried the necessary tools around with him on his marches. But that knowledge had vanished in the dark ages; and so it was for many centuries.

Roy Devereux (see further reading) tells us that in the Middle Ages when a herald announced the approach of uninvited guests the host called upon his tenants and villeins to throw fresh stone and gravel over the track. The roads of Britain were in a deplorable condition and remained that way until well into the 18th century. Many of the centres of communication were little more than dirt-tracks, and villages were completely isolated, when in winter the tracks were reduced to bogs and swamps. Even in the cities all was far from well. When Edward 111 rode to Parliament the holes in Westminster had to be filled with branches to allow the coach to pass over. The rich rode on horseback with their wives perched behind them. Normally Queen Elizabeth rode pillion behind the saddle of her Lord Chancellor. The poor walked. If any unfortunate being wandered out of London, or indeed out of any major city, in winter, he was liable to sink up to his thighs in mud.

The McAdams

The McAdams were a fairly wealthy family bearing the title Barons of Waterhead. This title was not a peerage but was given to landowners who held their lands under the Crown and until 1587 it carried with it the obligation to sit in parliament. After this date the barons were excused attendance and were permitted to elect representatives to sit in their place.

John Loudon McAdam was born in the town of Ayr on 21st September, 1756. His father, also John, Baron Waterhead, had married Susannah Cochran, a niece of Archibald Cochran, the 7th Earl of Dundonald. Cochran was eccentric but a brilliant inventor. Among many other achievments he was the first to distil tar from coal which was widely used, especially in the Navy, in which he was an Admiral, for the preservation of wood. McAdam was involved in the tar-making enterprise but never used it in his roadmaking. That was to come about, as we shall see, long after his death. The Earl was given the soubriquet 'Daft Dundonald' not because there was anything wrong with his wits, but because he had no head for business. He finished up bankrupt.

John McAdam senior was involved in the Bank of Ayr, and when it collapsed he felt its effects, losing much money and his estates, although not becoming bankrupt. He died soon afterwards in 1770 leaving about £7000 plus a widow and ten children of whom John was the youngest.

Off to New York

Due to the relatively impoverished state of the family John was sent that same year, at the age of 14, to New York where his father's brother had a prosperous mercantile business. Uncle William welcomed the boy who moved into his 'counting house'. And very successfully too. Ere long, John was on his way to becoming a very rich young man as 'agent for the sale of naval prizes'. His uncle founded the New York Chamber of Commerce, becoming its first President in 1772. John, at the age of 18, became its Treasurer two years later. In 1778, at the age of 22, he married Gloriana Nicoll 'a young lady of great Beauty and Merit with a large fortune, the great-great granddaughter of Matthias Nicoll who was appointed by the Earl of Clarendon as secretary and legal adviser to the expedition sent by Charles 11 to claim the territory of New Netherlands on behalf of his brother, Duke of York' (after whom it was named). Later the Duke succeeded to the throne as James 11. Gloriana's credentials were good! John's star was in the ascendancy.

But difficult times, which had been simmering even before John went to New York, were developing fast. The American Revolution (1765 - 1788), sparked by the issue of whether the British Parliament had the right to tax the colonists without representation, was gaining momentum and the American War of Independence (1775 - 1783) the very source of Uncle William's and John's wealth, held within it the seeds of their financial destruction. They were on the wrong side! John served for a period in the loyalist forces but was released from service on his appointment as Commissioner for Naval Prizes - another source of wealth.

In 1779, before the war was over, Uncle William died leaving his very considerable fortune to his nephew John. Unfortunately he had only one witness to his will and it was contested by his widow (from whom he was estranged). A previous will was upheld and Uncle Willam's widow inherited the lot. She promised to leave everything to John on her death. In the event she didn't, leaving it instead to her family.

Back to Scotland

By 1783 things were getting rather hot for John and his wife (whose family also supported the Crown) in America, and together they sailed for Scotland to live in 'Sauchrie' between Maybole and Ayr. His connections were good, he was appointed Deputy-Lieutenant of the County, and when the French threatened invasion he raised a corps of volunteers. It was during this period that, realizing the importance of communications and the need to move his troops quickly from place to place, he became very concerned about the condition of the roads - in his area they were in a deplorable condition and little more than muddy tracks through bogs and marshes.

He began the series of experiments that were to make him world famous. It was on the road leading to Sauchrie that he carried out his first trials.

Off to Bristol

McAdam spent 15 years in Ayrshire, before selling Sauchrie estate for £8,500 and moving with his family to Bristol where he was appointed Government agent for the victualling of the Royal Navy on the western coast of England. He also carried on the same kind of mercantile trade as he had in New York. Although his government service lasted only three years they were apparently very lucrative ones and he decided to stay on in Bristol where he had many influential friends.

Roads

It was now 1801, McAdam was 45 years of age, and he resumed his hobby of roadmaking, travelling some 30,000 miles (48,300 km.) throughout the country at his own expense making road inspection what he called 'a kind of business' enquiring about costs and methods of construction.

As in Ayrshire, he found that throughout the country the roads were in a deplorable condition 'loose, rough, and perishable, expensive, dangerous to travel on, and very costly to repair'. The Turnpike Act by which users had to pay for their upkeep was passed during the reign of Charles 11 (1630 - 1685) but was not brought into operation until 1767. Then turnpikes started sprouting up all over the country - gates, tollbars, toll houses, began to impede the traveller who was constantly having to pay out money to Trusts composed mainly of local dignitaries, who were then supposedly responsible for upkeep of the roads, but who in reality, spent very little money on them.

Roy Devereux, McAdam's biographer, tells us that for example on the 34 miles of road between Glasgow and Ayr, there were 10 turnpike gates which occasioned such delay and expense that the Postmaster General decided to discontinue running the coach carrying the mails for Ireland.

Despite the immense amount of money that was being taken in, the condition of the roads grew steadily worse. There were two reasons for this. The turnpike trustees were under no obligation to account for the money that they collected; and the money that they did expend on the roads was thrown away due to inefficiency, waste, and useless methods.

Bristol was a very important port and trading centre. It was essential that the 180 miles of roads radiating out and in, should be of good quality; but they weren't. In 1816 McAdam was invited by the Bristol Trustees to take charge of their roads as General Surveyor at a salary of £400 per annum. Immediately, with ten sub-surveyors at his command, he put his ideas into action improving the roads out of all recognition.

Advising Parliament

Later, in 1819 McAdam gave evidence to a Parliamentary Select Committee on Roads and laid before them his method of roadmaking which he recommended should be adopted throughout the country.

Roads, he said, should be composed entirely of a 10 inch (25.4 cm.) layer of stones none of which is more than 6 ounces (170 gm.)in weight. Under pressure of the traffic, the sharp angles of the stones unite into a compact mass which becomes entirely impervious to water. A road should be laid as flat as possible with just enough rise in the centre to allow the rain to run off it into ditches at each side. He advocated a three-inch (7.6 cm.) rise on a road eighteen feet (7.4 metres) wide. He did not believe that the weight of the vehicle mattered one whit - indeed the heavier the vehicle the better it would compact the stones and the more solid the road would be.

The size of the stones, preferably of granite, was critical for good compacting and prevention of moisture seepage, so he issued a two-inch

(5.1cm.) ring for measuring the stones and six-ounce (170 gm.)scales for weighing them. Before these implements were available however he gave instructions that the workmen should use their own mouths as guides. If a stone would not go into the mouth then it was too large for use. It is said that one day noticing that, despite his careful instructions, large stones were being used on a stretch of road, he remonstrated with the gaffer and accused him of laying the stones without testing them. Angrily the gaffer denied the charge and opened his very large mouth with no teeth in it!

McAdam absolutely forbade the use of earth, clay, or chalk, materials that had extensively been used before in road construction, because they would absorb water and be affected by frost.

"Nothing is to be laid on the clean stone on pretence of binding. Broken stone (of the correct size) will combine by its own angles into a smooth solid surface that cannot be affected by vicissitudes of weather or displaced by action of wheels which will pass over it without a jolt and consequently without injury". He objected strongly to a paved foundation or large stones as 'bottoming' such as was advocated by his arch rival and fellow-Scot, Thomas Telford. And this was true even when laying a road across a bog.

He recommended that the administration of road-funds should be put in the hands of trustworthy Commissioners who should employ trained surveyors instead of casual labourers

This latter advice was to little avail as too many vested interests were involved. But one very important recommendation was adopted - the appointment of surveyors to the Trusts.

Dynasty

The news of the great success that McAdam was having with the Bristol roads soon spread throughout the country and there were constant calls for his advice and help. He was lavish with both but he never asked for, nor received, any payment. He was now in his 60s, a national figure, and overwhelmed with work. But help was at hand.

William, his eldest son, left his post as manager of the British Tar Company and he brought his own son William with him to the West country. James, another son, who had been engaged in mercantile business, left it to become Surveyor General for 30 trusts. He was appointed Surveyor General for British roads in 1837 and was knighted (an honour which his father refused on account of old age and infirmity). A third son, also John, followed his brothers to England and became surveyor to 18 trusts covering 405 miles (651 km.)in counties as far apart as Somerset and

Yorkshire. W.J. Reader (see further reading) reports that between 1816, when John McAdam took up his appointment at Bristol and 1861 when William junior died, eleven McAdam kinsmen in three generations are known to have been surveyors of turnpike roads.

This raised considerable acrimony in road-surveying circles but the McAdams survived. Between them they transformed the road network of Britain. Without such a system the Industrial Revolution and the wealth that flowed from it would not have been possible. Their work ushered in the stagecoach and the mailcoach and the inns which sprang up all over the country. And they laid the way for the coming of the motor car.

In his old age McAdam petitioned the Government for financial recognition of his work. After much debate he was awarded £2000.

Return to Scotland

His wife died in 1825 and he resigned his post in Bristol soon afterwards. He settled in Hertfordshire, and in his 70th year married again, entered into the social life of London, and continued to make yearly trips to Scotland to visit the scenes of his boyhood. He travelled in a closed carriage drawn by two favourite horses. Behind the carriage trotted a pony, bridled and saddled, ready to carry him off into the byways to view a glen, a loch, a mountain. At the heels of the pony there was a Newfoundland dog whose duty it was to see that the pony did not lag behind.

McAdam lived to an active old age despite having suffered for much of his life from the 'spitting of blood'. He died, in November 1836, in his 81st year, returning south from such a visit. He was buried according to his wish to sleep amidst the mountains of Moffat beside his beloved grandmother, Lady Waterhead.

Tar Macadam

And so his name passed into the English language - an honour given to few. He was not however the inventor of the tar process that came to be known as 'tarmacadam' or 'tarmac'. Binding the stones with tar, although it was used in towns as early as 1832, really came into its own in 1901 when the County Surveyor of Nottinghamshire, E.P. Hooley, noticed that a barrel of tar that had burst and run over a road produced a dust-free, hard-wearing surface. He formed a company 'Tar Macadam' that was later abbreviated to 'Tarmac'. Soon every road in this country (and in many other countries) was transformed.

REFERENCES AND FURTHER READING

'Death of John Loudon McAdam'.' Ayr Advertiser' 8.12. 1836.
'John Loudon McAdam'. R. Devereaux. Oxford University Press, 1936.
'McAdam'. W.J Reader. Heinemann, 1980.
' John Loudon McAdam, Colossus of Roads'. Robert. H. Spiro Jnr. Ph.D. Thesis, University of Edinburgh, 1950.
'John Loudon McAdam' Dictionary of National Biography XXX1V, p 392 - 396.
'John Loudon McAdam - Centenary Celebrations' organized by the Institute of Municipal and County Engineers. Journal Institute of Municipal and County Engineers, Vol. LX111, No. 10, Nov. 19th., 1936.

PLACES TO VISIT

Scotland

McAdam's house 'Sauchrie' to which he moved from New York in 1783 is still there (and occupied) as is the road leading to it on which, it is said, he carried out his first experiments. There is a memorial bust to McAdam in Ayr Public Park.

THOMAS TELFORD (1757 - 1834)

Civil Engineer

'The Colossus of Roads' and 'Pontifex Maximus'
(Robert Southey Poet Laureate).

Early Days

Thomas Telford was born in a mud-walled, thatch-roofed shieling a few miles north of Langholm, Dumfriesshire, on 9th August 1757. He was an only child, his father, John, a shepherd, dying aged only 33, a few months after the boy's birth. Since it was a 'tied' cottage, mother and son had to move out into the single room of a two-roomed cottage nearby. Janet Telford was of hardy stock - she had to be - and she maintained them by milking, sheep-shearing and haymaking at adjacent farms. Soon Thomas was joining her in the fields.

Due to a little financial help from a relative, Thomas attended the local school until he was 14, when he was apprenticed to a stone-mason in Langholm, where he learned to carve gravestones, including one for his father's grave. He was a voracious reader, particularly of poetry (a habit that stayed with him all his life), his favourite writers being Burns and Milton.

London

A short stay in Edinburgh whetted his appetite for architecture and when, at the age of 24, he heard that a neighbouring landowner was sending a horse to London, he volunteered to ride it there. He was armed with a letter of introduction from an old friend, Miss Pasley of Langholm, to her brother John, an influential London merchant, who in turn introduced the young man to the two top architects of the time, Robert Adam and Sir William Chambers. Of the two, Thomas confessed that he preferred his countryman Adam; but it was Chambers who employed him as a mason.

However it was not Chambers who was destined to be his patron. That role was to be filled by Sir William Pultney, to whom he was introduced through the good offices of Sir James Johnstone whose horse he had ridden to London. Johnstone and Pultney were brothers, the latter having adopted his wife's name on marriage, through which he became a very wealthy landowner owning great estates throughout England. He took an immediate liking to the young fellow-Scot and was probably influential in Telford being asked to supervise the erection of a number of buildings at Portsmouth dockyards, including a very prestigious house for the Superintendent.

Shrewsbury

Pultney invited Telford to restore his home - Shrewsbury Castle. In itself it was not a big commission, but it led to Telford's appointment at the age of 30, as Surveyor of Public Works for the County of Salop responsible for the maintenance of roads and public buildings. Pultney's hand was probably behind it but it should not be assumed that this was blind patronage; Telford was on his way up; he was a very hard worker, rising at 5 am., studying and working through till 9pm when he had supper, with a short break to read and sometimes write poetry, then it was off to bed. He was also generous. Some of the money that he was earning was sent back home to be divided between his mother and Andrew Little, a friend of his youth who had trained as a surgeon but had been blinded by lightning during a visit to the West Indies.

During this period Telford constructed a new infirmary , a county gaol at Shrewsbury, a new church at Bridgnorth and, most importantly, a bridge over the Severn. The direction of his future career was taking shape, his reputation was growing, and he was creating a team of very talented men around him, led by Matthew Davison from Langholm. Between the years 1790-1796 he built 40 road bridges, in the construction of one of which he used iron.

The Ellesmere Canal

Then in the midst of this, in September 1793, came the first of his really big commissions. He was asked to become 'general agent, engineer and architect', at £300 per year, to the Ellesmere Canal Company, which had been formed to link the great trade-river, the Mersey, with the Dee at Chester and with the Severn at Shrewsbury. It was an enormous project that was to test his powers of engineering and his ingenuity to their limits; but it was also to be one of his great triumphs.

The whole story is told in many books, but it may suffice for our purpose to pick out one aspect - the bridging of the Vale of Llangollen at Pont Cysyllte by an aqueduct which carried the canal in an 11 ft. 10in. wide cast-iron trough supported by stone piers with 17 spans, over a length of 1000 ft. at a height of 127 ft. It has been described as "one of the greatest engineering achievments of all time". The opening ceremony took place on 26th November 1805; great crowds cheered and the Royal Artillery Company fired a 15 gun salute as six boats proceeded along the 'canal in the sky'. With this triumph, after 12 years, Telford resigned his post with the Ellesmere Company (though they retained him as a consultant) and handed over the remaining task of completing the canal to two of his assistants. He was ready to move on.

Scotland

When Bonnie Prince Charlie's army was defeated at Culloden in 1746, Cumberland exacted a terrible price, slaughtering men women and children indiscriminately, burning the houses, and destroying the clan system. The Highlands were left in complete disarray and although land was restored to some of the Clan chiefs in 1787, there was little improvement for they initiated the infamous 'Clearances', turning their own people off the land and replacing them with sheep. There was mass emigration and even the Government in London became concerned. The Highlands were becoming a wilderness. In 1788 Pultney with the Duke of Argyll and others formed the British Fisheries Society and built a series of small ports in an attempt to stimulate the Highland fishing industry. But they soon realized that this was useless as there were no roads and bridges over which the catch could be transported. The only roads indeed were the military ones, connecting the great forts, that had been built by General Wade when he was sent north to attempt to subdue the Highlanders in 1726. They were of little use for trade purposes.

The Industrial Revolution was being ushered in and with it rising living standards. These did not affect the Highlands directly, but they did indirectly, as with greater affluence in Lowland Scotland there was an increased demand for beef. The source of this was the Highland glens, from where the only way to supply it was 'on the hoof'. From time immemorial the Highlanders had brought their cattle to southern market towns such as Crieff, Falkirk and Lanark, along the 'drove roads', surviving on blood, drawn from the cattle, mixed with oat meal and whisky. When they came to a river they swam across with their animals.

A Government Commission

In 1801 the Government asked Telford, who was engineer to the British

Fisheries Society, to carry out a survey of Highland communications. In little over a month, perhaps to the Government's surprise, he had completed the job, going through the Western and Central Highlands to Cape Wrath and returning via John o' Groats down the east coast to Edinburgh.

Sheep, he found, were destroying the Highlands. Economically they were a financial success for the owners, but they were not creating jobs, and as long as sheep-rearing was the only industry then mass emigration would continue. The alternative was to create a better way of life through fishing and agriculture.

So well was his report received that he was asked to continue his survey in 1802. He found that 3000 Highlanders had left in 1801 and that 9000 were expected to leave in 1802. He emphasised that life could only be restored to the dying Highlands by improving the lines of communication - new roads, new bridges, new harbours, and a canal through the Great Glen to unite the east and west fishing grounds. These were massive, revolutionary and expensive proposals, but the Government acted promptly, setting up two Commissions, one for Highland Roads and Bridges, and the other for the Caledonian Canal through the Great Glen. The costs were to be shared between Government, local authorities, and landowners. Thomas Telford was appointed Engineer to both Commissions.

Transforming the Highlands

Over the next 18 years he was responsible for planning, designing, and building 929 miles of new roads and re-furbishing 280 miles of military roads. He concentrated mainly on communications to the north-west coast and the Islands, the major ones being from Fort William to Arisaig, from Loch Oich in the Great Glen to Glen Garry, from Dingwall to Loch Torridon, with a branch that ran across Sutherland to Tongue on the north coast; another branch ran along the Dornoch Firth to Wick and Thurso.

He created 1,200 new bridges in the Highlands, including the major ones crossing the Tay at Dunkeld, thus opening up the Central Highlands, the Dee, the Spey, and the Dornoch Firth. Harbours also came within his remit; he designed and improved those at Aberdeen, Banff, Cullen, Dundee, Fraserburgh, Kirkwall, Peterhead, and elsewhere. And the Highlanders' spiritual needs were not neglected - for good measure he constructed 42 churches, many of them in the Western Isles.

Telford made many tours of his 'Highland parish' including one with his friend Robert Southey, the Poet Laureate, who named him 'The Colossus of Roads' and 'Pontifex Maximus'.

Thomas Telford, perhaps more than any other man, changed the face and fortune of the Highlands of Scotland. Not only did he link them with the South and rescue them from isolation, but he also provided work for thousands, training the people in new skills, giving them a pride in that work and in their country. He effected a social revolution.

The Caledonian Canal

Telford now turned to the the biggest project that he undertook in Scotland - a canal through the Great Glen that would link the North Sea with the Atlantic Ocean. The Glen was threaded with lochs - Loch Eil, Loch Lochy, Loch Oich, Loch Ness - stretching from Fort William in the west to Inverness in the east - and he proposed to link them together by 22 miles of water to form the 60 miles long Caledonian Canal. It was a massive undertaking for the terrain was difficult. Construction began in the summer of 1804 and Telford again employed, as supervisors, the team that had been so successful at the Ellesmere project ; they in turn, recruited a massive labour force of 3,200 men. The building of the 28 locks, so as to reach the highest point on the canal, 100 ft. above high water mark, was in itself a heroic task involving excavations out of solid rock, scooping out the bases using steam bucket dredgers , draining on a huge scale involving Boulton and Watt engines, the quarrying and transport of granite and limestone and the erection of ironwork structures. Between Loch Eil, the southernmost point of the canal, and the loch next to it, Loch Lochy, the distance was only eight miles but the difference between their levels was 90 ft. They had to be connected by a series of eight gigantic locks to which Telford gave the name 'Neptune's Staircase'.

On 23rd October 1822, eighteen years after contruction had begun, the first boat passed through the canal from the North Sea to the Atlantic. The total cost of the canal was close to £1 million.

It was a magnificent achievement, but was it worth it? For various reasons, including the development of steam-power for ships, and the coming of the railways, the Canal never realized its potential; perhaps it was over-emphasised anyhow.

Lowlands

Telford's work, however, was not confined to the Highlands. In the Lowlands of Scotland he constructed 184 miles of roads including a major one from Glasgow to Carlisle with bridges at Hamilton and elsewhere en route. A road that he built through Lanarkshire connected Falkirk with the other great cattle markets of Crieff and Doune and with Carlisle in the north of England.

The Gotha Canal

Telford's fame was spreading. Four years after the Caledonian Canal project got under way, he received a letter from King Gustav Adolf IV of Sweden inviting him to take part in the planning and construction of a ship canal to link the North Sea with the Baltic. With the invitation there was also an enclosure from Count von Platen, who was the driving force behind the project and who had been working on part of it for four years, saying that he would welcome the opportunity to co-operate with so distinguished a man. Telford accepted and went across to Sweden for six weeks during which he drew up plans for the canal, including the locks; he and von Platen became good friends and colleagues.

The project in some ways resembled that of the Caledonian Canal in that its route lay along a string of lakes including the two major ones of Vanern and Vattern, but the Gotha Canal was much longer. Including an existing 52 miles already cut, 133 miles of lakes, and 53 miles of canal to cut, it made a grand total of 238 miles from sea to sea.

After his plans were accepted by the Swedish Parliament, Telford was surprised and delighted to be informed that the King of Sweden had created him a Knight of the Royal Order of Vasa.

The Holyhead Road

Ireland was still part of the British Isles and there was much coming and going between the two capitals. The road system from London to Holyhead was deplorable, a new one was needed, and a Commission set up by Parliament asked Telford to provide it.

This he did, taking his road through the mountainous regions of North Wales, despite the fact that there were some formidable obstacles in the way. One of these was at Betws-y-Coed where the road encountered the river Conway. Here Telford erected a single-span iron bridge, which has inscribed on the girders "This arch was constructed in the same year as the battle of Waterloo was fought". The span is decorated with cast emblems of the four nations - the leek, the shamrock, the rose and the thistle. Another, and even greater obstacle, was the Menai Straits, which he overcame by means of a suspension bridge - said to be one of his greatest engineering achievments. It was 15 years (January 1826) before the

Holyhead road was completed, but it was a magnificent job. Telford was now 70.

Other Works

He still had much work in him, including bridges at Tewkesbury and at Gloucester, the St. Katherine's Docks at London, the Dean Bridge at Leith, Edinburgh, the draining of the Fen country, and a bridge over the river Clyde, Glasgow.

As he became more successful Telford developed into a very sociable man. He did not marry and there is no mention of any women in his life other than his mother. He was a bachelor of the old school who held dinner-parties for his close friends, among whom he numbered the poets Thomas Campbell and Robert Southey. He was universally well-liked and was at home among both workmen and princes. He was, as we have noted, a Swedish knight, a Fellow of both the Royal Society of Edinburgh and of the Royal Society of London. He made Civil Engineering a 'respectable' subject and was the first President of the Royal Institute of Civil Engineering in 1820. He died aged 77 at his home, 24 Abingdon St. Westminster, on 2nd September 1834, and contrary to his wishes, was buried in Westminster Abbey where there is a statue of him in the east nave.

REFERENCES AND FURTHER READING

"The Life of Thomas Telford". Thomas Telford. ed. John Rickman, James and Luke G. Hansard, 1838.

"The Story of Telford - the rise of Civil Engineering". Alexander Gibb. Alexander Maclehose and Co. 1935.

"Thomas Telford". L.T.C. Rolt. Longmans, Green and Co. 1958.

"Thomas Telford". Brian Bracegirdle and Patricia Miles. David and Charles, 1973.

"Pioneers of Science and Discovery - Thomas Telford". Keith Ellis. Priory Press Ltd. 1974.

"Thomas Telford: Engineer" Ed. Alastair Penfold. Thomas Telford Ltd, 1980.

PLACES TO VISIT

Telford's Memorial, Westkirk, eight miles west of Langholm, Dumfriesshire.

But his memorial is of course also in the roads, bridges, canals, and harbours that he created. Among the more notable are:

Scotland

Caledonian Canal, Great Glen, Invernesshire. In summer you can cruise from Clachnaharry, Inverness, in m.v. Scot 11 through one of the most beautiful waterways in Europe.

Wales

'Waterloo Bridge' over River Conway, Bettws-y-Coed, Bangor, N.Wales.

Menai Bridge, Menai Straits, N.Wales.

Pont Cysyllte, Vale of Llangollen, N.E. Wales, over the River Dee.

ROBERT BURNS (1759 - 1796)

Poet

"There was a lad was born in Kyle".

"Our monarch's hindmost year but ane
Twas five and twenty days begun
And then a blast o' Janwir wind
Blew hansel in on Robin".

The 'hansel' (welcome) to the new-born son was not the only thing that the wind blew in on the Burnes's household, Alloway, Ayr, on that cold January night of 1759. It also blew in the gable- end of the clay biggin that William Burnes had built with his own hands, and the infant Robert (Robin) had to be carried through the storm to a neighbour's house (probably his grandmother's) where he could be kept until his father repaired the damage.

Early influences

Robert's father, William Burnes from Kincardine in the east of Scotland, moved to Alloway, Ayrshire to be head-gardener on the estate of a Dr. Ferguson. William was a stern, upright, humane man and when he married he was determined that his family would grow up independent, educated, and God-fearing. Although having little formal education himself, he was widely read and there was nothing that he enjoyed more than discussions of philosophical and theological matters with his neighbours. He was a very typical Scot of the period. His was a household with books in it.

William's wife, Agnes Broun (whom he wed when he was 36), daughter of a neighbouring tenant farmer in Ayrshire, couldn't read or write but she had a beautiful voice, a great store of Scottish songs, and there was nothing that Robert enjoyed more than having his mother sing to him. He was later to set new words to many of these tunes.

Another unlikely member of the household who influenced him was his mother's maid. "In my infant and boyish days," wrote Robert " I owed much to an old maidservant of my mother's who was remarkable for her ignorance, credulity, and superstition - she had, I suppose, the largest collection in the country of tales and songs concerning devils, ghosts, fairies, brownies, witches, warlocks, spunkies, kelpies, elf-candles, deadlights, wraiths, apparitions, cantrips, giants, enchanted towers, dragons, and other trumpery".

Surely this old maidservant provided him with material that he was later to use in his great narrative poem 'Tam o' Shanter':

> *And roars out:'Weel done, Cutty-sark!'*
> *And in an instant all was dark:*
> *And scarcely had he Maggie rallied*
> *When out the hellish legion sallied*

When Robert was six, his father, determined that his two sons should be well-educated, sent them to the local school where the dominie, John Murdoch aged 18, had been interviewed and appointed by William Burnes and four of his neighbours, to teach their children. The books that he used for their English lessons were 'The Spelling Book', the Bible, Fisher's 'English Grammar', and Masson's 'Collection of Prose and Verse'.

"Robert and his brother Gilbert" according to Murdoch "committed to memory the hymns and other poems in that collection with uncommon facility owing to the method pursued by their father and me of instructing them, which was to make them thoroughly acquainted with the meaning of every word in each sentence. I taught them to turn verse into natural prose order and to substitute expressions for poetical works." In later life Burns never had any difficulty in expressing himself clearly and precisely. He was to intermingle both of his tongues by writing in 'English tipped wi' Scots'.

When John Murdoch moved to a school in Ayr in 1771 William Burnes sent Robert, aged 12, with him to continue his education, to learn French, to study Latin, to read Shakespeare. He was reading everything that he could get his hands on and Milton was never far from his reach. But he was now also reading Scottish literature (it would be surprising if there was none in his father's house), Ramsay, Ferguson, and Blind Harry's 'Wallace'.

Peasant poet indeed! In literature, Robert was surely one of the educated young men of his generation.

There was a darker side to life. When he was six the family moved a few miles west to a neighbouring farm at Mount Oliphant, seventy acres of badly-drained ground where William struggled to make ends meet for twelve years. By the time that Robert reached the age of 15, when there were six younger children in the Burnes' household, he was doing a man's work on the farm. He later described it as "The cheerless gloom of a hermit with the unceasing toil of a galley slave". But there was some light.

His first love was Nelly Kilpartick with whom he knew the gaiety of the sun's rays in the harvest field in the autumn of 1773 when he was but 14. And she inspired the first song that he ever wrote. "I never had the least thought or inclination of turning poet till I got once heartily in love and then rhyme and song were in a manner the spontaneous language of my heart. I remember I composed it in a wild enthusiasm of passion and to this hour I never recollect it but my heart melts and my blood sallies at the remembrance":

> *"Oh once I loved a bonnie lass*
> *Aye and I love her still*
> *And whilst that virtue warms my heart*
> *I'll love my handsome Nell"*

Lochlie

All of the hard work at Mount Oliphant was in vain. In 1777 the family moved again, leasing at an inflated rental, the 130 acre farm at Lochlie which was ten miles away. Robert's life was alternating between drudgery and poetry. When not at the plough he was poring over the works of Pope and Shakespeare, Locke's essays, selections of English songs and Tull and Dickson on agriculture. He fell in love with a girl who worked on a neighbouring farm. She turned down his offer of marriage but inspired one of the loveliest of his early love songs - 'Mary Morrison':

> *"Oh Mary at thy window be*
> *It is the wished, the trysted hour*
> *Those smiles and glances let me see*
> *That makes the miser's treasure poor".*

And there was another interest in his life of which his father strongly disapproved. Nearby were the villages of Tarbolton and Mauchline and it was here that he found lively congenial company in the inns. In November 1780 he drew up the rules and regulations for the 'Tarbolton Bachelors Club', 16 members in number, and how he enjoyed his evening's drinking, carousing, discussing, and singing with them. Furthermore 'in absolute defiance of his father's command', he had joined the Tarbolton Dancing Class. Less controversially he joined the Masonic Lodge.

In 1784 William Burnes died, worn out, bankrupt. Robert was 24 and he and brother Gilbert moved the family to a rented farm at nearby Mossgiel. With the death of his father many of the moral restraints had gone and he was more free to indulge his demanding sexuality.

Fatherhood

He had a love affair in 1785 with a maidservant, Elizabeth Paton, and the resulting baby, Elizabeth, was handed over to his mother for upbringing. Not that Robert was displeased with the event:

> *"Welcome! my bonnie sweet wee dochter*
> *Though ye come a wee unsought for"*

He loved his baby and neither then nor later did he differentiate between those born in or out of wedlock:

> *The lisping infant prattling on his knee*
> *Does a' his weary carking cares beguile*
> *And makes him quite forget his labour and his toil.*

At this time he was beginning to have signs of the heart trouble that was to kill him. His doctor advised plunging into cold rivers when he felt fainting fits coming on. This advice probably shortened his life.

Jean

In 1785 Burns (he had long dropped the 'e') met Jean Armour the teenage daughter of a well-respected master-mason. Soon she was pregnant but when Burns proposed marriage the Armours would have none of it. He felt that Jean had betrayed him "my heart died within me".
He was in emotional turmoil - raging at the Armours, summoned with Jean to the the penitential stool on three successive Sundays by the Calvinist Kirk to publicly confess their sin of fornication. He was later to take his revenge on the hypocritical Kirk for its humbling of them, by writing the brilliantly biting, satirical, 'Holy Willie's Prayer'.

Highland Mary

After his rejection by the Armours he turned for comfort to Mary Campbell ('Highland Mary') with whom he might well have emigrated to the West Indies. But Mary died while tending her sick brother at Greenock. Burns makes no mention of the affair. It was only much later, when married to Jean, that she describes how he sat out one night, screening himself on a cornstack from the biting edge of the wind. He came in at dawn and wrote:

> *"That sacred hour can I forget*
> *Can I forget the hallowed grove*
> *Where by the winding Ayr we met*
> *To live one day of parting love.*
>
> *Eternity cannot efface*
> *Those seconds dear of transports past*
> *The image of our fond embrace*
> *Ah! little thought we 'twas our last!*

Was Burns feeling remorse? It is interesting to note that when Mary's grave was exhumed in 1920 an new-born baby was found buried at its foot. Had she died in childbirth and was the baby Robert's?.

A month before Mary's death, Jean bore him twins, Robert and Jean. Robert senior was happy to greet them.

The bonnie lass

But he was also interested in Miss Wilhelmina Alexander. He visited Ballochmyle in the south of Scotland and saw her from afar. "Twas evening and the fields were green". Miss Alexander was far above Burns's social status (the sister of Claud, the owner of the estate) and he had no opportunity to speak to her, but he sent verses in a letter:

> *"Oh had she been a country maid*
> *And I the happy country swain*
> *Though sheltered in the lowest shed*
> *That ever rose on Scotland's plain.*
> *Through weary winter's wind and rain*
> *With joy, with rapture I would toil*
> *And nightly to my bosom strain*
> *The bonnie lass of Ballochmyle".*

Wilhelmina was not interested. She took little notice of the letter or the poem, other than to demand an apology (which she got). Later she was to set high value on the compliment, but it was too late. Robert was dead. She lived, unmarried, until she was 90.

The Kilmarnock edition - and Edinburgh

In the midst of this turmoil, in 1786, Burns's 'Poems chiefly in the Scottish Dialect' (the copyright for which he later sold for 100 guineas to William Creech, publisher, of Edinburgh) was published by John Wilson of Kilmarnock.

It caused an immediate stir in literary circles. He was indeed 'the wonder of all the gay world' and the drawing rooms of aristocratic Edinburgh opened up to him in November 1786 (even if they hailed him as a 'heaven-taught ploughman'). Walter Scott, a boy of 16, was introduced to him and later said "His eyes were large and of a cast which glowed (I say literally glowed) when he spoke with feeling or interest".

It was in Edinburgh that he wrote his 'Address to a Haggis'. In the capital, among the 'Crochallan Fencibles' Burns amused his cronies with bawdy verses which would be published after his death as the 'Merry Muses of Caledonia'. It is strange that a man who could write so tenderly about women could also be so coarse about them, especially about Jean. It must throw doubts on his sincerity. Was he standing back, observing his poetry admiringly, as he wrote?

Soon he was off on a tour of the the Border country where, at Coldstream he crossed for a few days into England, going as far as Newcastle. This was the only occasion on which he left Scotland. Then he was off to the Highlands to be welcomed by the lairds, their wives, and daughters, before returning to Edinburgh. It was there that he met and fell in love, many say platonically, with Mrs. Agnes MacLehose whose husband had abandoned her and gone to Jamaica. A month later, in 1788, he returned to Mauchline and to Jean, with whom he had been in constant close contact, publicly attesting that they were husband and wife, a statement that was accepted by the Mauchline Kirk - and apparently by Jean's father, to whom Burns was now evidently much more acceptable. And a month after that she bore him twin girls both of whom died in infancy.

Ellisland

In 1788 Burns moved to the run-down 170 acre Ellisland estate in Dumfriesshire, which Patrick Miller had recently purchased and thought that Burns was the right man to run it. He advanced him £300 to build a house. It was at this time that he wrote what is probably the best known song in the world, 'Auld Lang Syne':

> *"Should auld acquaintance be forgot*
> *and never brought tae mind".*

He was also missing his wife:

> *"I see her in the dewy flower*
> *Sae lovely sweet and fair*
> *I hear her voice in ilka bird*
> *I hear her charm the air*
>
> *There's not a bonnie flower that springs*
> *By fountain, shaw or green*
> *There's not a bonnie bird that sings*
> *But minds me o' my Jean".*

In December of that year she joined him. Jean had a beautiful singing voice but she was virtually illiterate and she had little inkling of her husband's fame. But she was kind and long suffering, even taking in the illegitimate child, Elizabeth, resulting from his affair with a serving girl, Ann Park, and remarking "Oor Rab should hae twa wives". This was said just a month before she herself bore him a son, William (April 1791), followed by a daughter, Elizabeth Riddel (1792), and a son, James Glencairn (1794).

In poetry too, this was a very productive period including 'John Anderson my Jo' and 'Tam o' Shanter' in which he reflects on his own life:

> *"But pleasures are like poppies spread*
> *You sieze the flower, its bloom is shed*
> *Or like the snowflake on the river*
> *A moment white - then gone forever*
> *Or like the borealis race*
> *That flit ere you can point their place*
> *Or like the rainbow's lovely form*
> *Evanishing amid the storm".*

Dumfries

The Burns's moved to Dumfries in 1791 where Robert took up a job as exciseman, and from there he sent a flow of songs and poems to his publisher in Edinburgh for which he expected and got no payment.

After visiting the field of Bannockburn in 1787 he wrote the stirringly patriotic address 'Scots Wha Hae':

> *"Scots wha hae wi' Wallace bled*
> *Scots wham Bruce has often led*
> *Welcome to your gory bed*
> *Or to Victory!"*

It was during a visit to the Earl of Selkirk on St. Mary's Isle that he delivered (extempore) the famous 'Selkirk Grace':

> *"Some have meat and cannot eat*
> *Some cannot eat that want it.*
> *But we have meat and we can eat*
> *Sae let the Lord be thankit".*

Clarinda

He had, over the years, been sending a succession of letters, romantically signing them 'Sylvander', to 'Clarinda' (Mrs. Agnes MacLehose) in Edinburgh. When in 1791 she informed him that she was leaving to join her husband in the West Indies, Burns replied with 'Ae Fond Kiss':

> *Fare thee weel thou first and fairest*
> *Fare thee weel thou best and dearest*
> *Thine be ilka joy and treasure*
> *Peace, Enjoyment, Love, and Pleasure*
>
> *Ae fond kiss and then we sever*
> *Ae fareweel, alas for ever*
> *Deep in heart wrung tears I'll pedge thee*
> *Warring sighs and groans I'll wage thee*
>
> *Had we never loved sae kindly*
> *Had we never loved sae blindly*
> *Never met, or never parted*
> *We had ne'er been broken hearted.*

It was of these last four lines that Walter Scott said that they "contained the essence of a thousand love songs".

And yet there was anti-climax. In the Indies, Mrs MacLehose found that her husband had a Jamaican mistress and children. She returned to Scotland but she and Burns never met again; she survived him by 45 years, dying aged 82.

But it was for Jean that he wrote the most beautiful and touching love song ever written:

> "O, my luve is like a red red rose
> That's newly sprung in June
> O, my luve is like a melodie
> That's sweetly play'd in tune
>
> As fair art thou my bonie lass
> So deep in luve am I
> And I will luve thee still my dear
> Till a' the seas gang dry
>
> Till a' the seas gang dry my dear
> And the rocks melt wi' the Sun
> And I will luve thee still my dear
> Till the sands of life are run.

The cauld blast

And for Burns the sands of life had indeed almost run.

As he lay ill he was nursed by Jennie Lawars, a neighbour's daughter. On the piano she played one of his favourite airs 'The Wren'. She cared for him: in return, a few days before he died, he wrote for her, words to the song that she played:

> "O wert thou in the cauld blast
> On yonder lea, on yonder lea
> My plaidie to the angry airt
> I'd shelter thee, I'd shelter thee.

In his last days too, fearing that he would die a pauper, he wrote to his publisher in panic requesting £5.

And so on 21st July, 1796, at the age of 37 this complex, tormented genius died. He was not neglected in death as he had feared. His body was carried in its coffin to the Dumfries Council Chambers from whence he was given what amounted to a military funeral by the Royal Dumfries Volunteers. He was buried in St. Michael's Churchyard.

Jean bore him a posthumous son, Maxwell, a month later (in all, Burns sired 15 children, nine of them in 'lawful wedlock'). Jean outlived him by 38 years, her financial security assured by a special fund raised for her.

This erratic meteor, Robert Burns, flashed for a very short time across the barren landscape of southern Scotland, and yet he lit up the whole world. He never lived furth of Scotland, yet his poetry and song, had universal appeal.

RERERENCES AND FURTHER READING

So many books have been written about Burns and his poetry that it must appear presumptuous to pick out one or two. However among my favourites are:
'Robert Burns'. David Daiches. G. Bell and Sons, 1952.
'The Poems and Songs of Robert Burns'. James Barke. Fontana/Collins, 1985.
'The Complete Works of Robert Burns' (Official Centenary Edition). James Mackay. Alloway Publishing, 1986.

PLACES TO VISIT

Ayrshire is indeed the land of Burns, steeped in his folklore. At Alloway (Ayr) there is the Cottage in which he was born; an adjacent Museum of his manuscripts and letters; the Burns Monument amd Garden; the Land o' Burns Centre with video shows and exhibits; the Auld Kirk that was the setting for Tam o' Shanter and in whose kirkyard Burns's father is buried; the Brig over the River Doon which (with the help of Maggie) saved Tam's life. In the town of Ayr is the Tam o' Shanter Museum set in a mid 18th.-century inn. At the town of Irvine a few miles away is the Irvine Burns Club Museum devoted to the poet, his life, and books with letters from famous past-members of the Club, including Tennyson, Dickens, Garibaldi, Theodore Roosevelt and Eisenhower. The Burns' House Museum at Mauchline, the cottage in which he lived, displays relics; and at Tarbolton there is the famed 'Bachelor's Club' wherein Burns was initiated into Freemasonry; it is furnished with period items and contains memorabilia. Souter Johnnie's thatched Cottage at Kirkoswald displays Burn's relics and an interesting collection of cobblers' tools. The Burns Monument at Kilmarnock contains a small display on the life and times of the poet.

In the town of Dumfries there is Burns House in which the poet spent the last years of his life and where he died. He is buried in the kirkyard. Nearby is Ellisland Farm occupied by Burns from 1788 - 1791. The house contains writings and relics of the poet.

WILLIAM SYMINGTON (1763 - 1831)
PATRICK MILLER (1731 - 1815)
HENRY BELL (1767 - 1830)

Steamships

"On the 14th. inst.(Oct. 1788) a Boat was put in motion by a Steam Engine".

William Symington

No one knows who invented boats - that brave soul is lost in the mists of antiquity - but the first man to apply steam-power to them was William Symington. He was born at Leadhills in Lanarkshire and his father, who was an engineman employed in superintending one of Boulton and Watt's pumping engines at Wanlockhead mine, intended that William should enter the ministry of the Church of Scotland. But William had other ideas; his interests lay in inventing and in engineering.

While still in his teens he constructed a model of a steam road carriage that operated by a chain and ratchet system. This so impressed Mr. Meason, the manager of the Wanlockhead Lead Mines that he invited William to his Edinburgh home to demonstrate the model to some businessmen and to the science and engineering professors of the University. They in their turn were so impressed with the 20-year-old young man that they strongly recommended Mr. Meason to enter him as a student in the University.

Mr. Meason readily did so and William matriculated in 1786. The roads in Scotland were however in such poor condition that it was completely impractical to think of running a steam carriage over them, and Symington abandoned his idea.

Patrick Miller

A fellow student of Symington's in Edinburgh, who also knew of the model, was James Taylor who became tutor to the family of Patrick Miller of Dalswinton, a wealthy banker, merchant and landowner, who was carrying out experiments with boats on the loch of his Dalswinton Estate in Dumfriesshire in the south of Scotland. Patrick Miller was born in Glasgow. He spent his early years at sea and visited many parts of the world before settling down to become a banker in Edinburgh where, by dint of ability and hard work, he amassed a considerable fortune, being for some 30 years Deputy Governor of the Bank of Scotland. He purchased Dalswinton Estate and, building an elegant mansion on it, he devoted his leisure to the study of navigation, artillery and agriculture, making considerable advances in all three.

He invented and took out a patent for propelling boats by manually-operated paddle wheels and constructed a double ship with five masts and paddle wheels which he offered to the British government. His offer was declined so in turn he offered it as a gift to King Gustavus 111 of Sweden who was highly delighted, sending Miller a letter of thanks and a magnificent gold box within which was a small packet of turnip seed. In this way were Swede turnips introduced to Britain. They revolutionised agriculture by providing winter- feed for the livestock, many of which formerly had to be killed off with the approach of that season. He built the first drill plough ever to be used in this country, an iron plough, and a threshing machine. And he imported the very important agricultural grass, fiorin, from Ireland. He was the first man in modern times to construct guns with chambers and gave them the name 'carronades' after the Carron Iron Works, Falkirk, where they were cast, and in which he was the largest shareholder.

The world's first steamship

Acting on the suggestion of James Taylor, that he should substitute steam power for manual power, Miller employed Symington to design an engine for this purpose. Small engines were manufactured in Edinburgh, based on the design that Symington patented in 1787. Trials were carried out using one of these engines, and a boat 25 ft.x 7 ft. (7.6 metres x 2.1 metres) was constructed in October 1788. The engine was placed on one side of the boat and the boiler on the other side to balance it. There are conflicting reports as to performance, one suggesting that it chugged along beautifully at 5 miles (8 km.) per hour, another that it was less successful and that Miller's servants had to give it some help.

There was a report in a newspaper of the following day describing the result of an experiment. "On the 14th. inst.(Oct. 1788) a Boat was put in motion by a Steam Engine upon Mr. Miller of Dalswinton's piece of water at that place. It answered Mr. Miller's expectations fully and afforded great pleasure to the Spectators present".

This was an historic occasion - the launching and maiden voyage of the world's first steamship. There is also some controversy as to who viewed it. Certainly present were Miller, Symington, Taylor, and the Reverend Lawson of Kirkmaho, accompanied by his son, Archibald, who later became a magistrate in Glasgow and wrote an account of the event. Later other names were added including the artist Alexander Nasmyth who sketched the scene, and the poet Robert Burns.

Burns was at this time a tenant of Miller's on the farm at Ellisland and it would seem that Miller was well disposed towards him. "An unknown hand left ten guineas for the Ayrshire bard with Mr. Sibbald which I got. I have since discovered my generous unknown friend to be Patrick Miller Esq of Dalswinton" (Robert Burns, Dec. 1786). He wrote several letters to Miller.

After the trial, the engine was taken into Miller's house where it was kept for many years before being sold for scrap. Many parts went missing but it was bought by a Mr. Bennet Woodcroft who had it reconstructed and displayed in the Science Museum , Kensington, London, where it can still be seen today.

Miller opts out

Miller had a larger boat, ninety feet (27 metres) in length, built at Leith and he commissioned Symington to prepare a suitable engine. He placed the order for the engine at the Carron Iron Works, and in trials carried out on the Forth and Clyde Canal, speeds of 7 miles (11.3 km.) per hour were attained. Miller was not completely satisfied with the engine and he applied to Boulton and Watt for one of proper construction. The response from Watt was not encouraging. He had no great hopes for steamships and he was probably instrumental in Miller withdrawing from the venture.

The 'Charlotte Dundas'

Symington had lost his main support and for nearly ten years the idea of steamships lay practically dormant though some unsuccessful experiments by others were carried out elsewhere. Then, in 1801, Symington got another chance. Lord Dundas, Governor of the Forth and Clyde Canal, asked Symington if there was any possibility of substituting steam-power for horse-power to move barges on his canal. Symington took out a new patent employing a piston-rod guided by rollers, with a connecting rod to a crank which was attached directly to the paddle-wheel, a system that has been used for paddle-steamers ever since that date. By June 1801 the first trials with the 'Charlotte Dundas' were carried out on the Rivers Carron and Forth.

These trials were not particularly successful and the boat was replaced by a second 'Charlotte Dundas' designed wholly by Symington. There was more success this time and on 28th March 1803 the boat, trailing two barges, travelled along the 20 miles (32 km.) of the canal to Port Dundas in Glasgow in six hours, against a strong headwind.

The best laid schemes

Lord Dundas was so delighted with the results that he introduced Symington to Lord Bridgewater, the great canal proprietor in England, who ordered six boats of the same design to be made as speedily as possible. Symington's star was in the ascendancy. But other powers were at work and in the moment of his apparent triumph, all was snatched from him - "the best laid schemes o' mice and men, gang aft agley". The proprietors of the Forth and Clyde Canal were worried that the banks of the canal would be seriously undercut and washed away by the waves from the paddles, and they prohibited all further experiments. On top of this, Symington was told that the Duke of Bridgewater had died and all his orders were suspended.

Symington, a disappointed and disillusioned man, had lost all of his money in the venture. He gathered together such parts of his boat and engines that he could find and sold them for scrap. Later he brought his claims as the inventor of steamships to the attention of the Government and although unsuccessful, he received £100, and later £50, from the Privy Purse. In poverty, completely destitute, he and his wife moved to London where they were dependent on members of their family for the last years of their lives. When he died he was buried in St. Botolph's, Aldgate, London, where there is a memorial tablet:

> He constructed the Charlotte Dundas, the
> first steamboat fitted for practical use;
> dying in want, he was buried in the adjacent
> churchyard, March 22nd 1831.

It is ironic that Taylor also petitioned, in 1824, for a reward for his services in connection with the invention of steam navigation and although he too was unsuccessful, a renewed application after his death, resulted in his widow being awarded £50 per annum.

Among the many visitors who inspected the 'Charlotte Dundas' on her trials was the American artist, engineer, and inventor, Robert Fulton, who, obtaining an engine from Boulton and Watt, launched his vessel the 'Clermont' which went from New York to Albany, a distance of 150 miles (241 km.) in 32 hours, in 1807.

Henry Bell

There is a myth around, certainly in Scotland, that Henry Bell invented steamships. He didn't; but he certainly played a prominent part in developing them. Like Fulton, he too was aboard the 'Charlotte Dundas' taking notes. Henry Bell was born at Torpichen, near Linlithgow in 1767. The course of his future interests was probably influenced by the fact that his uncle gave him a present of a model of a full-rigged ship when he was a schoolboy and he spent many hours sailing it on the nearby River Avon. His father was a millwright and he apprenticed young Henry, aged 13, as a mason and a millwright to a relative of his mother. After working for several engineers in London, Henry returned to Scotland in 1790. He knew of Symington's work and was resolved to build a practical sea-going steamship. In 1808 he moved to Helensburgh where his wife superintended the Public Baths and ran the Baths Hotel. In time Bell became Provost of the town but his main interest still lay in ships.

He tried to interest the Government of the day in 'Transmarine Navigation' but could get little support, although no less a person than Lord Nelson tried to persuade them. He is reported to have said, "My Lords and Gentlemen if you do not adopt Mr. Bell's scheme other nations will and in the end vex every vein of this Empire. It will succeed and you should encourage Mr. Bell".

The 'Comet'

In the meantime Bell launched his own boat, the 'Comet', built by John Wood and Company, on the river Clyde in January 1812. It was 42 ft. (13 metres) in length, and was driven by a 3hp. engine made by himself, and a boiler constructed by David Napier. This was the first European steamship in service. The following notice appeared in the 'Glasgow Chronicle' 5th. August, 1812.

The Steamboat 'Comet'
Between Glasgow, Greenock, and Helensburgh
For Passengers Only

The subscriber, having at much expense, fitted up a
handsome vessel to ply upon the river Clyde from
Glasgow, to sail by the power of air, wind, and
steam, intends that the vessel shall leave the
Broomielaw on Tuesdays, Thursdays, and Saturdays
about mid-day, or such an hour as may suit the
state of the tide, and to leave Greenock on
Mondays, Wednesdays, and Fridays in the morning
to suit the tide. The terms are for the present fixed
at four shillings for the best cabin and three shillings for the second.

The subscriber continues his establishment at
Helensburgh Baths (Hotel) and a vessel will be in
readiness to convey passengers by the 'Comet' from
Greenock to Helensburgh.
Henry Bell
5th. August, 1812

Thus began the trips 'doon the watter' on paddle steamers, that were to become such a feature of the life of the Glaswegian in the years ahead. The 'Comet' was the forerunner of the succession of paddle steamers from the 'Columba' to the 'Waverley' that were to endear themselves to generations of Scots.

But the 'Comet' did more than ply the Clyde. It blazed a trail for the shipbuilders - 30,000 ships of importance were launched on the Clyde between 1810 and 1980, ranging from the Cunard wooden paddle ship 'Britannia', built at Greenock in 1840, that sailed from Liverpool to Halifax in twelve days, to the glorious 'Queens' of John Brown's shipyards, Clydebank.

The 'Comet' continued service until 1820 when she sank off the Western Isles. Her wheel can be seen in Hermitage Public Park, Helensburgh, and there is a monument to Henry Bell near the sea- front. A replica of the 'Comet' was built in 1962 at Lithgow's East Yard where the original was launched 150 years before. It sailed to Helensburgh and back and is now on show near the seafront, Port Glasgow, as a 'memorial to Henry Bell and the expertise of Port Glasgow craftsmen'.

REFERENCES AND FURTHER READING

"Life of Henry Bell". Edward Morris. Glasgow, 1844.
Dictionary of National Biography:
  Henry Bell, 11, p159, 1909.
   Patrick Miller, X111, p 417, 1900.
   William Symington, X1X, p 169, 1909.
   James Taylor, X1X, p 419, 1909.
   Chambers Biographical Dictionary of Famous Scotsmen.
   "The Scottish Nation" 2 vols. William Anderson. A. Fullerton and Co. 1871.

PLACES TO VISIT

Scotland

Monument to Symington, Symington St, Leadhills, Lanarkshire.

Monument to Henry Bell on Clyde Street, Helensburgh; Wheel of original 'Comet' in Hermitage Park, Helensburgh.

Replica of 'Comet' on coast road, Port Glasgow.

It is good to report that the present owner of Dalswinton Estate, David Landale, proposed that Dumfries and Galloway College of Technology should construct a replica to mark the 200th anniversary of Symington's original vessel. By researching the history of the original, computer plans were drawn up and with the help of the Manpower Services Commission, newly sawn timber from Dalswinton, and the advice of a professional boatbuilder, from Kirkcudbright, the job was completed by college staff, students, apprentices, and groups of young unemployed people and the splendid replica went on view at the Glasgow Garden Festival in 1987.

England

Science Museum, Kensington, London , where there is a reconstruction of the engine that Symington used on Miller's paddle steamer on Dalswinton Loch, 14th. Oct. 1788.

Aldgate Cemetery where Symington is buried and where there is a memorial tablet.

CHARLES MACINTOSH (1766-1843)
Dyes and Rubber

"I fear that the development of the railways will destroy the need for waterproof coats"

Charles Macintosh was born in Glasgow, the son of a wealthy manufacturer, George Macintosh. His mother, Mary Moore, was a cousin of General Sir John Moore, killed in the retreat from Corunna during the Napoleonic Wars.

After attending classes at the Grammar School, Glasgow and a school in Yorkshire where he made a number of influential friends, Charles started his working life as a clerk in the firm of a Mr. Glassford but he had little interest in that side of business. He had devoted much of his spare time to the study of chemistry, attending classes in Glasgow and Edinburgh, and soon he joined his father George in his manufacturing chemist business.

Cudbear

The Macintosh firm became heavily involved in the production of dyestuffs, one of their main products being 'cudbear', a well-known dye for silk and wool, an invention of the Leith firm that it had earlier taken over. Cudbear was prepared by mashing up a special species of lichen plant ('*Lichen tartareus*', got mainly from the Highlands of Scotland) in wooden troughs with ammonia and lime for 14 days. The quality of the ammonia was very important and Charles believed that the best for his purpose was got from human urine.

In those days there were no toilets in the homes of the people - even later, in Queen Victoria's time, a chamber-pot had to be brought into her room for her use - and the method of disposal was primitive. In our 'gardez-loo' cities if you were a little hard of hearing, or not very nimble of foot, then the deluge from the window was liable to descend upon you. Charles Macintosh decided that the urine could be put to better use.

He sent his men round the houses of Glasgow where they collected as much as possible, sometimes 3000 gallons a day (for which he paid them the equivalent of 1d (1/2p) per gallon). They were furnished with special hydrometers so that they wouldn't be given watered-down urine, so to speak.

The urine was heated and the ammonia distilled off. Depending upon the proportions of the various ingredients that were used, the cudbear produced beautiful shades of pink, red, purple, and blue. It was used throughout the world. He was also in touch with Boulton in Birmingham to see if he would be interested in the urine residue for the extraction of chemicals. He wasn't.

It is not surprising that the Macintoshes did everything in their power to hide the secrets of their manufacturing process. Industrial espionage is not new. They built walls 10 feet high around their factory and the only workmen that they employed were Gaelic-speaking Highlanders so that they could not pass on secrets to rival firms.

The demand for cudbear was so great that 250 tonnes of lichen was required annually; when the Scottish stock was exhausted it was imported from Norway, Sweden, the Canary Islands, and Malta. Sweden alone exported 130 tonnes annually from 1770, and in 1793 Charles Macintosh visited King Gustavus Adolphus 1V to get the export duty removed. As the supplies of lichen became more difficult so the price rose progressively from £3 to £25 to £45 a tonne. It is estimated that between the years 1778 -1838 over £300,000 was spent on this lichen alone. As it became more scarce a different species of lichen - '*Lichen pustulatus*' - was substituted.

The end of the cudbear trade came about, not because of shortages of lichen or urine, but simply because of a change in fashion. Instead of wearing bright clothes, men and women started wearing clothes of grey and black. Black was the 'in' colour. Why was this so? The most likely reason is that with the advent of the Industrial Revolution, people began to live in an atmosphere polluted by soot from the manufacturing industries. The Macintosh cudbear works closed in 1852.

Alum

All vegetable dyes require a 'mordant' - a substance that 'fixes' them and brings out the true colours. A number of chemicals can act in this capacity among them alum, a complex aluminium salt. Macintosh, who was a very able chemist, knowing of a considerable seam of aluminous shales to he found at Hurlet, near Glasgow, and noticing that those shales that had been thrown up in coalmining, decomposed on exposure to air to yield a bloom of iron and aluminium on the surface, realized that it should be possible to extract alum from the shale by treating it with alkali. He opened the first alum factory in Scotland in 1797 which soon became the largest in Britain. A second factory at Campsie in Stirlingshire followed in 1808.

As well as being a mordant, alum was used for a number of other industrial purposes such as tanning of hides, in the purification of sugar, for treating paper so that it was suitable for carrying gunpowder, for hardening tallow. It was also used in the purification of water and still is today.

By 1822 these factories were producing 1000 tonnes of alum per year. By 1835 it had risen to 2,000 tonnes and the price fell progressively from £28 to £9. 10s. a tonne.

Prussian Blue

At his alum works at Campsie, Charles Macintosh dissolved calcined blood, hooves, hair, woollen rags, and potash in sulphuric acid. When iron sulphate was added to this witches brew there emerged crystals of the dye, Prussian Blue. He did not invent the dye but "his crystals of prussiate of potash are unrivalled for their beauty and purity, and his Prussian Blue cannot be excelled" said one observer. And his process reduced its price from 6 shillings an ounce to 1/5d a pound. It was outstanding as a dye.

Bleaching

In 1774 a Swedish chemist, Scheele, discovered the new element chlorine and 11 years later a French chemist, Berthellot demonstrated its bleaching power. He communicated his finding to James Watt who was in France at the time. Watt in turn told his father-in-law, Mr. McGregor, a bleacher, who became the first in Britain to use it. The strong chlorine smell was a drawback and attempts were made to alleviate it by passing potash through the liquid but this interfered with its bleaching powers.

At the turn of the 19th. century, Charles Tennant of St. Rollox, Glasgow, who had manufactured it as a liquid for the bleaching of linen, passed lime through the liquid to form a powder and took out a patent for 'chloride of lime' - bleaching powder - and marketed it as such. But it is clear that it was Charles Macintosh (who was in partnership with Tennant at the time) who, in 1799, devised the process and the patent was put in Tennant's name as a convenience. The value of this development to the country was recognised by the Glasgow Chamber of Commerce who petitioned Parliament for a financial award to the inventors, citing that not only was it saving the country several thousand pounds annually, but it was also creating work and thus increasing the country's wealth. Nothing was forthcoming and Macintosh withdrew from association with Charles Tennant in 1814. It has been calculated that the total saving over a period of 46 years was more than £423 million. Little wonder that Charles Tennants became one of the most important chemical manufacturers in Britain.

Disease

Mackintosh took no part in the development nor in the profits of chloride of lime, but, in 1804 we find him writing to his relative Francis Moore, Deputy Secretary at the War Office, proposing that chlorine would be a very effective preventative in the spread of contagion and disease. Although his letter was placed before the Medical Board no action was taken on it, but more than 25 years later, in 1831, we find Henry Warburton M.P. consulting Macintosh about the approaching threat of cholera in this country and asking him whether chlorine might help to stay its spread.

This was long before Pasteur put forward his germ theory of disease but the authorities ignored Macintosh leaving countless thousands to die needlessly in subsequent epidemics.

Rubber and Macintoshes

But Macintosh's most important discovery, one that was to make his name a household word, was yet to come. His thoughts had turned to rubber.

Rubber, the juice of a South American tree (*Hevea*), the plaything of the Aztec Indian children, had been brought back to Europe by the Spaniards. Joseph Priestley, the famous English chemist, had determined its chemical composition and he used it to erase pencil marks; but by and large it remained a hard useless lump. No one yet could find a solvent to make it more malleable, turpentine and chloroform, among others, being tried without success.

Ammonia was an important material in a number of Macintosh's manufacturing processes and as business expanded he looked around for new sources. In 1819 he bought all the tar from the newly-formed Glasgow Gas Company. From the tar he distilled off ammonia. By further distillation he separated off naphtha which Dr. James Syme, Professor of Surgery at Edinburgh used as a solvent to make rubber gloves and tubes. But it was waterproofing that Macintosh was chasing. He dissolved the rubber in the naphtha to make a gluey substance and made a 'sandwich' of two layers of cloth stuck together by the liquid rubber which penetrated the pores of the cloth. The naphtha evaporated off leaving the cloth waterproofed. The waterproof or the 'mac' was born.

In 1823, the year that this remarkable man patented his waterproofing invention, he was elected a Fellow of the Royal Society. After an experimental period in Glasgow, Macintosh set up a company in Manchester for the manufacture of coats, capes, inflatable goods, cushions, pillows and beds. Thomas Hancock who was involved in the vulcanization of rubber by the addition of sulphur became a partner. In 1824 Sir John Franklin ordered considerable supplies of various waterproofed fabrics for use in an Arctic expedition, even using some in the construction of his boats.

The Company prospered and "accumulated a very handsome fortune". One little cloud that appeared on the horizon was the development of the railway system. It was felt that since people did not now have to travel on horseback and on the outside of coaches, they would not have the same need for waterproof clothing. The Company need not have worried - people weren't always aboard trains and when they weren't the British weather saw to it that they needed protection!

The hot blast process

Charles Macintosh wasn't quite finished yet. In 1825 he patented a process for converting iron into steel. This technique proved to be uncommercial but James Beaumont Neilson (another Scot) assigned to Macintosh a share of his patent for 'the Hot Blast Process' in appreciation of the assistance rendered to him.

Charles Macintosh died in Glasgow in 1843 aged 77.

REFERENCES AND FURTHER READING

'Biographical Memoir of the late Charles Macintosh F.R.S.'. George Macintosh. 1857.
'The Chemical Revolution'. A.Clow and N.Clow. Batchworth Press, 1952.

MUNGO PARK (1771 - 1806)

Explorer

"I shall set sail for Africa with the fixed resolution to discover the termination of the Niger or perish in the attempt"

Mungo Park was born in a little hamlet, Foulsheils, five miles west of Selkirk in southern Scotland. He was the seventh child of a family of thirteen, five of whom died in childhood, and he attended the local grammar school in Selkirk after a period at home with a private tutor. He showed considerable promise and his father, a farmer with a great belief in education, had high hopes that he would become a minister of the Church. But Mungo was a strong-minded boy and made it clear that he wanted to become a doctor.

At the age of 15 he was apprenticed for three years to Dr. Thomas Anderson, a doctor in Selkirk, where he pursued his medical and classical studies. But he did more than that - he met Dr. Anderson's daughter who twelve years later was to become his wife. His apprenticeship completed he moved on to Edinburgh University for a further three years to complete his qualification. Thus at the age of 21 young Mungo was a doctor. But not for him a quiet country practice; he had his eyes on more distant horizons. Like so many Scotsmen before (and after) him he set off for London there to confer with his brother-in-law, James Dickson. Dickson was the son of a Scottish farm-worker who went to London to become a nurseryman in Hammersmith, studying botany in his spare time and, by his abilities, attracting the attention of Sir Joseph Banks, a famous plant collector who had accompanied Captain Cook on his world expedition. Sir Joseph who was from a very different backgound - Harrow, Eton, and Oxford - from that of Dickson, warmed to the young man, gave him the free run of his library and encouraged him in every way. In time Dickson became a botanist with a European reputation.

Off to Sumatra

He introduced his young relative to Sir Joseph who got Mungo the job of assistant surgeon on one of the East India Company vessels en route for

Sumatra, Indonesia. Park made many observations, collected plants, and on his return a year later read a paper to the Linnean Society concerning eight new fishes that he had discovered. Banks was impressed by this earnest hard-working young man and offered him the prospect of an exciting adventure. Would he be willing to lead an expedition into West Africa to trace the course of the River Niger? This was a difficult and dangerous trip, but Park did not hesitate - he accepted the commission immediately.

It was a problem whose solution had eluded some of the most eminent explorers for more than 200 years, but Park jumped at the chance; he was young and strong, fearless, energetic, and full of the spirit of adventure. He had tasted foreign travel and was keen for more.

The Gambia

He sailed from Portsmouth on the 22nd May, 1795. His ship entered the River Gambia, West Africa, one month later and continued the voyage up river to the small village of Bisania where there was a British trading post. He was well looked after, settling down during the months of the wet season, when the rain was torrential, to study the country through which he would travel and to learn the language, Mandingo, of the area. Twice he was laid low with fever, for this was a highly malarious area, but with the coming of the dry season his spirits rose and he was ready to be off.

Into Africa

Bidding farewell to his friends on 2nd December, 1796, he struck east, astride his horse, into the interior. He had two African helpers mounted on mules as his companions. All three travelled light - provisions for two days, some beads, amber, and tobacco, for trading, a few changes of clothing, an umbrella as shelter from sun and rain, a compass, a thermometer, two pistols, and some money. Thus they travelled hundreds of miles into the unknown, into the teeth of danger.

They did not get off to a good start having barely travelled three miles when they were set upon by a mob, who had no doubt been monitoring their intentions, and who deprived them of some of their money before allowing them to continue their journey.

They met many friendly people on their way but also many thieves and robbers. The King of Wuli, a venerable old man, not only gave them permission to travel through his territory and provided a guide, but also sent up prayers for the success of the expedition.

Park planned to go east through the kingdoms of Kaarta and Bambarra till he reached the Niger, but these two countries were at war with each other and so he had to make a detour through the Moorish kingdom of Ludamar. This was dangerous country and one of his servants, Johnson, fearing that the Moors would make him a slave, deserted. Park and his other servant, Dembha, were indeed captured and suffered from terrible hunger, thirst, and cruel treatment. And Park was racked with fever. For weeks they were marched north, more dead than alive, through the hot sandy country, to meet Queen Fatima of Ludamar who, Park was told, would likely order that his eyes be gouged out.

Eventually they reached the camp of Behaun where women and children swarmed over Park examining him with great curiosity and wondering at the whiteness of his skin. He was installed as barber to the Royal family but after making a poor job of the hair of one of the princes he was relieved of his post. His faithful servant was sold as a slave and never heard of again.

A week after his arrival a council of the elders met to decide Park's fate which teetered between death, having his right hand cut off, or having his eyes gouged out. But no final decision could be taken until the arrival of Queen Fatima who was up north on business. When she did arrive, two months later, he was dragged before this enormously corpulent lady who was surrounded by her ladies-in-waiting. Like the Queen they were huge and fat and Park later related that no woman who could walk without two slaves under each arm to support her could have any pretentions to distinction and loveliness. As the Queen pondered his fate, and he suffered from thirst and hunger, he began to have hallucinations. "No sooner had I shut my eyes than fancy would convey me to the streams and rivers of my native land - there as I wandered along the brink I surveyed the clear stream and tried with haste to swallow the delightful draught but alas disappointment awakened me and I found myself a lonely captive perishing of thirst amid the wilds of Africa."

But help was at hand from an unexpected quarter. News arrived that the country had been invaded by a neighbouring country. The Moors were thrown into confusion. Queen Fatima had more important things to concern her than the fate of a skinny white man. In the confusion, Park escaped and stealing a horse he rode into the desert passing en route the long lines of slaves fastened neck to neck with thongs of hide being whipped along through the Sahara desert to the slave markets of North Africa. He reached the jungle and in the villages he traded wisps of his hair (treasured as a charm against evil) in return for food.

Talking with the villagers, he knew that he was approaching his target and reaching Dego, the capital of Bambarra, he saw before him the Niger "glittering in the morning sun, as broad as the Thames at Westminster and flowing slowly eastwards. I hastened to the brink and having drunk of the water gave up my fervent thanks in prayer to the ruler of all things for having thus far crowned my endeavours with success".

Home

But his quest was far from over. He followed the river east for a short distance but overcome with fever and exhaustion he had to turn back. He decided to make for the coast, a march of 3,220 kilometres through swamps and rivers still clinging to his precious notes. It took him seven months and how, with his fever-tormented body, he did it is beyond comprehension. He was fortunate to fall in with some Arab slave-traders who helped him over the last 800 kilometres. Even then his troubles were not over. He had to sail to America aboard a slave ship and then re-cross to Britain. After an absence of two years eight months he was home again; but he was so altered by his sufferings that none of his friends, not even James Dickson his brother-in-law, recognised him.

Once it was established who he was, however, his return caused a sensation. An abstract of his travels was prepared and published by the Africa Association, and Park returned to the quietness of Foulshiels to be reunited with his mother and to write his book. It was published in the Spring of 1799 and was an immediate success. He proposed marriage to Ailie Anderson the doctor's daughter who had waited for him and to whom he was devoted; together in 1801 they settled down to a country practice in Peebles. One might have thought that that was the end of Park's story. Far from it!

Back to Africa

Africa is like a fever in the blood that lies dormant for a long time then suddenly erupts. So it was with Park; he had to go back. It was his friend Sir Walter Scott who first recognised the symptoms as he watched him throwing stones into the River Yarrow. A harmless pursuit, but Park confessed that this was the technique that he used to determine the depth of rivers in Africa; and there was longing in his eyes.

When he was given the chance to lead an expedition to locate the mysterious city of Timbuktu, a Muslim centre that had been founded in the 11th. century, near the banks of the River Niger, he jumped at the chance. In the Spring of 1805, accompanied by an officer, 35 soldiers, and a number of carpenters whose job would be to build boats on the Niger, Park sailed from Portsmouth for the Gambia. He was 34 years of age, and he left behind a wife and family whom he would never see again.

It was an ill-fated expedition; within a few months most of them were dead or dying of fever. By November the party was down to Park ('the man with the great beard'), the officer, two soldiers, and one carpenter. They set off up the River Niger in a large canoe which Park named the 'Jolliba' (the African name for the Niger) in search of Timbuktu; but they never made it. Before sailing he gave letters to an African guide with instructions to take them back to the Gambia for onward transmission to Britain.

On the banks of the Niger, the Africans were hostile so that Park and the remnants of his expedition were unable to land; their food ran out. The end was near; their canoe overturned; Park and his men were engulfed in the torrent and were never seen again.

But one African in the party survived and vanished, it was he who later revealed how and where Park had died. They had navigated 1,600 kilometres of the river (its total length is 4183 kilometres).

There are three footnotes to the story:

Mungo Park's son refused to believe that his father had died; he sailed alone up the Gambia in search of him and he too disappeared into Africa.

Another Scot, Major Laing, following the course of the Niger, entered Timbuktu and was murdered there in 1827.

The marshy delta through which the River Niger seeps its way into the Gulf of Guinea was discovered in 1830.

REFERENCES AND FURTHER READING

'Travels in the Interior of Africa' Mungo Park. 1799.
'Mungo Park'. T. Banks MacLachlan. Famous Scots Series, Oliphant, Anderson, and Ferrier, 1898.
'Great Scots' John. F. Houston. Robert Gibson, 1951.
'Life of Park'. L.G.Gibbon, 1934.

PLACES TO VISIT

Scotland

At Foulshiels the ruins of Park's house are preserved as a memorial. There is a plaque on the wall:

MUNGO PARK
BORN 10th. SEPTEMBER 1771
KILLED AT BOUSSA
ON THE NIGER, AFRICA, 1805
Foulshiels, 1885.

Nearby is the beautiful River Yarrow where Park played as a boy.
In Peebles the houses where he lived and worked have been marked.
Statues of Mungo Park are to be seen in Selkirk and Moffat.

WALTER SCOTT (1771-1832)
Novelist and Poet

"O Caledonia! stern and wild,
Meet nurse for a poetic child!
Land of brown heath and shaggy wood,
Land of the mountain and the flood"

Walter Scott was the creator of the historical novel combining past events with the sense of adventure. But he did more than this. He mined a rich seam. Before his Waverley novels, and his ballads, the Scots were almost completely ignorant of Scotland's past. Following his writings there was a great resurgence of interest in Highland and Border history and many learned societies sprang up to uncover and to publish documents relating to the subject. It is also said that his writings were responsible for the Romantic movement in France which yielded such writers as Victor Hugo, de Musset, and Gautier, and painters such as Corot and Millet.

Walter Scott, born on 15th August, 1771, in the family home at the head of the College Wynd, Edinburgh, was the ninth child of Anne Rutherford, wife of Walter Scott, Writer to the Signet, the highest rank in Scotland in the profession of solicitor. Childhood was a hazardous state in 18th century Britain and the Scotts had already lost their first five children.

Illness

Until he was about 18 months old, Walter was a healthy, active baby. Then a paralysis struck and he lost all power of his right leg. His mother's father, Dr. John Rutherford, Professor of Medicine in the University, advised that the baby should be sent, for the sake of his health, to his grandfather, Robert Scott, who had a farm, 'Sandy Knowe', in Roxburghshire. Fresh air was about the only prescription that doctors had for all illnesses. And so young Walter became a Borderer. He spent three very happy years there, absorbing Border stories and legends, until his grandfather died.

It was decided that his maiden aunt, Miss Jenny, who had kept house for her father, should take the boy to test the medicinal waters of Bath. They sailed from Berwick on the twelve-day voyage to London aboard 'The

Duchess of Buccleuch'. The boy enjoyed his 12 months stay in Bath amid the splendour of Neo-Georgian England and although the waters did nothing for his paralysed leg it is said that he acquired "a perfect English accent!" On his return to Edinburgh, to his parents' new home in George Square, bathing in the waters of nearby Prestonpans didn't help either. A withered shrunken leg was to be a legacy for the rest of his life.

School and University

He attended Edinburgh High School where, though he was not an outstanding pupil, he began to show talent as a story-teller with a delightful sense of humour. Completing his studies, he spent a few months in the Borders, joining his Aunt Jenny at Kelso, which he later described as "the most romantic village in Scotland", where she now lived. He was reading all that he could lay his hands on, and he was wandering the countryside.

But all too soon, at the age of 12 it was time to leave that enchanted airt for the more disciplined Edinburgh University where he studied Latin, Logic, Metaphysics, History and Mathematics.

A meeting with Burns

In November 1786 Edinburgh was agog with the news that the Ayrshire poet, Robert Burns was to visit the city. A reception was to be held for him at the home of Professor Adam Ferguson. Among others, the chemist Professor Joseph Black, and the geologist Professor James Hutton, were to be there, and through Ferguson's son, young Scott, aged 13, got an invitation too. When Burns stopped before an engraving of a soldier lying dead in the snow with his dog sitting miserably beside him and his wife with her baby on the other side, Burns was moved to tears when he read six lines of verse below, and he enquired about the identity of the author. Only Scott knew that it was John Langhorne. "I whispered my information to a friend present, who mentioned it to Burns who rewarded me with a look and a word."

Completing the course at University, Scott at the age of 15, was apprenticed to his father's office, where he felt 'caged up like a cobbler's linnet'. Any money that he earned he spent on books. He longed for the country and an unexpectedly severe illness, a haemorrhage of the bowel, allowed him to escape to Kelso, this time to stay with his bachelor uncle, Captain Robert Scott of the Honourable East India Company, who had retired and bought a cottage there.

Returning to Edinburgh he studied Scots Law with a view to becoming an Advocate and in his spare time he toured the Scotland that he loved so well - Perthshire, Forfarshire, Aberdeenshire - staying mostly at country houses and visiting places of historical and romantic interest - Loch Lubnaigh, the Carse of Gowrie, St. Andrews and at Dunsinane, the room in which King Duncan was murdered. And romance was looming.

Marriage

Miss Charlotte Carpenter of Carlisle met Scott when, as a member of the Edinburgh Light Dragoons he found himself in that airt. Charlotte was a French refugee - "a lovelier vision - could hardlier have been imagined" and she had a fortune. After a fairly short wooing Scott proposed and was accepted. They were married in the nave of Carlisle Cathedral on Christmas Eve 1797; they set up home at 50 George Street, Edinburgh, later moving to Castle Street, and they hired a country cottage in the village of Lasswade on the river Esk, about six miles south-west of the city.

It was in Castle Street that their first child, a boy, was born about a year later, but he died almost immediately. It was a sore blow to them, but within a year a little daughter, Charlotte Sophia brought them solace.

Scott, now a qualified advocate, had his eye on the Sheriffdom of Selkirkshire and in December 1799, due to the influence of his friend the Duke of Buccleuch he was appointed.

To their great joy Charlotte gave birth to a son on October 28th 1801. He was christened Walter but Scott nicknamed him "Gilnockie". He was destined to be a soldier and a great source of pride and happiness all his life to his father. His second daughter, Anne, followed only sixteen months later.

Border Ballads

Scott meantime was moving in aristocratic circles, something that he enjoyed very much. He was dining with the Duke of Buccleuch and he spent Christmas 1801 with the Duke of Hamilton and his family. In amassing poems for the 'Minstrelsy of the Scottish Border' he met James Hogg, the Ettrick Shepherd, who drew his attention to some old ballads, and who contributed verses himself. The two men of such different background, training and temperament, became good friends and Scott did all that he could to promote Hogg's interests.

The first two volumes of the 'Minstrelsy of the Scottish Border' were published in 1802 and were an enormous success. But already he was planning a long narrative poem of his own and he had written the first four cantos, when, in September 1803 he had visitors from the Lake District. William Wordsworth and his sister Dorothy were on a tour of Scotland and they walked into Scott's cottage at Lasswade. A friendship was struck though Wordsworth was rather cool about Scott's poetry. 'The Lay of the Last Minstrel' was a romance of Border chivalry which was completed in 1803. Sales were prodigious and within two weeks of its publication Scott was famous. Yet still he looked on writing as merely a pleasant way of adding to his income.

It was becoming ever more necessary that he should live within his shrievalty and in 1804 he gave up 'Lasswade' and moved into 'Ashestiel', a farmhouse on the banks of the Tweed.

Marmion

One might have thought that following on the success of 'The Lay of the Last Minstrel' Scott would immediately produce another epic poem. Not so. Instead he undertook to edit, with a full biography, an edition of Dryden's works, and as soon as it was finished, a similar edition of Swift, both for a series on 'British Poets' being published by Constable. They entailed an enormous amount of work. And still intent on his career in law he obtained the Clerkship of the Court of Session. Only then, 18 months after the 'Minstrel' did he turn to his second great epic poem - 'Marmion' - a tale involving the Battle of Flodden, but leading on to the exploits of Nelson, Pitt and Fox. Again it was a winner. Things looked good; but he entered into a close financial partnership with the publishers, John Ballantyne, including support for a new newspaper, 'The Edinburgh Annual Register'. These dealings were later to spell trouble for him.

The Lady of the Lake

At first, however, all went well. Scott's third great poem 'The Lady of the Lake' was published in May 1810 and as well as getting 2000 guineas as author, Scott was also entitled to half of the publisher's profits. It was said by Ballantyne that "no book of Scott was ever more keenly looked for in Scotland or more ardently received". But not only was the book successful; suddenly 'The Trossachs' was the place to visit.

Abbotsford

Scott was now nearly 40 years of age, with a good income from his writing, and he proceeded to spend money as fast as it came in - mainly on his new house. The lease for Ashesteil had run out. For £4000 he bought a 110 acre estate with a farm and a cottage on it, on the banks of the Tweed, renamed the complex "Abbotsford" and was proud to be the 'The Laird'. He had to borrow heavily from Ballantyne to raise the money and as a result was now tied into writing to finance the venture.

But of course he wasn't satisfied with a farmhouse; he set out to have a mansion built and over the years 'Abbotsford' was to develop into a house of great beauty, a drawing room, a handsome dining-room, a conservatory, a study, an armoury, a chapel, all with magnificent antique furnishings; and he was extending his land holdings. The costs were very high.

Financial worries

Warning bells were ringing. Ballantyne, who was no business man, informed him that the 'The Edinburgh Register' had been steadily losing £1000 a year; he got financial support from Scott to the tune of £200 a week; and Ballantyne was pleading with Constable to take the publishing business off his hands. For their part, Constable's terms were that £4000 must be raised; and there would be no place for Ballantyne in the new set-up. Scott was worried. He turned to the Duke of Buccleuch for help, and he was not found wanting; he guaranteed the £4000 which tided them over for the time being.

Whistling down the wind

Scott now turned his thoughts to a novel that he had started long before. It was 'Waverley', the centrepiece of which was Bonnie Prince Charlie and 'the Forty-Five' narrated, interestingly enough, through the eyes of a young Englishman, Edward Waverley. But Scott did not put his name to it. The novel as a form was not quite 'respectable'. "I am not quite sure that it would be considered quite decorous for me, as a Clerk of Session, to write novels - I shall whistle it down the wind and let it prey at fortune." It did more than whistle; it was a tornado. The world buzzed with interest. 'Waverley' was the most successful anonymous novel ever published; 5000 copies were sold within the year.

Leaving success behind however, the anonymous author 'disappeared' on the evening of August 1st. 1814. He was off, from Leith in the Firth of Forth, on a yachting trip round Scotland with the Commissioners of the Northern Lights whose chief executive, in charge of the trip, was Robert Stevenson, the grandfather of Robert Louis Stevenson. They viewed the Bell Lighthouse off Arbroath, called in at Aberdeen, Fraserburgh, and

Lerwick; they inspected Pictish forts and castles; visited the knitters of Fair Isle; landed at Kirkwall in the Orkneys; viewed Cape Wrath and moved into the Atlantic. Fortified with fresh herring, haddocks, eggs and butter, barley bannocks, oat cakes, tea, coffee, and, of course, whisky, they headed for the Isle of Skye and Dunvegan Castle presided over by the Laird of MacLeod. They visited Staffa and Fingal's Cave; a few days later they were in Greenock, on the Firth of Clyde.

Out of this trip there emerged, in January 1815, the long narrative poem 'The Lord of the Isles'. It was good, but it did not have the impact of his earlier poems. Little over a month later the novel 'Guy Mannering', set in the Borders, appeared. Many believe that the eponymous hero is based on Scott himself; and that it is his best novel.

Now he was travelling again, sailing from Leith, but this time to London, to be entertained by the Prince Regent, by his brother the Duke of York, and by Lord Byron. As always, Scott charmed all of them. No sooner was he back in Edinburgh than he was off to Paris to a dazzling reception. The long war with France was over and the Duke of Wellington, the foreign crowned heads, and the Ambassadors welcomed him there.

He was now in a flurry of prose-writing. Back home in Edinburgh he produced 'The Antiquary', a slow-moving fisherman's tale, followed by, in 1816 'The Black Dwarf' set in the time of Queen Anne. This was to be one of his few failures. But it was followed by the successful 'Old Mortality' whose heroes were Claverhouse on one side and the Covenanters on the other. All novels were anonymous but no one doubted who the author was. In quick succession, in 1817, there followed 'Rob Roy' featuring the 'Highland rogue' and Bailie Nicol Jarvie, and, in the following year, 'The Heart of Midlothian' set in his beloved Edinburgh.

Sir Walter

Towards the end of 1818 he got his due reward when the Regent conferred a baronetcy on him. His daughter Sophia married the promising young lawyer John Lockhart. These were happy times for Sir Walter and Lady Scott. To add to his pleasure, he had obtained the Regent's permission to uncover the Regalia of Scotland - the Sword of State, the sceptre of James V, and the silver mace of the Treasurer of Scotland, which had lain, locked away in Edinburgh since the Union of Parliaments in 1707. Only one thing clouded his pleasure. He had recurrent severe attacks of gallstones.

Both Oxford and Cambridge offered him honorary degrees, but he could not face the journeys; besides he was too busy to accept. But he did accept the prestigious Presidency of the Royal Society of Edinburgh. Scott was in full flow, he had given up his anonymity, and in 1819 he published 'The Legend of Montrose' and 'The Bride of Lammermoor'. He dictated the latter from his sickbed as he suffered agonies of pain and it is noticeable that it is the only one of his books that has a savage, tragic ending. Soon another, 'Ivanhoe' - a knights-in-armour story and the first of his novels in which the action is outside Britain - followed a year later. Then in 1821 came 'Kenilworth' set in the time of Queen Elizabeth, and ranked among his best.

The King visits Edinburgh

In 1822 there came exciting news; the newly-crowned George IV was to visit Edinburgh and Scott was to stage-manage the affair. He did so to such effect that the 60 year-old King, fitted out in Stuart tartan, after a two-week visit, was reluctant to leave. Before he did so, Scott extracted from him the promise that the historic 'Mons Meg' cannon, which had been presented to Scotland by her biggest trading partner, Flanders, in 1457, would be returned from the Tower of London to its rightful place in Edinburgh castle, and that Scottish peerages, forfeited in the Stuart uprising, would be restored. In time they were.

He took up his pen again. 'Quentin Durward', the story of a Scottish archer in the guard of Louis XI, established Scott's reputation on the continent. In 'St. Ronan's Well' he returned to contemporary life in his native Borders, in 'Redgauntlet' he tells the tale through a blind fiddler; while 'Wandering Willie's Tale' was later considered by Robert Louis Stevenson to be one of the best short stories ever written. It was followed by 'The Talisman'; a make-believe tale of the Crusades. 'Woodstock', an imaginary story of Charles II's flight after the battle of Worcester, followed in 1826. And he had in mind "the most wonderful book", 'The Life of Napoleon Buonoparte.' Before that however his fortunes were to reach a low ebb.

Desolation

Early in 1826 the London market took a bad dip; Constable the publishers found themselves in grave difficulties, and Scott was heavily involved in Constable. Among other things he owed them literary work, as yet unwritten, to the value of £10,000 which he had already received and spent on 'Abbotsford'. But that was the least of it. Hurst and Robinson, Constable's London agents went bankrupt for £300,000; Constable themselves went bankrupt for £250,000 and Ballantyne's owed £117,000. Scott, as a major shareholder, was heavily involved with the latter firm; and Ballantyne's was involved with Constable. Ballantynes could have declared themselves insolvent, in which case Scott would have lost all of his personal property, including the furniture and books at Abbotsford. But then he would have been free to start again. Instead, with the agreement of the trustees, Scott elected to write himself out of trouble; all of his future earnings would go to the trustees until his debts were paid off. He closed his Edinburgh house. He was 55 and in ill-health; it was an enormous undertaking and the last six years of his life were devoted to it. In the midst of his troubles, on 11 May 1826, his wife died. He was desolate.

Restitution

He had written innumerable articles in many papers and journals and he continued to do so. But his main task was to write more novels. Hardly surprisingly he produced little of outstanding merit during this period, though they did yield money. The 'Chronicles of the Canongate' contained three stories - 'The Highland Widow', 'The Two Drovers', and 'The Surgeon's Daughter', but he will not be remembered for these. They were followed by two much better stories, 'The Fair Maid of Perth' a story of feudal times, and 'Anne of Geierstein' set in Switzerland.

His 'Bonnie Dundee' (in which he reverted to verse):

> *'Come fill up my cup, come fill up my can,*
> *Come saddle your horses and call up your men*
> *Come open the West Port and let me gang free,*
> *And it's room for the bonnets of Bonny Dundee!'*

is a rousing song that lives to this day, and shows that his spirit was not dead.

With his daughter Anne he visited London where he was received and feasted by the King. In Paris he was welcomed by Charles X, and lionised wherever he went.

He was now working on 'Napoleon' and he finished the massive task in 18 months, in 1827. Its sale yielded £18,000. But it almost involved him in a duel with a General Gourgard who felt slandered and who, it was said, was a crackshot. In preparation for the event, Scott chose Napoleon's pistols from his armoury. Fortunately for Scott, Gourgard did not appear.

For his little grandson, Johnny Lockhart, Scott wrote, 'Tales of a Grandfather', a four volume history of Scotland. Not only did Johnny enjoy it - the general public did too. Scott was now earning £20,000 per year but it all went to his creditors. Meanwhile 'Magnum Opus' - the 48 volumes of his novels under the heading 'The Waverley Novels' - was bringing in £5,000 a year.

A last journey

To celebrate, he and his daughter Anne paid a visit to Italy but on his return journey, in Holland, he suffered a cerebral haemmorhage which paralysed him and he was carried, first to London, where he was attended by two royal physicians, and then home to Abbotsford, where within a few weeks he died. He was buried at Dryburgh Abbey.

REFERENCES AND FURTHER READING
"The Life of Walter Scott." J.G. Lockhart. Robert Cadell, 1842.
"The Life of Sir Walter Scott". Stephen Gwynn. Thornton Butterworth, 1932.
"The Journal of Sir Walter Scott". Edited by W.E.K. Anderson, Clarendon Press, 1972.
"The Wizard of the North'. Carola Oman. Hodder and Stoughton, 1973.
"Walter Scott and Scotland" Paul Henderson Scott. Saltire Society. 1994.

PLACES TO VISIT
Scotland
'Abbotsford', Melrose, Still family-owned but open to the public.
Dryburgh Abbey where Scott is buried.
Lady Stair's House, Lawnmarket, Edinburgh has portraits and manuscripts relating to Scott (as well as to Burns and Stevenson)

JAMES YOUNG (1811 - 1883)

The World's First Oil Man

"With one distillation it gives a clear colourless liquid of brilliant illuminating power". (Lyon Playfair)

In a shady corner of a graveyard near the church where he worshipped, in the little village of Inverkip on the Firth of Clyde, there lie the remains of the world's first oil man.

James Young was born on 13th July 1811, in the Drygate, an old street near Glasgow Cathedral. His father was a carpenter and cabinet-maker and James had but a scanty education spending his days assisting his father at the workbench. But, like many Scots of the period, he had a thirst for knowledge and he was fortunate in that nearby was the Andersonian University founded in 1796 in accordance with the will of John Anderson to make science education available to artisans.

When he was 19 years of age James began to attend evening classes and he fell under the spell of the professor of chemistry, Thomas Graham. It was there too that he formed friendships that were to be with him all his life, friends who were to play a major role in his future. They included fellow students - David Livingstone who was studying medicine at the Andersonian, Lyon (afterwards Baron) Playfair, Hugh Bartholemew, later manager of the Glasgow Gas Works, and Angus Smith, who was to become assistant to Playfair when he was professor at Manchester University, and later to succeed him.

A move to London

Professor Graham quickly recognised Young's potential and within two years he appointed him his assistant. Occasionally Young would take Graham's lectures and his success may be gauged by the fact that in 1836 he was presented with a gold watch and a year later with a testimonial by the Mechanic's class in appreciation of the quality of his teaching. It is also interesting to note that "a galvanic battery constructed by two young men on a new principle, under Mr. Young's instructions, became an object of great attraction, and among those who came to see it and its effects, were two sons of the Professor of Mathematics at the University. Although but boys, both were fired at this first interview, with enthusiasm for electrical science. Both have been for many years Professors in the University of Glasgow. The elder, who has now retired, Professor James Thomson, is well known for his useful inventions and ingenious papers on many branches of science. The younger, Sir William Thomson, ranks over the world as prince of electricians, and second to no living man in scientific reputation" (W.G. Blaikie 'The Life of David Livingstone'. 1910). William Thomson went on to be Lord Kelvin.

When Graham left the Andersonian in 1837 to take up a similar post at University College, London, he took his young assistant with him. A year later Young married his sweetheart, Mary Young who subsequently bore him three sons and four daughters.

Manchester

In 1839 Young left the academic life behind and after working for five years as a manager of Muspratt's chemical works near Liverpool, he joined the great chemical engineering firm of Charles Tennant in Manchester in 1844. He entered readily into the intellectual life of that city, being an active member of the Manchester Literary and Philosophical Society, starting a local Chemical Society, and setting afoot the movement for the establishment of a new liberal newspaper.

The world's first oil well

It was during this period, on 3rd December 1847, that Young received an interesting letter from his friend Lyon Playfair, who in the interim had become Professor of Chemistry in the Royal School of Mines, and had married a Miss Oakes, daughter of the owner of the Rissins Iron Works and collieries at Alfreton, Derbyshire. In this letter Playfair told Young that a spring of naphtha had been discovered on an estate near Alfreton belonging to his brother-in- law. "It yields at present about 300 gallons (1364 litres) daily. The naphtha is about the consistency of thin treacle and with one distillation it gives a clear colourless liquid of brilliant illuminating power". He went on to say that he had advised his in-laws not to develop this product since it would be " an industry foreign to their occupation". He offered to send a gallon (4.5 litres) for examination. "Perhaps you could make a capital thing out of this new industry and enable my friends to do the same".

Young put this proposal to his employers but Tennant's thought that this was too small an enterprise for them, and gave him permission to go ahead on his own and so in 1848, enlisting the aid of the work's chemist, Edward Meldrum, and a young lawyer, E.W. Binney, as partners, Young bought up the yield from the spring and began to produce lubricants for the Manchester cotton mills. Illuminating oils were also produced.

It was noted that a fraction of the oil turned cloudy in cold weather and Playfair pointed out to Young the similarity between this material and the 'earth oil' from Burmah which Christianson in Edinburgh had extracted as a solid and named 'petroline', and the solid 'paraffin' which Reichenbach in Germany had got from beechwood tar. Experimentally, but not commercially, the wax (for such it was) was extracted from Alfreton oil, purified, and converted into candles which were used by Playfair during a lecture on petroleum.

Other sources

The supply of oil from the Alfreton spring was drying up and Young's thoughts turned to other possible sources. He had deduced that the oil was produced by vapours from coal condensing in porous sandstone. He set to work to reproduce these conditions artificially, experimenting with the production of paraffin from the dry distillation of coal. In this he was following in Murdoch's footsteps.

We now know that he was wrong - oil in the earth is formed, not from ordinary coal, but from the remains of marine unicellular plants being compressed over millions of years by accumulating overlying sediments. But his mistaken deduction didn't matter; indeed it was probably helpful since it led him on to the discovery of the extraction of oil because 'coal' of the right kind is a rich source.

The world's first oil works

On 17th October, 1850, he took out a patent for the process of extraction and he coined the word 'cracking', the thermal splitting of paraffins into substances of lower molecular weight, e.g. petrol, a term that is still used in today's oil industry.

Now a second friend from his Andersonian days played his part. Hugh Bartholemew, who had become manager of the Glasgow Gas Works, knowing of his investigations, sent him a sample of cannel coal - a Boghead parrot coal which was being used by the people of Armadale and Bathgate, West Lothian, in little braziers beside their main ordinary coal fires to provide light in their houses. It is of interest here to note that cannel coal had been in regular and continuing use since 1635 as a lighthouse fuel on the Isle of May in the Firth of Forth.

·Cannel was found to give a better yield of oil than any other coal and in the summer of 1850 Young gave up his post at Tennants and, in partnership with Meldrum and Binney, works were erected at Whiteside, Bathgate. A contract was made for supplies of Boghead coal and operations began in 1851. Thus was established the first commercial oil works in the world producing lubricants and naphtha as a solvent for rubber and paint manufacture. A year later Young moved permanently to Scotland and soon he was in business with a large installation, at Addiewell in West Calder, mining and refining and turning out a whole range of products including lubricating oils, illuminating oils, solid paraffin, and candles. Oil lamps were being manufactured in Glasgow and Birmingham.

In Court

The great success of this business gave rise to an immense amount of litigation. Attempts were made to prove that the material from which Young extracted the oil was not true coal and was therefore not covered by his patent of 1850, and in addition that many had preceded him in the distillation of coal. After much conflicting scientific evidence from very distinguished chemists and geologists, it was decreed that the material that he used was indeed a kind of coal. Regarding precedence, it was decided that Young was the first who by gradually bringing coals to a low heat and purifying the products suitably afterwards, made the process a commercial success. His patent was upheld.

In one case concerned with infringement of his patent, the defending company maintained that laboratory methods of preparing paraffin wax were well known before Young took out his patent. Under examination, Young agreed that he had seen paraffin wax while a student at the Andersonian, but that had been a laboratory curiosity, brown in colour and about the size of a walnut. He then produced a 60 lb (27.24 kg) block of white wax and told the court that this was how his company produced it. The ensuing judgement was that whoever could bring a useful commodity from the plane of a laboratory curiosity to that of a commercial product was certainly entitled to the benefit of a patent.

In America

In 1859 Young, accompanied by his wife, went to America to collect royalties due to him from manufacturers who were using his methods of oil extraction. He also viewed, no doubt with considerable apprehension, the great Drake well in Pennsylvania that was ushering in the petroleum age.

The move to shale

On his return to Britain his interest moved to shales ... slate- like compressed sediments containing a good deal of oil within them. After prospecting and finding that there were large deposits in the West Calder area he bought up half a dozen properties, all rich in oil shale. A new company was formed in 1865 with Playfair, Bartholemew, and others on the Board. A plant was erected at West Calder and Young's friend, David Livingstone, laid the foundation stone. Other companies opened up under licence and the paraffin industry spread. Things did not work out well however; among other worries there was severe competition from petroleum and Young retired from the board and management in 1870.

At its peak the mining of oil shale involved some 13,000 men in the county of West Lothian alone. Throughout the area the mining and the manufacturing of products at 120 works were responsible for the employment of 40,000 people turning over 3.75 million tons of oil shale per year. They were producing naphtha for dry-cleaning and India rubber manufacture; batching oils for the spinner and weaver; paraffin wax for candles, tapers, and matches, for waterproofing and for electrical insulation; sulphate of ammonia for our fields in peace time and to provide explosives in war; power oils for the farm tractor and the fishing boat; lighthouse and long-burning oils for the important duties of lighthouse and railway signal lamps.

The discovery of oil wells in the USA, the Middle East, and elsewhere was casting a shadow over the oil shale industry and driving prices down. The number of plants was reduced to 30 by 1873 and to 13 by 1905 though some companies began moving with the times producing fuel oil for furnaces and diesel engines. In 1919 the six surviving companies were brought under one management, Scottish Oils Ltd, a subsidiary of the British Petroleum Company. Competition and high production costs killed the industry and the last of the shale mines closed in 1962.

Retirement

When he retired in 1870 Young was a very rich man owning many large estates and houses in Scotland and England which he gifted to members of his family. He fitted out laboratories in two of his houses, 'Limefield' in West Calder, and 'Kelly' near Wemyss Bay, on the Firth of Clyde and he carried out experimental work at both. In later years he spent most of his time at 'Kelly'.

In the year of his retiral he expressed his thanks for opportunities given in his early life by founding the Young Chair of Technical Chemistry in the Andersonian University, now the University of Strathclyde where the Chair is still in being, and endowing it with £10,000, which was a considerable sum in those days. He also provided a lectureship in Geology but omitted to put this on a permanent footing. He was President of his old University from 1868 -1877. He also presented to the City of Glasgow a bronze statue of his former professor, Thomas Graham, and it stands today in George Square, not far from the statue of James Watt. He also had Graham's researches published privately; these were edited by another old friend, Angus Smith, with whom he spent many vacations.

Young and Livingstone

He did not forget his friend and fellow-student David Livingstone, who had visited him often at 'Limefield'. While Livingstone was exploring in Africa, Young allowed him to draw on him financially as he pleased and any monetary promise made by Livingstone whether to a Portuguese trader or an Arab slave trader, was honoured by Young. He gave generously towards Livingstone's second and third expeditions, contributed £1000 towards his last Zambesi exploration and financed an expedition to Africa under a Lieutenant Grandy to find Livingstone; but it was too late to find him alive.

In his books Livingstone makes many references to his generous and anonymous friend who funded his trips and looked after his family. It is undoubtedly true that without support from Young, Livingstone would not have been able to carry out his later explorations.

Honours

In 1873 Young was elected a Fellow of the Royal Society. In 1879 he was awarded an Honorary LLD of St. Andrews University and in the same year he was elected Vice President of the Chemical Society.

In his later years he enjoyed cruising on his yacht 'Nyasa' with his friend of student days, Angus Smith, visiting the Mediterranean, the island of St. Kilda, and Iceland. The latter two trips were chronicled by Smith and it is clear that Young had not lost his enquiring spirit. Noticing that the bilgewater in his yacht was acid he suggested that the addition of caustic soda would neutralize it and prevent rusting. This idea was later adopted by the Royal Navy.

James Young died at 'Kelly' on 13th May, 1883.

REFERENCES AND FURTHER READING

"James Young." Dictionary of National Biography. Vol. XX1.

"Dr. James Young - a brief biography". H.R.J. Conacher. 'Oil Shale and Cannel Coal'. Institute of Petroleum. 1938.

"Paraffin Young". David Murray. Pall Mall Press, 1959

"James Young" - John Butt PhD. Thesis, 1964, Unit of Glasgow

"The World's First Commercial Oil Industry - where it all began". Anon. Livingston New Town, West Lothian, Scotland.

PLACES TO VISIT

B.P. Information Centre, Grangemouth where there is an excellent shale- oil mining exhibit and where you can get information and a booklet on the 'Paraffin' Young heritage trail, a tour through places of interest relating to Young and the shale oil industry. It includes Young's home 'Limefield' in the grounds of which there is a sycamore tree planted by Livingstone, and in the river, a miniature 'Victoria Falls'.

Inverkip Church Graveyard is on the coast road between Greenock and Largs where Young is buried. Unfortunately his house 'Kelly' is no more. The estate was purchased by Alexander Stephen of Linthouse in 1883. He built a new mansion there which was burned down during suffragette riots in 1913.

DAVID LIVINGSTONE (1813 - 1837)

Missionary and Explorer

"The smoke of a thousand villages, where no white man had ever been before".
(Dr. Robert Moffat)

The Early Years

David Livingstone was born on 19th March 1813 in the little village of Blantyre, eight miles from Glasgow, where his father, Neil, of Highland stock, a deeply religious man steeped in the Calvinist tradition, worked as an itinerant tea vendor, passing out religious tracts with his tea packets. Their home was a single room in Shuttle Row, a three-storey tenement, the property of the mill- owner; David with his two brothers and two sisters attended the village school.

At the age of 10 he was apprenticed in the local cotton mill as a piecer, his job being to join together the broken threads. This was a tough life. He and the other workers, 75% of whom were children, worked from 6 a.m. till 8 p.m. with two breaks half an hour for breakfast and one hour for dinner. But the employers considered themselves 'enlightened'; they provided a school for the boys in their employ where classes were held from 8 p.m. till 10 p.m. David revelled in this opportunity.

He read An Appeal (for medical missionaries) to the Churches of Britain and America on behalf of China' by a Mr. Gutzlaff. Now he knew where his future lay; he would become a medical missionary and go to China. Aged 20 he was off to Glasgow in the winter of 1836 - 37 to study medicine at Anderson's University.

The Missionary Society

During his second session (1837 - 38) he was provisionally accepted by the London Missionary Society and was sent for a three months probationary period to the Rev. Richard Cecil in Essex where he was given instruction in Theology, Latin, Greek and Hebrew. At the end of this period, at his own request, he was sent to London for specialist medical trainmg.

A meeting with Dr. Robert Moffat, a fellow Scot, at the Missionary College determined his future life. Moffat was on leave from his South African Mission from which, he told Livingstone, he had looked north and seen "the smoke of a thousand villages, where no white man had ever been before" and he persuaded the young man that that was where his destiny lay. Livingstone was also fired by a public lecture given by Thomas Buxton, the slave- trade abolitionist, who proclaimed that Africa must be explored, commerce encouraged. Henceforth Livingstone's creed was to redeem Africa by Christianity, Colonisation, and Commerce.

He returned to Glasgow, to pass his exam for the Licentiate of the Faculty of Physicians and Surgeons of Glasgow. Back in London he was ordained as a missionary and on 8th December 1840, aged 27, he sailed for Cape Town, acquiring a knowledge of navigation from the ship's Captain as he went. It was to be 16 years before he saw home again. Arriving in South Africa he made his way 700 miles up country by ox-wagon to Dr. Moffat's station at Kuruman, Bechuanaland where he fell in love with and married Moffat's daughter Mary.

Together they moved north to Chonuane, the village of the Bakwain tribe, whose Chief Sechele, a close friend, had a house, church and school built for them. Sechele was his only convert to Christianity. The remainder of the tribe resisted. "There is no good talking to them", said Sechele, "that will achieve nothing. I have found that the only way to persuade them to do anything is to thrash them. If you like, I will call my head-man and with our whips of rhinoceros- hide, we will soon make them all believe together". Livingstone declined the offer!. During this period Mary had two children - Robert and Agnes.

Due to persistent droughts, the Livingstones and the tribe were constantly on the move crossing the Kalahari Desert in search of better conditions, eventually reaching the marshy shores of Lake Ngami (the first recorded visit by a European). Livingstone wanted to strike off to the north-west where he was sure there was fertile land for the establishment of a Mission, but the river Zouga was a barrier.

They were forced to retrace their footsteps.

A Second Journey

But Livingstone was itching to get back to the Ngami area and beyond. He set off in April 1850, again making the extraordinary decision to take his family of a pregnant Mrs. Livingstone, Robert aged 4, Agnes aged 3, and Thomas aged 1 year, with him. He achieved nothing. His oxen, bitten by the tsetse fly died of 'nagana'. More seriously his children developed malaria, though fortunately Livingstone had a supply of quinine with him and their lives were saved. He noted that "the mosquitoes were so bad that

I could not touch a square half inch of the bodies of the children unbitten after a single night's exposure". Crossing the Kalahari desert they suffered agonies of thirst and the children were so ill, that Livingstone decided to retreat. En route Mary had her overdue baby who died within six weeks.

A Third Journey

The family recuperated with the Moffats for four months, but later Mrs. Moffat, getting a letter from her daughter stating that Livingstone was again planning to go north on a further family expedition, reacted violently and told Livingstone so in no uncertain terms in a letter. "O Livingstone, what do you mean?—all the world will condemn the cruelty of the thing - it is preposterous". She was wasting her breath. The letter merely stiffened Livingstone's resolve to take Mary with him - "Who that believes in Jesus would refuse to make a venture for such a Captain?" In April 1851 they set out, with Mrs. Livingstone again pregnant, but this time they went due north. This meant a longer desert crossing and the family suffered agonies of thirst for five days. But crossing the river Chobe, which Livingstone later discovered was a major tributary of the Zambesi, was easier than the Zouga. Livingstone pressed on to the Zambesi, which it was said, lay 100 miles to the north. When he did reach it he was overcome with wonder it was more than 300 yards wide and very deep. He immediately visualised it as a great commercial highway into the heart of Africa. He also thought that this would be an ideal site for a mission. Livingstone left for the south in August 1851 and on the way, Mrs. Livingstone gave birth to her third son, William.

You are in His care

They arrived in Cape Town on 16th March 1852. Livingstone had previously written to the Missionary Society saying than he was proposing to open up a route into Central Africa that would be shorter than the 1,300 mile trek from the Cape. Furthermore he was sending his family home, and would the Society look after them?.

In April, Mrs Livingstone and her four children sailed for England. When Mrs. Moffat asked what provision had been made for them, Livingstone who had had no reply from the Society, calmly replied that he had no idea! He told his children that Jesus was now their father. "I have given you back to Him and you are in His care". With a small allowance from the Society, Mary and her family became wanderers in Britain staying with her hus-bands's family and then with friends in various parts of England. As the

Dr Livingstone, I presume? The famous meeting between David Livingstone and Stanley

The Explorer as a young man   *As a boy at the mill*

Livingstone with his family

The interior of the house in which Livingstone was born.

Sir James Young Simpson, pioneer in the use of chloroform

Physicist James Clerk Maxwell with his wife and their family pet dog

Andrew Carnegie was born in this room at the family's home in Dunfermline

The author inspects a model display showing Carnegie at work in his study

A portrait of Carnegie who later gave much of his fortune away

Dunlop with his family

*Tyre pioneer John Boyd
Dunlop cycles off*

*Telephone pioneer
Alexander Graham Bell*

*Thomas Edison whose
modifications to the telephone
extended its range*

Telecommunications... how it all began.

Robert Louis Stevenson and (in foreground) a letter in his own handwriting

Scenes from RLS – from left one of his most famous characters Long John Silver, the Young Fol
and the front

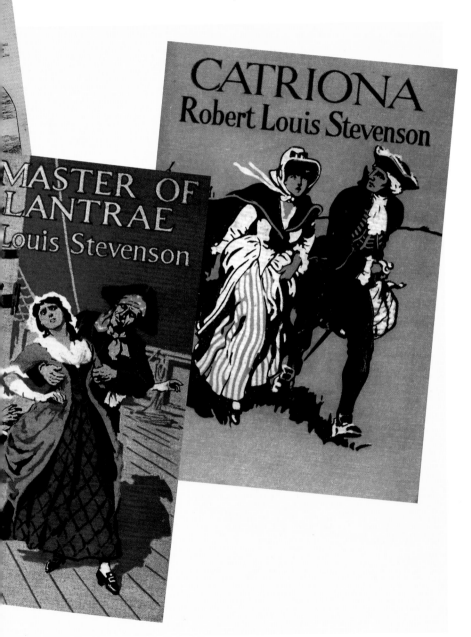

ay 1, 1886, in which *Kidnapped* made its first appearance, *The Master of Ballantrae* in 1916,
iona in 1915

Arthur Conan Doyle posing as his most
famous character Sherlock Holmes

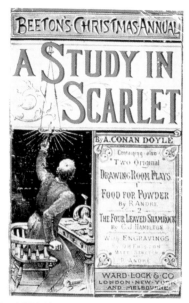

An 1887 Christmas annual in which Holmes
and Watson make their first appearance

A portrait of J. M. Barrie

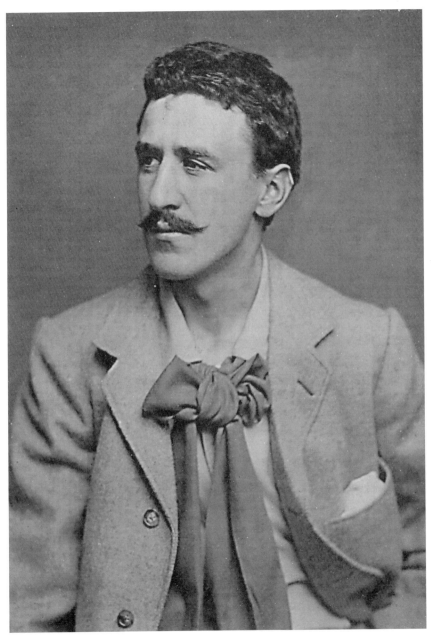

A portrait of Charles Rennie Mackintosh

*Famous high-backed chair designed by Mackintosh
for the Argyle Street Tearooms in Glasgow*

*The Board Room at Glasgow School of Art – 1887–1899. It was later renamed the
Mackintosh Room*

John Buchan pictured at Reuters Ltd

Mairs School at Darvel where he was a pupil

Memorial in Darvel to Alexander Fleming who discovered penicillin

John Logie Baird, who invented television

A memorial bust to Baird at Helensburgh

A demonstration of pioneering colour television broadcast in the 1920s

An early working model of Baird's television

A replica of the first bicycle with front-wheel steering and the rear wheel driven by pedals.
Invented by Kirkpatrick Macmillan. (See chapter on John Boyd Dunlop).

years passed she gave up hope of ever seeing her husband again. She found solace in the bottle.

Across Africa

Now Livingstone was free to undertake his great dream; to cross Africa from Luanda, Angola, on the Atlantic coast to Quelimane, Mozambique, on the Indian Ocean, determined to find a pathway by land or river for traders to penetrate from either coast into Central Africa. It was a journey of 6000 miles and it took him four years during which he suffered recurrent bouts of malaria, and faced many hostile tribes.

Along the Zambezi river he encountered 'Mosi-oa-Tunya' (the smoke that thunders) - 90 ft. across and twice as deep as Niagara - and renamed it the 'Victoria Falls'.

He reached the port of Quelimane, Mozambique on 20th. May 1856 and from there he sailed to England.

Return to Britain

Arriving in London on 9th December 1856 he found himself the most famous man in the country. He had been away 16 years but the story of his travels had spread and had gripped the public imagination. He came back to a hero's welcome, being lauded on all sides as the country's greatest explorer and missionary. His name rang equally through the learned societies and through the churches of the land. But he resigned from the London Missionary Society, much to the chagrin of the Directors.

He was given the Freedom of London and of Glasgow, the latter city also giving him a £2000 testimonial. Oxford, Cambridge (where his speech was received with such enthusiasm that a combined Universities Mission to Central Africa - U.M.C.A. - was formed) and Glasgow universities, gave him honorary degrees. He wrote and had published, his enormously successful 'Missionary Travels' which made him a rich man. He was received by Queen Victoria who 'graciously accepted a copy'. He and his wife were feted wherever they went.

He was invited to make speeches throughout the country, their centrepiece being that the evil of slavery could be overcome by commerce and that the way into central Africa was by the Zambezi river. This theme was taken up by the British government and he was appointed Consul for the East Coast of Africa at £500 per year with Lord Clarendon, the Foreign Secretary, saying "Just tell me what you want and I will give it to you".

God's Pathway to Central Africa

On 10th March 1858, the small steamer 'Pearl' carrying the Zambezi Expedition, sailed for Africa with Dr. and Mrs Livingstone, with their youngest child Oswell, and six assistants, aboard. Mrs. Livingstone being unwell was dropped off at Cape Town to make her way to her parents' home at Kuruman. The 'Pearl' headed for the mouth of the Zambezi where they unloaded and assembled their launch, the 'Ma-Robert' (named in honour of Mrs. Livingstone). Contrary to his expectations, the way was barred by waterfalls and rapids; and sometimes the river dried up to a mere stream. The promises that Livingstone had made in England were in tatters. The Zambezi was not navigable; it was not the easy path to central Africa. He was devastated.

But Livingstone was resilient. He believed himself to be in God's hands, carrying out His purpose. He diverted along the Shire river and on 16th. September 1859 they reached Lake Nyassa.

A letter from the new Foreign Secretary, Lord John Russell, lifted Livingstone's spirits. He was providing a more powerful steamer 'The Pioneer' which arrived on 31st January 1861, to replace the 'Ma-Robert'. Russell also informed him that Bishop Charles Mackenzie, with a band of Anglican missionaries, under the auspices of the U.M.C.A. would be arriving aboard the new ship. Livingstone decided to settle them in the Shire Highlands to form the nucleus of what he hoped would, in time, become a large settlement.

Muscular Christianity

As the 'Pioneer' with Livingstone, the Bishop and his team aboard, steamed up the Zambezi towards the Shire Highlands, it ran into difficulties. Livingstone had a difference of opinion with its Master, who there- upon left for England, and he happily took over command of the ship.

Sometimes they had to haul it over sandbanks and eventually they left the boat behind and set off on foot to find that the Highlands were awash with slave-traders whipping their human cargo along the trails opened up by Livingstone. He found this difficult to take and, at the point of a rifle, freed 84 men, women and children. The Bishop weighed in too and over the next two days 64 more captives were released at gun point. Not only that: the Yao tribe were among the most notorious slavers and Livingstone led an armed attack on one of their villages during which six Yao were shot and the captives released. Livingstone fired the village. Later, when the

Mission was installed at the village of Chigunda, the Bishop, between prayers, led similar raids. This was indeed muscular Christianity, and there were mixed reactions when the news reached England.

Tragedy

Mackenzie had sent a message home for his elderly spinster sister to join him, accompanied by the young bride of Henry Burrop, a new recruit to the Mission. Livingstone approved the idea and to complete the party, he asked his wife Mary to come over with them from Britain, where she had gone from Kuruman to look after their children. When Miss Mackenzie, Mrs. Burrop and Mary arrived in harbour aboard the 'Gorgon', Livingstone, who had returned to the coast, was waiting to greet them.

The captain of the IGorgon' escorted Miss Mackenzie and Mrs Burrop to the Mission. But what should have been a happy arrival was instead a very sad one; they were met with the devastating news that the Bishop and Henry Burrop had earlier died of fever. And that was not the end of the tragedy. Three months later, Mary Livingstone who had long been in poor health, also died of fever. Livingstone, overcome with grief, buried her beneath the shade of a large baobab tree.

The Lady Nyassa

As well as bringing the ladies, the 'Gorgon' had brought the sections of a steamship, the ILady Nyassa', paid for by Livingstone to the tune of £6000. He set to work to have it assembled but surprises were in store for him. The new Bishop from England, who had come to replace Mackenzie, decided that the Mission was not in a suitable site and he moved it west to safer and healthier country. This was a blow to Livingstone's pride since he had chosen the original site; but a bigger blow followed. There was a dispatch from Lord Russell recalling the Zambezi expedition and ordering that the Pioneer' was to be handed over to the navy. This was done. Livingstone decided to sell the 'Nyassa' which he owned, but the only offer came from the Portuguese, who would have used it as a slaver, and Livingstone was not having that. So, on 30th April 1864 he set off on an incredible 2,500= mile, three months voyage across the Indian Ocean to Bombay. He left the vessel to be sold there and made his way to England arriving on 21st July .

Home again

His welcome this time was not as ecstatic as on the the first occasion. Although the Prime Minister, Lord Palmerston, was "very affable" the

Foreign Secretary, Lord Russell was "cool". He got offers (£500 each) from the Government and from the Royal Geographical Society, to trace the source of the Nile. It was fairly niggardly, but it was subsequently topped up by another £1000 from James Young a friend of his 'Andersonian' days, and Livingstone jumped at the chance.

Back to Africa

Arriving at Bombay he sold the 'Lady Nyassa' for £2600 which he proceeded to lose by investing it in the Indian Bank. In January 1866 he saile for Zanzibar to the mouth of the river Rovuma. With the exception of two, Susi and Chuma, his helpers were not up to the job, and gradually deserted him as he penetrated inland by foot in search of the lakes that might be the source of the Nile. Everywhere he went he met slavers and, although he found the trade abhorrent and cruel, eventually he was so weak with rheumatism, dysentery and malaria, that he had to accept help from them.

The one bright spot was the arrival at Ujii on 10th November 1871, of Henry Morton Stanley who had been sent out by the 'New York Herald' to find him. The two men struck up an immediate rapport, but all attempts by Stanley to persuade Livingstone to return to England with him failed. It was a sad parting, for Livingstone's health was deteriorating and both men knew that they would never see each other again.

The end was approaching for the elderly African traveller; he was becoming ever weaker and during his last expedition, Susi and Chuma had to take turns of carrying him on their shoulders. It was these two who found him dead, kneeling by his bedside, at Ilala on 1st May 1873.

Three of his servants remained faithful to the end - and beyond. They removed the contents of his chest and abdomen and buried them under a tree on which one of them, Jacob Wainwright, inscribed Livingston's name. He also conducted the burial service and then made a careful inventory of his master's possessions. The remainder of the body was embalmed by drying it in the sun and was then carried by Susi, Chuma, and Wainwright through 1,500 miles of dangerous country, through swamp and desert, to the coast of Zanzibar, whence it was carried by ship to England to be buried in Westminster Abbey.

Jacob Wainwright was wrongly identified as leader of the group and was taken to London to play a prominent part in the service. Susi and Chuma were virtually neglected but were brought later to Britain by Young.

Epilogue

In his day, and well beyond it, David Livingstone was acclaimed by the

Protestant Church as one of its greatest missionaries, and by the Geographical Society as one of its greatest explorers. Yet he was neither. In the course of his work in the mission fields of Africa he converted only one man, Chief Sechele, to Christianity and most of the places that he 'discovered' had been visited before by white men. And yet the myth lives on to the present day. Why? Well quite simply the Victorians needed and demanded heroes. And there is no doubt but that Livingstone was heroic. Why should he be included in this book? The reason is that he changed the world. His influence was enormous. His stories inspired many young men and women to enter the mission field; others to become explorers; British and other governments colonised Africa in his wake; and trade missions were established. The face of Africa was changed out of all recognition. And he persuaded white men to look anew at the horrors of slavery.

REFERENCES AND FURTHER READING

'Missionary Travels and Researches in South Africa'. D. Livingstone. John Murray, 1857.

'Narrative of an Expedition to the Zambezi and its Tributaries'. D. and C. Livingstone. John Murray, 1865.

'Last Journals of David Livingstone in Central Africa:1868-1873'. Horace Waller. 1874 (2 vols.)

'David Livingstone'. Thomas Hughes. Macmillan and Co. 1889.

'The Life of David Livingstone'. William. G. Blaikie. John Murray, 1910.

'Livingstone' R. J. Campbell. Ernest Benn Ltd, 1929.

'Livingstone'. Tim Jeal. Heinemann, 1973.

'David Livingstone - The dark interior'. Oliver Ransford. John Murray, 1978.

"Journey to Livingstone: Exploration of an Imperial Myth". Timothy Holmes. Canongate Presss. 1993.

PLACES TO VISIT
Scotland

Livingstone's birthplace at Blantyre, near Hamilton, where 'Shuttle Row' has been converted into a splendid musem, including the room in which Livingstone was born and in which he and the family lived. There is also a series of illuminated scenes of his African journeys.

Royal College of Physicians and Surgeons, 234-242 St Vincent St, Glasgow where many of his instruments are exhibited. (By arrangement).

JAMES SIMPSON (1811 - 1870)

Anaesthesia

"This is far stronger and better than ether"

James Young Simpson was born on 7th June 1811 in the little weaving town of Bathgate some 18 miles west of Edinburgh where his father, David, was the Main Street baker. His mother was of Huguenot extraction and bore David one daughter and seven sons of whom James was the youngest.

James was a very able pupil at school, becoming Dux, but he always maintained that his mother, to whom he was devoted, was his best teacher. Her death while he was still a boy, was a sore blow to him, but his sister, Mary, became his 'second mother' and looked after him well. He never forgot his mother and he could never see a woman mending her child's dress without a tear coming to his eye. He was very fond of children which may have led him into his specialist medical field and when, at the height of his fame, he visited his old school, he offered an annual prize for the best darner, reckoning that there were already enough prizes for academic pursuits.

But that was in the future.

University

In view of his scholastic ability his elder brothers decided that they would support him at university so, at the age of 14, off he went to Edinburgh, carrying his traditional sack of oatmeal and a goodly supply of eggs, to enrol for a Master of Arts degree. He was young, poor, and very lonely away from his loving sister but she kept him well-supplied with food and clothes. He took some time to settle to the unfamiliar life but gradually, as he gained confidence, his worth began to show and he won the Stuart Bursary of £10. He shared accommodation with two hard-working Bathgate lads who were studying medicine and young James fell into their work habits.

Medicine

He also absorbed their love of medicine and some evenings he would go with them to hear lectures by Dr. Knox who was to become notorious as a receiver of corpses from the grave-robbers and murderers, Burke and Hare.

James switched to the study of medicine in 1827 when he was 16 years of age.

He wasn't long into his studentship when he almost gave it up, so terrible were the sights that he had to endure in the operating theatres. There were no anaesthetics so that the patient had often to be dragged screaming to the theatre and held down by four or five men while the surgeon performed the operation with the patient fully conscious. Not only had the patient to endure terrible pain; sometimes the shock of the operation was fatal. Surgeons had to work fast!

Fortunately Simpson decided to continue and, as we shall see, it was he who was to take the terror out of operations. He graduated M.D. in 1832. After three months travelling in Europe, with money generously provided by his brothers, he settled down to general medicine in Edinburgh and in time built up a large and very successful practice. But always his eye was on midwifery and when the Chair in that subject fell vacant he applied for the post and was appointed professor in 1839. Perhaps he did not have stiff opposition. Midwifery was considered the lowliest of subjects - birth was considered a fairly routine matter despite the attendant deaths, and womens' medical problems were not considered worthy of any special attention.

Success

Professor Simpson was an immediate and brilliant success. Students flocked to his classes, so that soon it was a case of 'standing-room only'. From being the Cinderella of medical subjects the Midwifery class became the largest in the University. The numbers were swollen by people who had long-since left the University, but who returned to sit at the feet of the brilliant young professor. Since this was a time when students paid their fees direct to the professor who taught the class, Simpson was on his way to becoming rich. He married, moved into a splendid house, and could now afford a carriage.

His fame was spreading. His patients now numbered princesses, marchionesses, and countesses. He was attending duchesses in London. And, crowning glory of all, in 1847 he had a letter from the Duchess of Sutherland telling him that the Queen had appointed him one of Her Majesty's physicians in Scotland. But his feet were firmly on the ground. His sister had married and moved to Australia, but he kept up a correspondence with her and with his eldest brother in Bathgate. "Flattery from the Queen is perhaps not common flattery; but I am far less interested in it than in having delivered a woman this week without pain while inhaling sulphuric ether. I can think of naught else".

Hypnotism

He had long been interested in ways of relieving pain and suffering, and had even dabbled in hypnosis finding that he had considerable powers in this field. One of his great successes was manifested at a dinner party. He hypnotised a young lady sitting next to him and then forbade her to speak until he gave her permission to do so. Unfortunately he was called from the room and when he returned some time later he found the young lady literally and metaphorically speechless. She had expressed her anger in writing! He gave up the idea of applying hypnosis to medicine, not because of this incident, but because he found that it was very erratic in its application.

Laughing gas

He turned to the use of anaesthetics. Exciting news was coming out of America. Although the distinguished chemist, Sir Humphrey Davy in England, experimenting on himself, had shown that nitrous oxide was "capable of destroying physical pain - and may be used with advantage during surgical operations", this finding had lain dormant for about 40 years till a Mr. Colton, lecturing on nitrous oxide gas at Hartford, Connecticut, impressed a dentist, Mr. Horace Wells, a member of the audience, by demonstrating its properties on a subject who fell and bruised himself without apparently feeling any pain. Next day Wells offered himself as a guinea pig and had Colton administer gas to him while a fellow dentist, Dr. Rigg, extracted a tooth. Wells suffered no pain and this was certainly a landmark in dentistry.

Ether

But it was more than that. It led to the testing of other gases and a very brave young dentist named Morton, in 1846, tried out ether on himself, and was insensible for eight minutes. Later, he administered ether to a patient and extracted a tooth. He realized that it could be used for bigger and longer operations than tooth extraction and within a few weeks it was being used for surgical operations in Boston with Morton as the anaesthetist.

Simpson knew of this work that was going on in the U.S.A. and he used ether as an anaesthetic on the mother while delivering a child on 19th

January 1847. It was a landmark and it went well; but still he was not completely satisfied. Ether had a disagreeable smell and was inclined to irritate the lining of the nose. Like Morton before him, Simpson experimented on himself in his search for a 'drowsy syrup' and he went around inhaling all sorts of vapours, putting his own life at risk in the process. Happily he survived.

Chloroform

Mr. Waldie, a chemist from Liverpool sent him a small quantity of the chemical 'perchloride of formyle' (chloroform) and suggested to him that it might be worthy of trial. The scene that followed was described by a neighbour, Professor Miller in his book Principles of Surgery (1852):

"Late one evening - it was the 4th November 1847 - on returning home after a weary day's labour, Dr. Simpson with his two friends and assistants, Drs. Keith and Matthews Duncan sat down to their somewhat hazardous work in Dr. Simpson's dining room. Having inhaled several substances without much effect, it occurred to Dr. Simpson to try a ponderous material which he had formerly set aside on a lumber-table and which, on account of its great weight, he had hitherto regarded as of no likelihood whatever. That happened to be a small bottle of chloroform. It was searched for and recovered from beneath a heap of waste paper. And with each tumbler newly charged, the inhalers resumed their vocation. Immediately an unwonted hilarity seized the party; they became bright-eyed, very happy, and very loquacious - expatiating on the delicious aroma of the new fluid. The conversation was of unusual intelligence and quite charmed the listeners - some ladies of the family and a naval officer, brother-in-law of Dr. Simpson. But suddenly there was a talk of sounds being heard like those of a cotton-mill, louder and louder; a moment more, then all was quiet, and then - a crash. On awakening, Dr. Simpson's first perception was mental - 'This is far stronger and better than ether' he said to himself. His second was to note that he was prostrate on the floor and that among the friends about him there was both confusion and alarm. Hearing a noise, he turned round and saw Dr. Duncan beneath a chair; his jaw dropped, his eyes staring , his head bent half under him; quite unconscious and snoring in a most determined and alarming manner. More noise still and much motion. And then his eyes overtook Dr. Keith's feet and legs making valorous efforts to overturn the supper table, or more probably to annihilate everything that was on it".

It is not surprising to learn that the party went on till 3 a.m. The onlookers who were so alarmed were Mrs. Simpson, her sister Miss Grindley, her niece Miss Petrie, and her brother-in-law, Captain Petrie. Simpson's daughter Eve who wrote a biography of him writes: "My aunt often spoke of Dr. Keith's ghastly expression when, ceasing to kick, he raised his head to the level of the table and stared with unconscious eyes on them. She had such a horror of chloroform she refused ever to try it".

Well, Miss Grindley may never have used it but many were willing to extol its virtues. Among them was the Duchess of Argyll who wrote to congratulate Simpson within a month of its discovery. By 1895, Duncan and Flockhart, the firm that had supplied the first sample of chloroform to Simpson, were producing three-quarters of a million doses a week.

The first child to be born while her mother was anaesthetized was the daughter of a medical colleague and she was christened 'Anaesthesia'. When she was 17 she was photographed and she sent a print to Simpson. It is said that he was delighted, but there is no record as to what she thought of her name.

One of the first surgical cases, a soldier, on which chloroform was used, enjoyed the experience so much that on waking up "he seized the sponge, with which administration had been made and thrusting it into his mouth, again resumed inhalation more vigorously than before, as if it were too good a thing to be stopped so soon".

But not all were so deliriously happy, and in childbirth cases, Simpson had to face some pretty stiff opposition, especially from men, who did not feel that it was right to 'interfere with Nature'. There was also a storm of invective from those who believed that the use of chloroform undermined religion. Many churchmen held that "to try to remove the primal curse on women was to fight against divine law". Some doctors believed that the cold steel of the surgeon's knife was a good tonic!; some believed much more realistically, that a number of deaths were due to the use of chloroform.

Simpson was shaken by the opposition to his discovery, but he hit back by collecting figures on the results of births and operations using chloroform, and he met the religious bigots on their own ground by finding suitable quotes from the Bible. But it was not until Queen Victoria gave birth to Prince Leopold, while anaesthetized by chloroform, that the opposition began to wither away. What was good enough for the Queen was good enough for everyone! Surgery without chloroform became unthinkable. The alleviation of pain and suffering due to its use is incalculable.

Honours began to pour in on Simpson. Queen Victoria made him a baronet in 1886. He received the Freedom of Edinburgh, and was given an Honorary degree by Oxford University. He was made an Associate of the Imperial College of Medicine, Paris; he received the Order of St. Olaf from the King of Sweden; and he was awarded the Monython Prize by the French Academy of Sciences. Many attempts were made to entice him away from Edinburgh; but he loved it too much to go. Besides he was close to Bathgate and perhaps he loved that even more.

His personal life was sad in that he lost four members of his family - his first child Maggie the "beloved Marmazette" lived for only four years; a son Jamie suffered from progressive blindness before he died; David, the eldest son graduated M.D. but died soon afterwards; and his sister "darling little Jessie" delicate from birth, followed him. And so, despite all his triumphs, Simpson suffered crushing blows. He said of the honour that had been bestowed upon him, "I felt this baronetcy such a bauble in health and now when sick and heartsore what a bauble it is".

The long years of hard work and the great sorrows, were taking their toll. His health was failing, and he died on 6th May, 1870. His family were offered a resting place for him in Westminster Abbey, but his wife declined the honour, feeling that he would prefer to be buried in Edinburgh.

REFERENCES AND FURTHER READING

"Memoir of Sir J.Y. Simpson (Bart.). John Duns. 1873

"Sir James Young Simpson". Eve B. Simpson. in Famous Scots Series. Oliphant, Anderson, and Ferrier, 1896.

"Sir James Young Simpson and Chloroform". H.L. Gordon, 1897.

PLACES TO VISIT

A room at Simpson's home, 52 Queen St, Edinburgh, is now a museum containing many items of interest. There is a statue of Simpson in Princes St, Edinburgh.

JAMES CLERK MAXWELL (1831-1879)

Physicist

*"He mounted one of his students on a stand and pumpit him
him fu' o' electricity so that his hair stood oot on end"*

(R.V. Jones)

Within both the Clerk and the Maxwell families in southern Scotland, there was a long history of outstanding medicine, science and technology, stretching back to the 17th. century. And it all seemed to peak in one unlikely lad, James Clerk Maxwell. He has been described as one of the finest mathematicians who ever lived, but he is best known for his contributions to physics, in which subject he has been placed second only to Einstein.

James's father, John, although a qualified barrister, had a deep interest in technology, devising a bellows to deliver a continuous blast of air, and writing a paper on 'A plan for Combining Machinery with the Manual Printing Press'. He was also an active Fellow of the Royal Society of Edinburgh. He was married at the age of 36 in Edinburgh, to Frances Cay, the sister of a close friend and fellow enthusiast for technology.

Early Days

Their first child, Elizabeth, died in her infancy, and James, their only surviving child was born on 13th.June 1831 at 14 India Street, Edinburgh. Soon afterwards they moved to the very substantial family home at Glenlair, Galloway, where James spent a happy childhood. He was an eager, questing boy and he constantly bombarded his father with questions ranging from the working of the Universe to "How do you know that that pebble is blue?".

A lesser man might have evaded such difficulties. Not so John. He treated his son as his intellectual equal and attempted answers to the questions that came in from all sides. A deep bond of affection and respect was forged between the two, a bond that lasted throughout their lifetimes. Unlike many of his neighbours, James would not shoot or fish. Instead, he observed. Thus the boy grew up and developed in a scientific atmosphere.

His mother redressed the balance with Bible instruction and James remained a devout Christian all his life.

His mother died, aged 48, when he was only nine. His father, keen to retain the company of his son, brought in a private tutor, only 16 years of age. This was disastrous. The tutor, convinced that James was a dunderhead, used his belt liberally, banged his head, and pulled his ears. How James must have longed for his gentle mother. But James had a few tricks himself - he was not above putting a live frog in his mouth and allowing it to pop out when speaking to someone.

Schooldays

His early days at Edinburgh Academy were miserable ones. As a result of being tutored at home he came 'late' to school and found that 'cliques' had long since formed. Maxwell was an 'outsider' and, due to his withdrawn manner and country dress, he fell easy prey to torment and bullying. His schoolmates seemed to reach the same conclusion as his erstwhile tutor; James was nicknamed 'Daftie'. He was not helped by the fact that he held on to his 'rustic' Scottish accent. James retained it all his life, and resisted all attempts to have it flattened into 'Standard English'. Well done James! He didn't shine in classes either, seeing little logic in the Latin that was taught.

It was only in his senior years at school, as he gained confidence and his short-sightedness was diagnosed, that he began to shine; Latin began to unfold before him and mathematics revealed its true beauty. In his spare time, with his father, he attended lectures at the Royal Society of Edinburgh, and the Society of Arts, and the day came when he himself contributed a paper 'On the Description of Oval Curves, and those having a Plurality of Foci'. He was but 14 years of age and adjudged too young to make a presentation. His paper was read for him by Professor James Forbes, who was later to become his friend and teacher at university.

Edinburgh University

Leaving school, Maxwell moved on to Edinburgh University, though he was by no means sure as to whether he would specialize in Law or in Science. One of the great advantages of the Scottish university system was that he didn't have to make an early choice. There was a strong thread of Philosophy running through both in the generalist degree, and within the Philosophy there was much science. The Law seemed to offer the better chance of a reasonable living but Maxwell fell under the influence of Philip

Kelland, Professor of Mathematics, Sir William Hamilton whose Philosophy veered towards Science, and Professor James Forbes of Natural Philosophy who, it will be recalled, read Maxwell's paper for him at the Society of Arts. There were no practical classes for undergraduates in Natural Philosophy in those days, but Forbes gave James the free run of his private laboratory where he could carry out experiments of his own. In addition, through one of his relatives, James visited the distinguished scientist, William Nicol, the deviser of the 'Nicol Prisms', beloved of geologists, for analysing polarised light. Nicol gave him a pair of prisms, which stimulated his interest in light, and which he cherished all his life. James decided that he was going to be a scientist.

Cambridge

It was time to move to Cambridge, and here his true worth showed and was appreciated. So too was his Scottish accent. It had an air of authority. He was recognised as being close to genius. At Cambridge, unlike Scotland, there was no compulsion about attending lectures, and the more general practice was for the students to employ tutors. Despite his earlier experience, Maxwell soon fell into this scheme of things and this time he was very lucky with his choice. William Hopkins was very experienced, accepted only 14 of the best, of which James was one, and had a high record of success in the maths 'Tripos' - that peculiarly Cambridge system of attaining a degree. It consisted of seven days of examinations made up of some 200 questions. The questions for the first three days consisted of bookwork (Euclid and 'Principia') at the end of which most participants opted out with enough for a degree. For Honours awards, however, there were four more days of questions, at the end of which the top student was declared the 'Senior Wrangler'. It was followed by one further exam for the very prestigious 'Smith Prize'.

Students trained hard for the Tripos and none more so than Maxwell. He had one period of ill-health - 'brain-fever' - but made a good recovery. It was expected that he would be Senior Wrangler but in the event he came second and he was First equal in the Smith Prize. It was at Cambridge that he began his work on electromagnetism.

In the winter of 1855/56 his father, to whom he was very close, fell ill. Maxwell welcomed the invitation to apply for the position of Professor of Natural Philosophy at Marischal College, Aberdeen. It was prestigious and it also would mean that he could be near his father. But his father died in April 1856, before his son was appointed.

Marischal College

Life in Aberdeen was very different from the leisurely life that he might have had as a don in Cambridge. The Scots were great believers in lots of lectures and lots of examinations.

Professor Maxwell had to take students through the degree course almost single-handed and had to give them tests weekly. In addition he introduced something entirely new - practical classes for undergraduates. It was a tall order, but there were compensations. The Scottish session ran from November to April. Thereafter, professors (and students) were free to 'gang their ain gait'. For Maxwell this meant heading for Glenlair to look after the estate that he had inherited from his father and which he looked upon as a sacred trust. He still found time to initiate his research on gas theory; and to be awarded the Adams' Prize of St. John's College Cambridge, for his demonstration, involving much mathematical calculation, that Saturn's rings were composed of particles of matter. This established him as a front-rank scientist.

It was in Aberdeen (1858) that he also found time to meet and marry Katherine Dewar, seven years his senior, daughter of the Principal of the College. She encouraged him in his research, and looked after him well when he contracted smallpox in Galloway and in his last illness in Cambridge.

He made one bad calculation. It was proposed that the two Aberdeen colleges - Marischal and Kings - should unite, with both sets of professors remaining, or fuse with one set of professors becoming redundant. Maxwell came out strongly in favour of the latter and it won the day. It was assumed that Maxwell would retain the Chair. In the event, he didn't, and Professor David Thomson of King's took over. Maxwell was redundant!

He applied for the recently-vacated chair at Edinburgh University, but was beaten to it by Professor P.G. Tait of Belfast, an old Edinburgh Academy and Cambridge friend whom he had earlier beaten for the Marischal post.

But he didn't have long to wait. The Professorship of Natural Philosophy at King's College, London, fell vacant, and Maxwell was appointed in 1860.

London

Maxwell spent only five years at Kings but they were among his most productive. It was here that he drew together the threads of his work on electricity and magnetism and united them into four simple mathematical formulae - what we now know as Maxwell's equations. He also drew optics into this great electomagnetic unification. As well as having enormous implications for fundamental science, his findings paved the way for the later practical development of X-rays, radio, and television. His work was but one of the many manifestations of the value of 'pure' research.

In optics he carried out fundamental investigations on colour vision and colour-blindness, showing that the eye has three sorts of receptors - one sensitive to red light, another to blue, and a third to green, and that colour-blindness was due to the absence of one of these receptors. He contributed to the great Victorian pastime of photography by taking the first colour photograph.

Back to Glenlair

In 1865, Maxwell resigned his Chair at King's and moved back to Glenlair in Galloway. He wanted to look after the property and to devote much more time to his researches and to complete his book 'A Treatise on Electricity and Magnetism'. He kept up a massive three-way correspondence with Thomson (Kelvin) in Glasgow, and Tait in Edinburgh, in which the three sparked ideas off each other, dealing with the most abstruse problems in Natural Philosophy. They also met from time to time in the rooms of the Royal Society of Edinburgh. What a triumvirate that was! Three of the most distinguished physicists in the world, two of them Scottish (Tait and Maxwell) and one Irish/Scottish (Kelvin)

Maxwell applied for the Principalship of St.Andrews University but did not get the job. Perhaps it was fortunate that he didn't because it would have involved him in administrative work to the detriment of his science and in 1871 he was winkled out of Galloway and persuaded to become the first Professor of Experimental Physics at Cambridge.

One of his duties was to organize the construction of the Cavendish Laboratory, the money for which was put up by William Cavendish, Duke of Devonshire, one of the few members of the aristocracy to take a deep interest in Science; in the years to come the Cavendish was to stand for all that was excellent in physics.

Another was to encourage research, and this he did to such good effect that he published more than 50 papers during this period, including the final ones on the dynamics of gas movement, the monumental work that he had begun in Aberdeen. Many of his research students attained high office in the scientific and academic world.

Perhaps he wasn't quite so successful with his undergraduate lectures. On occasions it is said that only two students attended. But then, as Maxwell would recall, attendance wasn't compulsory!

Maxwell died on November 1879 of cancer of the colon. He was only 48 years of age.

REFERENCES AND FURTHER READING

'The Life of James Clerk Maxwell' Lewis Campbell and William Garnett. 1882.
'Clerk Maxwell and Modern Science' ed. C.Domb. 1963.
'The Demon in the Aether - The Life of James Clerk Maxwell'. Martin Goldman. Paul Harris Publishing, 1983.

PLACES TO VISIT
Scotland
Glenlair Country House, Galloway, where there are portraits and many items of his scientific apparatus.

England
Cavendish Laboratorie, Cambridge.

ANDREW CARNEGIE (1838 - 1919)

Industrialist

"Never stop a man making money but remember that during his lifetime
he should always give it back"

"The King sits in Dunfermline toon
Drinking the bluid-red wine
Where will I get a skeely skipper
To sail this ship o' mine?"

Dunfermline, established as the first capital of Scotland by Malcolm Canmore (1031 - 1093), whose father had been slain by Macbeth, houses the bones of another Scottish king, Robert the Bruce (1274 - 1329), discovered in 1818 still wrapped in their shroud of gold and linen cloths.

It is also the birthplace of Andrew Carnegie, destined to be the richest man in the world. The Carnegies were a poor, radical, anti-royalist family. His father, William, was a weaver, but the change from hand-loom to steam-loom weaving (not recognised early enough by William) was disastrous, and although the family income was supplemented by a wee shop kept by his wife (a formidable but loving woman) the Carnegies on occasions knew real poverty.

Dunfermline days

Andrew had a scanty education, not going to school until he was eight, because his parents felt that he should not go until he decided that he wanted to! But he has written that when he did go there "it was a perfect delight to me", although he was sometimes late in the mornings through having to fetch water from the well. He came under the benign influence of the headmaster, Mr. Robert Martin, who gave him the first penny that he ever earned, for reciting Burns' 'Man was made to Mourn'. Another marked influence on him was 'good Uncle Lauder' who told him stories of the great patriots Wallace and Bruce, of the poets Blind Harry, Burns, Scott, Ramsay, Tannahill, Hogg, and Ferguson, creating in the boy a fierce patriotism that never left him.

Even in those early days Andrew was beginning to show his entrepreneurial spirit - when his father gave him a couple of rabbits he offered his pals the chance to have them named after them provided they fed them.

Off to the New World

A letter came from his mother's sisters in America inviting the Carnegies to join them and so in May 1848, William Carnegie sold his looms and his furniture, borrowed £20, and with his wife and two sons, Andrew (12) and Tom (4) sailed all the way to Pittsburgh, Pennsylvania. They took the cheapest possible route – by rowing-boat to a steamer in the Firth of Forth that took them up the Clyde to the Broomielaw, Glasgow, where they boarded the 800 ton sailing ship 'Wiscaset' which was to be their home for 7 weeks. After a short stop in New York to change boats, they sailed up the Hudson river to Albany, to Buffalo, to Cleveland; then three weeks on a canal-boat to Beaver, and by paddle-steamer up the Ohio to Pittsburgh. They had arrived after travelling 4000 miles of sea voyages.

Pittsburgh

The Carnegies were warmly welcomed by their relatives. But they lived in the poorest quarter and Andrew had to find work. Through his father, who got a job in the cotton mill with a Scotsman who employed only immigrant Scotsmen, Andrew got a job as a 'bobbin boy' at $1.20 a week. In time he moved to the factory of a Mr. Hay, another fellow Scot, who manufactured bobbins, to run the steam-engine and fire the boilers. Mr. Hay was a good business man but not a good writer. Andrew was, and he was also good at figures and when the paper work came in, Andrew helped him out. Soon he was taken off the shop floor to become a clerk at $2 a week. He attended evening classes and got a job as a message boy in a telegraph office at $2.50. In his spare time he read voraciously the books belonging to a Colonel James Anderson who made his 400 volumes available, free, every Saturday, to any poor boy who wished to borrow a book for a week. Carnegie was to remember this and act on it in later years.

He was very bright. Soon he was relieving telegraph operators and after three years he had a regular job at $20 a month. He repaid the £20 debt back in Scotland. His mother was always behind him, encouraging and urging him on. As we shall see, she remained a powerful influence all the days of her life.

A railway appointment

Business men praised his prowess, and when the Philadelphia to Pittsburgh railway line opened, the newly appointed Superintendent, Thomas Scott, appointed Andrew, aged 16, his personal operator. Andrew thrived in the job and when Scott was absent from the office on business,

Andrew took decisions, even anticipating a strike and averting it by sacking the leaders. Here was a foretaste of his future attitude to strikes.

With the money that he earned he bought shares in the Railway Company and in the newly-developing sleeping-car carriages . At the age of 24 he succeeded Scott (who was moved up to Vice-President) as Superintendent (at $1,500 a year). The young Scot had come far - but he had further to go.

He was not really interested in salaries - he had discovered that shares were the real way to make money. He was only 5 ft. 3" tall but he was very tough. In the Civil War he made no secret of where his sympathies lay - he was a strong supporter of the Republican North. Scott had moved on to bigger things after leaving his job as Superintendent. He was now organizing railways for Abraham Lincoln and he summoned young Carnegie to Washington to assist him. When that job was completed Andrew returned to his job with the railways at $2,400 a year. But that was chicken feed. Almost in passing he made a few million dollars by investing in the Drake Oil Well discovered in Pennsylvania; but that was not where his main interests lay. He was hooked on railways, and through railways, on steel. At the age of 30 he resigned his post as Superintendent, and was soon arranging telegraphy for the new Pullman Car Company and building bridges, deducing that if railways were to succeed, America needed bridges. He was also busier than ever buying and selling shares. He had become very wealthy. Early bridges were made of wood, but Carnegie, realizing that they would not carry the heavy locomotives and carriages that were developing, moved in, bought the Keystone Bridge Company, and created the Union Iron Mills.

He made a foray into politics. Linking the two countries that he loved, he tried very hard for the post of American Consul in Glasgow, but in this one he failed. He retired, at least temporarily, from the political field.

The Steelmaster

More and more of his time was now devoted to the manufacture of iron and when Henry Bessemer in England in 1856 developed his process for making steel from pig-iron, Carnegie realized that the world was entering the Steel Age. He built a massive steel mill in Pittsburgh and during the Depression he bought up cheaply, all the iron, low in phosphorous, that he could lay his hands on. He was ready for the boom when it came and instead of paying his employees high wages, he encouraged them to take shares in the Company, always keeping 55% to himself so that he had total control. Construction costs never worried him - it was operational costs that mattered - and that was one of the reasons for his success. That and returning only a small profit to shareholders - he kept dividends low, ploughing profits back into the Company, buying and expanding in recession - because recessions don't last. He looked on recession as a time of opportunity. He made his brother Tom Chairman and by 1880 Carnegie Bros. and Company Ltd. was making $2 million a year profit.

A visit to Scotland

With his mother he visited Scotland. In Dunfermline he donated a swimming baths to the town, and his mother opened there the first library that he gave outside the U.S.A. Carnegie was emotionally deeply attached to her, and determined that she should have all the good things in life that had been denied her as a young woman. He also loved his native country and the town of his birth "Ah, you suit me Scotia, and proud I am to be your son. What Benares is to the Hindu, Mecca to the Mohammedan, Jerusalem to the Christian, all that Dunfermline is to me". He was really a remarkably emotional man.

Marriage and Scotland

In 1883, when he was 48 years of age, he became secretly engaged to Louise Whitfield, but they did not marry until his mother died three years later. Immediately after the wedding they sailed for Scotland taking over the tenancy of Cluny Castle near Kingussie. From the first Louise fell in love with Scotland and for the next ten years they spent the six summer months here when their daughter Margaret was born in 1897. Then Louise insisted that they must have their own home in the Highlands and so Skibo Castle on the Dornoch Firth, Sutherland, was bought. Carnegie threw himself into British politics, becoming a friend of Gladstone and a supporter of the Liberal Party. He bought up seven daily and 10 weekly newspapers expressing his views through them. He was anti-monarchist, pro-Republican, anti-House of Lords, anti-Imperialist, pro-Home Rule for Ireland. He roused the unemployed, the miners, and the mill-hands to action; he supported strikes which was curious considering his later actions when faced with strike-action at his own works. He considered becoming a Member of Parliament, but thought the American system 'perfect'. A friend, the novelist William Black, called him the 'Star Spangled Scotchman'.

Back in the USA

He was steadily becoming richer and he was pouring out money in new machinery and plant. As mentioned, capital costs did not worry Carnegie; but he worried about operational costs. When railway companies in the USA would not give him lower freight charges he threatened to build railways for himself. The companies lowered the charges! For his steel works he bought his own iron-ore fields.

But one major error was made and it was fatal to his reputation. There was a strike at one of his steel works at a time when Carnegie was in Scotland and his manager, a Mr. Frick, brought in the 'Pinkerton National Detective Agency' to break it.

The 'Pinkertons'

This was an extraordinary organization started up in the United States by Allan Pinkerton a young man of 23, who had emigrated from Glasgow in 1842. He built up a team of detectives who were available for hire. One of their great coups was the capture of the key men involved in the robbery of $700,000 from The Adam Express Company in 1866. Another was the breaking of the 'Molly Maguires', an Irish Secret Society that had taken over the Pennsylvanian coalfields by terrorizing the workers. But perhaps their most notable success was the foiling of a plot to assassinate President-elect Abraham Lincoln. One of their major ways of operating was to infiltrate the organizations that they were investigating.

Much has been made of the fact that Carnegie was absent when the decision was taken to enlist the aid of the Pinkertons in 1892, but there is also evidence that wherever Carnegie was he was constantly in touch with his enterprises. It seems hardly likely that such an important decision was taken without his knowledge and assent.

Be that as it may, the Pinkertons arrived and so great was the strikers' anger that in the ensuing battle four Pinkertons were killed and many people were wounded. The State Militia had to move in to restore order.

The 'St. Louis Post Dispatch' reported "Three months ago Andrew Carnegie was a man to be envied. Today he is an object of mingled pity and contempt".

'The Richest Man in the World'

Nine years later, in 1901, he sold out all his interests in Carnegie Steel to the financier J. Pierpoint Morgan for $480 million who, as they shook hands remarked, "Mr. Carnegie I want to congratulate you on being the richest man in the world". For his part Carnegie, at the age of 63, had taken up golf and now he had time to enjoy it, becoming quite a fanatic!

But he did more than that. He proceeded to give all of his money away because he thought that it was a rich man's duty to the community to do so. "Never stop a man making money, but remember that during his lifetime he should always give it back — a man should be ashamed to die rich". He also believed that if you want to destroy your family, leave them plenty of money. Giving money away he considered much more difficult than making it. But he tried.

Politics
He strongly supported the idea of a union between the U.S.A. and Canada. When the U.S.A. took over the Philippine Islands from Spain he offered to buy them from the U.S. President and set them free. This was one of his unsuccessful ventures.

Libraries and Organs
Remembering his 'Colonel Anderson days' he donated 2811 public libraries of which 1946 were located in the USA, 660 in Britain, 156 in Canada, 23 in New Zealand, 11 in South Africa, 6 in British West Indies, 4 in Australia, and 1 each in Seychelles, Mauritius, and Fiji. He gave buildings, not books; these had to be supplied by the local authority. He loved opening libraries, particularly in Britain where he usually got the Freedom of the town, which he also loved. In all he collected 57 Freedoms. He liked to donate church organs too - more than 7689 of them costing $6.5 million of which over 1000 were in Scotland. Indeed a 'kist o' whistles'!

Education
But nearly $300 million went to education. No wonder his friend Mark Twain nearly always referred to him as 'St. Andrew'. In 1901 he set up the Carnegie Trust for the Universities of Scotland with a grant of $10 million, half of which was to encourage developments in Science which he felt was being neglected, Medicine, and the Arts; the other half was to pay the University fees of students of Scottish birth or extraction. He arranged that the Principals of Scottish Universities should meet annually at his Skibo Castle in Sutherland, which he had purchased for $85,000 and spent £1 million renovating. He did not forget his old town, creating the 'Dunfermline Trust', funded to the tune of four million dollars, to bring

'sweetness and light' to the town. He had little time for Oxford and Cambridge believing that they got too much money anyhow. But he was happy to accept an Honorary degree from Oxford, and one from St. Andrews where he was twice elected Rector by the students.

In the United States he felt the same antipathy towards the 'Ivy League' of Yale, Harvard, and the like. In Washington, DC, he considered setting up a University but changed his mind and built an Institute to further knowledge for all the universities, and endowed it with $10 million, thus ensuring an annual income of $0.5 million. In it he established Departments of evolution, marine biology, history, economics and sociology. He was urged to start a university in Pittsburgh but instead set up schools to produce skilled craftsmen; these later amalgamated and evolved into an Institute of Engineering.

He kept a few surprises up his sleeve. The President of Princeton University, Woodrow Wilson, later to be President of the USA, was rather surprised, following his request for help, when Carnegie donated a rowing lake to divert interest from American football, which he hated. "I asked for bread and he gave me water," said Wilson of the $400,000 gift.

Being surprised to find that American university teachers did not have a pension on retiral he set up a $10 million pension fund. But there were strings; the universities and colleges would have to meet certain criteria - they must be non-sectarian and non-denominational and must have appropriate entrance requirements. This revolutionized American education, not only at college and university level -they raised their entrance requirements and many did away with discrimination - but also at school level where they raised their standards to meet entry requirements.

Heroes and Peace

He established a 'Hero Fund Trust' to award gold, silver, or bronze medals, plus a pension, to people who were injured, or their families if they were killed, in an endeavour to reward the saving of lives in peaceful pursuits. Based in Dunfermline the fund has made over 6000 awards in the 75 years of its existence.

By 1910 Carnegie had given away $179 million. By 1913 it had risen to $332 million. International peace had become one of his objectives. He built Temples of Peace costing $25.5 million, The 'Carnegie Endowment for International Peace' costing £10 million, and the 'Church Peace Union' costing $2 million. He visited the Kaiser whom he admired and, considering him a man of peace, he arranged a meeting between him and Theodore Roosevelt, who had just retired as President. This plan however was disrupted by the death of King Edward V11 in 1910 when all nations concerned went into a period of mourning. He was increasingly drawn to the idea of a coalition of the Great Powers - the U.S.A., Great Britain, Germany, Russia, and France, to police the world. The outbreak of war in 1914 was a sore blow to him, but he later supported America's entry in 1917 as a quick way to bring about peace.

He fell ill with pneumonia and died aged 84 at Lenox, Massachusetts, on 11th August, 1919, leaving his wife Louise who continued to visit Scotland annually until the outbreak of war in 1939. She died in New York on 24th. June 1946. Carnegie was buried at Sleepy Hollow, North Tarrytown, N.Y. where his grave is marked by a Celtic Cross cut out from stone quarried near Skibo.

He had given away $350,695,650. He left $30 million in his will of which $20 million went to the Carnegie Corporation in New York. Of the remaining $10 million, $4 million was set aside for pensions of $5-10 thousand for Dunfermline relatives and old friends, including Mrs. Theodore Roosevelt, and lesser amounts to tenants and servants at Skibo. The remaining millions were divided among a number of Institutes. He had already made provision for his wife and daughter Margaret.

Thus Andrew Carnegie paid back his debt to mankind.

REFERENCES AND FURTHER READING

'Andrew Carnegie'. Joseph Frazier Wall. Oxford University Press NY, 1970.
'Andrew Carnegie - My Own Story' reprinted for the Carnegie Dunfermline Trust by permission of Houghton Mifflin Company. 1984.
'Mister Carnegie's Lantern Lecture' W. Gordon Smith. Carnegie Dunfermline Trust, 1985.

PLACES TO VISIT

Scotland

Andrew Carnegie Birthplace Museum, Moodie Street, Dunfermline, Fife.

This is a treasure trove of Carnegiana including his birthplace cottage, a recreation of Carnegie sitting at his desk, the Roll of Honour of the Hero Fund Trust, an audio-visual sequence, a Memorial Hall donated by Mrs. Louise Carnegie to house his collection of freedom caskets, university degrees, medals etc. And much more.

Skibo Castle, Dornoch Firth, Sutherland. Formerly Carnegie's home converted by its owner into a Private Country Club retaining many of the decorations installed by Carnegie.

JOHN BOYD DUNLOP (1840 - 1922)

The Pneumatic Tyre

"There's a demon in that machine!"

John Macadam's method of roadmaking had opened up the roadways of the world for travel. The mailcoach and the stage coach carried people beyond their own little towns and village inns, where people might stay during their sojourns, had sprung up all over Britain. But travel was laborious and painful, for the vehicles were fitted with wooden, metal, or at best, solid rubber tyres.

John Boyd Dunlop, whose name was to become a household word, provided the solution. He was born on 5th February 1840 at Dreghorn, Ayrshire, where his family had been successful farmers for generations. John was destined for the farm too, but he was of rather a sickly disposition, and so instead was sent to Edinburgh University, where at the age of 19, he obtained his qualification as a veterinary surgeon. He worked for a time in Edinburgh to gain experience and then, at the age of 29, moved to Belfast, where he built up a very successful practice, one of the largest in Ireland, in the course of the next 20 years.

Early experiments

Dunlop moved around the countryside a lot in the course of his veterinary practice and uncomfortable rides they were in his horse-drawn gig. It occurred to him that there was one way in which the pain could be eased, and the speed increased; it could be done by using better tyres on the wheels. His little son Johnny was a keen cyclist and it was a wheel from his tricycle that was used for the first experiment. Dunlop took a strip of elmwood, bent it into a hoop, equivalent in diameter to one of the tricycle wheels, and riveted the ends together. He made a rubber tube which he fitted over the rim of the elmwood disc, inflated the tube and protected it with a canvas covering. Taking one of the tricycle wheels he rolled both wheels along his backyard, and found the the elmwood wheel with the inflated tube easily outdistanced the tricycle wheel.

The next step was to fit Johnny's tricycle with three of these new tyres and test out their effect. "I told him to to ride it over my newly-laid macadam. He was very enthusistic about the tyres". Not only did Johhny have a much more comfortable ride, but in a race against his pals, who were on their bikes with traditional wheels, he left them trailing in his wake.

The pneumatic tyre

John Boyd Dunlop had invented the pneumatic tyre in 1887. Or rather he had re-invented it. Unknown to him, a man from Stonehaven, R.W. Thomson, had invented and patented it more than 40 years before, in 1846. Unfortunately for Thomson no real use could be found for his invention. He was a man ahead of his time. It did however lead to considerable litigation but, as a result of having patents for rims and valves, Dunlop was given the all-clear to proceed.

In 1842 another Scot, Kirkpatrick Macmillan, a blacksmith at Keir, Dumfriesshire, had invented the first bicycle with front-wheel steering and the rear wheels driven by pedals. He made a cycling trip from his village to Glasgow which took two days, and as the wheels had solid iron tyres Macmillan confessed that he was rather sore at the end of the 80 mile journey!

By Dunlop's time the bicycle had become popular, and he persuaded the captain of the Belfast cycling club to ride one fitted with his new pneumatic tyres. He won the race easily against his competitors riding traditional machines. "There's a demon in that machine!" yelled an onlooker. "At the end of the race," said Dunlop, "I was asked to explain the nature of my new invention. The immense crowd cheered me".

Dunlop patented his invention and went into partnership with W.H. Du Cros, a wealthy paper merchant. Together they formed a company in 1889 to market pneumatic tyres. Du Cros was enthusiastic and energetic and he travelled the British Isles extolling the virtues of the new product. He was so enthusiastic indeed that he raised the ire of the penny-farthing brigade who saw this as a threat to their livelihood. Many bicycle shops slammed their doors in his face and on one occasion he was booed and harassed by penny-farthing enthusiasts.

One aspect of his enthusiasm also angered Dunlop, who in his retiral had taken up cycling and could be seen, with his long white beard, top hat, and eyeglass, speeding through the Belfast streets. He was very angry when an advertisement appeared for Dunlop tyres showing this self-same old gentleman as the centrepiece. So much so in fact that he resigned from the

Company and took no further part in its activities. The Dunlop Rubber Company went on to become an international force.

Dunlop retired to Dublin, where he bought a draper's shop, and he lived there until he died, aged 81, in 1921.

He had set a transport revolution in train. His invention paved the way not only for the motor car, but also for the aeroplane. It is difficult to envisage the development of either of these without the pneumatic tyre.

REFERENCES AND FURTHER READING

"History of the Pneumatic Tyre". Jean McLintock. Thom. 1923.

Two Good Men of Ayr" . Helen Freeman. Scotland's Magazine, Jan. 1969.

PLACES TO VISIT

There are memorials to Dunlop at Belfast, Edinburgh, and Fort Dunlop, Birmingham.

A tyre made by Dunlop can be seen at the Royal Scottish Museum, Edinburgh.

The Transport Museum, Kelvingrove, Glasgow, has a wealth of material relating to transport through the years, including a replica of Kirkpatrick Macmillan's bicycle.

ALEXANDER GRAHAM BELL (1847 - 1922)

The Telephone

"Mr. Watson please come here I want you".

Alexander Graham Bell was born in South Charlotte St., Edinburgh, the son of Alexander Melville Bell, a well- known and highly respected teacher of elocution and speech production, who as well as lecturing in Edinburgh University also coached teachers, ministers, and private pupils.

Young Alexander did not particularly shine at the two schools that he attended (McLaren's Academy and Edinburgh High), being described as 'lazy', although he did show considerable interest in science (particularly zoology and botany) and in technology (inventing a device with rotating blades for de-husking cereal grains). He left school at the age of 13, and went off to polish up his education by spending a year with his paternal grandfather who was Professor of Elocution in the University of London. It is not surprising that under the influence of his grandfather and his father, his interest in speech therapy was developing apace. And he was growing up in a stimulating environment. Back in Edinburgh, when his father challenged him to produce a 'speaking machine' he obtained a lamb's larynx from the local butcher, dissected it (his knowledge of zoology came in handy) and noting the position of the vocal organs, he built a model in which mechanical 'organs' could be manipulated by levers. Blowing through a tube linked to them he made a fair shot at producing human sounds.

Reis's telephone

It was in Edinburgh that he came across a piece of apparatus that was to change his, and our, lives. A schoolteacher, Philip Reis, had made what he called a 'telephone'. It consisted of two boxes connected to each other by electric wires fed from a battery. In one of the boxes was a metal knitting needle and if someone spoke or played a musical instrument into the empty box then the sound was transmitted along the wire causing the needle to vibrate and give off sounds resembling the speech or music. It was primitive, and it was not a piece of apparatus that aroused a great deal of interest at the time. Bell reflected on its possibilities without at that time realizing its enormous potential.

London

When his father was appointed to succeed his own father as Professor of Elocution at London University, Alexander moved with them, after a short spell of teaching elocution and music at Elgin in the north of Scotland and at Bath in the south of England. In a nearby school he taught four little deaf girls by means of 'Visible Speech,' a method using symbols to represent words and letters, that had been invented by his father. He also became his father's assistant and when Professor Bell was invited to the U.S.A to give a series of lectures at the Lowell Institute, Boston, young Alexander stood in for him in London.

Canada

Unfortunately, the family scourge, tuberculosis, that had already swept away his two brothers, looked like manifesting itself in Alexander too. He was 21 years of age and the family doctor advised that only a complete change of climate would save his life. The Bells could not bear to be parted from their only remaining son. So, after some discussion, deciding that all three would go off together, they packed their bags and emigrated to Canada where the air was pure and the climate bracing. It certainly did the trick so far as Alexander was concerned and almost from the time of landing, his health began to improve.

Boston

He began teaching again and in 1872 he was appointed Professor of Vocal Physiology in Boston University, Massachusetts, to continue the work that his father had begun with 'Visible Speech'. It was here that he met his future wife, Mabel Hubbard, who had been stone deaf from birth, and who had been sent by her father, a wealthy business man, to learn the new language that was being taught by Bell.

Bell had become intensely interested in deafness from a very early age. Not only was it his father's specialism: his mother was deaf, and although she was a very talented pianist, she could only make sound contact by reversing her hearing tube and attaching the ear-piece to the soundboard of the piano.

Early attempts

Boston was the leading centre of American science and technology. It was not surprising that Bell's inventive spirit was stimulated in such an atmosphere. His great ambition was to devise an instrument by means of which the deaf could hear. To this end he obtained from the mortuary, parts of a human ear that had been cut from a corpse. He attached one end of a light reed to the eardrum and to the other end of the reed, a glass plate coated with carbon. He shouted into the ear hoping that sound vibrations would be carried along the reed and its quivering would etch out patterns on the smoked glass. He did have partial success but the drum was not nearly sensitive enough to convey meaningful patterns.

He set to, to construct an artificial ear. He found that if an iron diaphram were made to vibrate near a magnet with a coil of wire round it, with the aid of a battery, a current was induced in the coil. Thus the vibrations of air caused by human speech (or music, or any other sound) could be converted into varying electrical current and conveyed along an electric wire. At the other end of the wire the sound could be reconstituted by means of the current affecting another magnet and thus vibrating another diaphram to produce the original sounds that had been fed in. In his attempts to produce a 'hearing aid' he had invented a system for transmitting sound.

Success

But this was only the beginning. On the 2nd. June 1875, Bell and his assistant, Thomas Watson, were tinkering with the apparatus when Bell found, to his utter astonishment, that it would transmit sounds along an electrical wire without help from a battery. He had invented the telephone (as he called it, remembering Philip Reis and his Edinburgh days).

Several months later, he and Watson fitted up a transmitter in the attic of his house and a receiver in a room downstairs. Watson stood by the receiver while Bell spoke into the transmitter. The words that he spoke have become almost as famous as Stanley's "Dr Livingstone I presume?". They were "Mr. Watson, please come here, I want you". One minute later Watson was bounding up the stairs. "I could hear you" he cried "I could hear you!".

Bell was no business man, so wisely he turned for help to Mr. Hubbard, his prospective father-in-law. He was not disappointed. Hubbard quickly had the invention patented and then persuaded Bell to demonstrate it at the International Centennial Exposition which had opened at

Philadelphia. Bell took three telephones there but they attracted little attention as people drifted past his exhibit. He was on the point of going home, but Hubbard persuaded him to stay a few days more. A very important group, including the Emperor and Empress of Brazil, Sir William Thomson (later Lord Kelvin) who had succeeded in laying the first transatlantic cable, and Professor Hendry of New York, inventor of the electric bell and of A.C/ D.C. fame, was to pay a visit on the Sunday.

When the Emperor Pedro entered the hall he immediately recognised Bell, having attended one of his classes in Boston a few years before, and moved over to see his invention. Giving Pedro the receiver and instructing him to put it to his ear, Bell moved to the far end of the hall with the transmitter and spoke into it. It is reported that Pedro jumped. "Great Heavens" he said "the thing talks!".

Salem

Despite the enormous interest that followed within the Exhibition, recognition was slow to develop in the big world outside. Bell and Watson decided to put on a public demonstration by establishing a line between a house in Boston where Watson was stationed, and a hall in Salem, some 15 miles distant, where Bell took up his position. An organ thundered out 'Yankee Doodle Dandy' and 'Auld Lang Syne' in Boston and was appreciated and loudly applauded in Salem. Mr. Watson made a neat, witty speech over the 15 miles distance and was loudly applauded by the audience in Salem. The demonstration ended with a conversation between the two men. This was in fact the first broadcast programme. They received 85 dollars for their efforts.

Marriage

Bell spent his share on a little silver telephone for Mabel Hubbard. Perhaps the gesture won her heart; perhaps she loved him anyhow. They were married in August 1877. For their honeymoon they sailed for Britain, and Bell, of course, took his telephones with him.

Success in London

His invention was a big hit in London. A telephone wire was set up between the high steeple of Bow Church and the street below. Londoners queued up and paid one penny to say "How do you do?" to a man on top of the steeple, and hear him reply "Very well thank you".

The Queen is amused

For Queen Victoria, who had expressed great interest, Bell established telephone connection between Osborne House and Osborne Cottage on the Isle of Wight. The queen was so delighted with the result that she had connection established between her residence at Cowes and London, so that she was able to enjoy an organ recital from the capital.

Expansion

A week later Bell installed a telephone in the gallery of the House of Commons, and from there a reporter dictated the course of a debate on the floor below to his newspaper in Fleet Street. Within a few months, telephone communication was established between the mainland and the Island of Jersey, between Dover and Calais in France, between Holyhead and Dublin in Ireland. Sir William Thomson was enthralled by the vast steps that had been made in the development of the then relatively primitive instrument that he had first seen in Philadelphia little more than a year ago. He called the telephone "one of the most interesting of the scientific inventions made in this century, or that has ever been made in the history of Science". He personally supervised a number of experimental transmissions, one of which was at Preston Colliery. Connection was made between the office and the coal-face by means of 600 yards of electric wire. Questions were asked in the office and immediately responded to by the miners . Small wonder that the latter cheered. They now had a life-line if anything went wrong underground.

Boom time

In 1878 Bell and his wife returned to the United States to find that the telephone was booming there too. In New Jersey a switchboard, the first telephone exchange in the world, had been set up for 100 subscribers so that fires and burglaries could be reported immediately. A year later one was set up in London with seven or eight subscribers. More and more companies were adopting the system as the revolutionary idea of instant communication caught on. Telephones were soon found in every civilized country in the world and all were to Bell's specification. It is perhaps not surprising that, with so much money involved, there was immense litigation. The Bell Company had to fight more than 600 law suits and they won them all. The biggest of them all was with the Western Union Telegraph Company, who had as their technical adviser the redoutable Thomas Alva Edison who had improved on Bell's invention by developing a more efficient transmitter and receiver. The Bell Company won that one too. Incidentally it was Edison who 'invented' the word 'Hello' in the 1860's. When using the telephone, he wanted a word that would immediately attract attention and so he used 'Hello' ('Ahoy' was also considered) instead of the word 'Hallo' that had been in common use as a form of greeting for centuries.

Other interests

Bell was by now an immensely rich man. He took little further interest in the telephone (he would not even allow one in his study!). He settled down in Washington and resumed his earlier work of teaching the deaf which was really his consuming passion. With a prize of 50,000 francs which he had received, he set up the Volta Laboratories to develop and spread knowledge relating to the deaf.

Flying machines

In later years, when Bell went to live in Nova Scotia, he became interested in the new science of flying machines that had been developed by the Wright brothers, Wilbur (born Indiana, 1867) and Orville (born Ohio, 1871) who had made their first flight on 17th. December, 1903 at Kitty Hawk, North Carolina (though this was ignored until they made their first public flights in 1908 when Wilbur flew in Europe and Orville at Fort Mayer in the U.S.A.).

Bell could be seen running across the fields flying his large kites as he studied aerodynamics. He formed a club to build the first Canadian aeroplane and in this machine, which he called a 'Double deck Aerodrome', two Canadian fliers, in 1908, made the first flight in the British Empire. He realized the tremendous potential of the aeroplane as a weapon of war and he advised the British Government to make Britain strong in the air, warning that the day might come (prophetic words!) when aeroplanes of a foreign power might destroy London from the air. It is of interest to note that his admirer, Lord Kelvin, did not agree with him. In response to a query from General Baden Powell, Kelvin replied "I have not an atom of faith in heavier than air machines. The future of air transport lies with balloons". A few years later young men were fighting to the death over the Western Front in their 'wonderful flying machines'.

Coast to coast

In 1915 coast-to-coast telephone communication was established in a link-up between New York and San Francisco. Alexander Bell was asked to open it. He insisted that his former assistant, Thomas Watson, should also take part and should be stationed at the end of a telephone in San Francisco. Bell in New York repeated the famous words that he had spoken forty years before in the little house in Boston "Mr. Watson, come here, I want to see you". It is said that Watson laughed. "Thanks for the invitation boss, but it would take me a week now".

Family life

Bell had taken out American citizenship in 1874, but he also loved Canada. As noted, in the 1880's (as he moved into his 40's), he bought a house in Nova Scotia. He gave it the Gaelic name 'Bienn Bhreagh' (beautiful mountain) and here he spent his summers with his family. They had two daughters, Elsie and Marian (known to the family as Daisy). Elsie's husband was Gilbert Grosvenor, the founder of the National Geographic Magazine. They had seven children, one of whom, Gilbert (who succeeded his father as head of the National Geographic), was a great favourite of his grandfather's. Daisy and her husband, the noted botanist, David Fairchild, added three more, so that in summer Bienn Bhreagh reverberated with life and laughter.

Bell made many visits to Scotland during one of which he set up a school for deaf children. There was one sadness; despite his great success, he never succeeded in making Mabel hear. While all the world reverberated to the chattering through his telephone lines, Mrs. Bell remained isolated in her silent world.

Thomas Graham Bell died, aged 75, at Cape Breton Island in Nova Scotia on 22nd. August, 1922. All the telephones in the United States and Canada were kept silent for a short period as a tribute to him.

REFERENCES AND FURTHER READING
'Alexander Graham Bell'. C.D. Mackenzie. 1928.
'The History of Bell's Telephone'. Kate Field (editor). Bradbury Agnew and Co. 1952.
'Alexander Graham Bell'. Robert. V. Bruce. National Geographic. Vol. 174, No. 3, September, 1988.

PLACES TO VISIT
Scotland
There is a plaque on Graham Bell's birthplace in South Charlotte St. Edinburgh.

Canada
Graham Bell Museum, Nova Scotia.

U.S.A.
Bell's Room, National Geographic Society, Washington DC.

ROBERT LOUIS STEVENSON (1850 - 1895)
Novelist and Poet

"But I, when I am stronger, and can choose what I'm to do
O, Learie, I'll go round at night, and light the lamps with you".

Illness

From his infant days Robert was a delicate sickly child and was 'spoiled' not only by his mother and father, but also by Alison Cunningham, who was brought in when he was 18 months of age to be his nurse and teacher. Suffering from the tuberculosis that was to plague him all his life, he could not go out in winter and in Cummy's arms he watched the lamplighter through the window:

"But I, when I am stronger and can choose what I'm to do
O, Learie, I'll go round at night, and light the lamps with you".

Schooldays

He had a very erratic 18 month's schooling at Edinburgh Academy, playing truant, and being absent due to spells of ill-health. Thin, narrow chested, stooped, spindle- shanked, long-faced, with lank fair hair topped with an old straw hat, he was the butt of satire and torment from his schoolfellows; but he made no attempt at retaliation. Instead, he played the fool which was perhaps the only weapon he had. After a short spell at a boarding school in London he returned to a little private school in Edinburgh 'for backward boys' where he took no part in games, but he published, and contributed to, the school magazine.

University

His father was keen that he should become an engineer like himself and so, aged 16, 'Lou' became a student at Edinburgh University. During this period he founded the 'Edinburgh University Magazine'. He was reading essayists - Hazlitt, Cant, Defoe - and developing his writing skills which did not come easily to him; his talent developed slowly. Much to his father's delight he read a paper before the Royal Society of Arts on 'a New Form of Intermittent Light for Lighthouses' for which he received a silver medal and £3. But that was his last effort in this field; he made it clear that he did not wish to be a lighthouse engineer like his father. As a concession to his parents who were deeply disappointed, he agreed to study law and, at least nominally, he became a law student.

For them, however, there was further disappointment. Lou pronounced himself an atheist. His father, who was a devout Christian felt it bitterly but Lou went his own way believing himself to be a re-incarnation of Robert Fergusson, the Scottish poet who died insane at the age of 23. He began to visit the low dives and the 'houses of ill-repute' of Edinburgh. His dress was bizarre; today he might well have been a punk.

France

At the age of 23 he fell very ill and his parents sent him off to the Riviera to regain his health. From there he made his way to Paris where, clad in his long purple cloak, he immersed himself in the bohemian life. He turned to opium for solace and used it all his life, though he did not become an addict. Strangely enough his health improved.

Returning to Edinburgh he passed his final Law examinations at the age of 25 and he was called to the Scottish bar. Dressed "like a drunken Irishman returning from a funeral", he 'put up his plate' at 17 Heriot Row, but getting clients was another matter. He was now writing essays and short stories, and developing an interest in fiction.

Marriage

On a second visit to France he met Fanny de Grift Osbourne, an American lady of 36. Separated from her husband, she was studying art, and was accompanied by her daughter aged 17, and her young son Lloyd aged 5. It was love at first sight. When Fanny returned to California, Stevenson consoled himself with a trip through the Cevennes, with the strong-willed Modestine, which he described in 'Travels with a Donkey', but when he heard that Fanny was ill he set sail for America.

They met in Monterey, south of San Francisco where she obtained her divorce from Osbourne, and they were married on 19th May, 1880. He was close to death, but under her care he improved and took on a new lease of life. They had no money, but his father made him an annual allowance of $250. After a short stay in California, Stevenson, his wife, and her son Lloyd, set off for Britain to be met at Liverpool by his mother and father. Stevenson senior had no great hopes for his daughter-in-law but she, for her part, was determined to win his family over. And she did so to such good effect that he was enchanted and thought her an ideal wife for his errant and ailing son. Off they all went together to tour the Highlands.

Treasure Island

It was at Braemar in the Highlands, that his writing career took off. It was a wet, windy day, and to amuse his step-son Lloyd, Stevenson drew a map which he named 'Treasure Island' and he began to weave a story round it at the rate of a chapter a day. It was noted by an American editor, Alexander Japp, who was visiting the Stevensons and he submitted it to a boys' paper, 'Young Folks' in which in 1881, it appeared in 17 instalments under the authorship of 'Captain George North', a pseudonym that Stevenson thought gave it greater authenticity. Thus 'Treasure Island' first appeared in print.

But as a serial it was a flop. There was not enough action in the early chapters and the hero, Jim Hawkins, did not make any impact until instalment six by which time most of the young readers had given up. Stevenson learned his lesson. Thereafter his two succeeding serials in the same paper, 'The Black Arrow' and 'Kidnapped' had action from the beginning.

He began the slow process of writing, re-writing, and re-casting 'A Child's Garden of Verses' which was in time to endear him to a world of readers. But his health was deteriorating. In October 1881 he went to Davos in Switzerland and spent his 31st birthday there with his wife and stepson. There was little improvement in his health, and his wife was ill too, but the stay was notable for good work. He wrote several essays and stories that were printed later, and he set up a little printing-press of his own - the 'Davos Press' - to amuse and occupy Lloyd. They both 'published' little stories and illustrated them with woodcuts.

In May of the following year, 1882, the family left Davos, without regret. They visited Edinburgh, but the state of Stevenson's health was such that he could no longer live in a northern clime. He was hit by a further haemorrhage and they left for the south of France, but his ill-health continued; haemorrhages with intermittent bouts of fever continued to plague him. Often he was at death's door, but always he struggled back.

Bournemouth

In the summer of 1884 they paid a visit to England. He was staying at Richmond in Surrey, and his play 'Deacon Brodie' was being put on in London but sadly, Stevenson was too ill to attend the premiere. They planned to take up permanent residence in Bournemouth and Stevenson's father bought a house there which Stevenson, still longing for Scotland, named 'Skerryvore'. But he was a virtual prisoner in it, though he made many friends and had a constant flow of visitors.

In March 1885 'A Child's Garden of Verses' was published which, to her great delight, was dedicated to his old nurse 'Cummy'. It was at Bournemouth that he wrote the immensely successful eerie tale 'The Strange Case of Dr. Jekyll and Mr. Hyde', the essence of which, it is said, came to him in a dream, but which may in part reflect his 'double life' in Edinburgh where he drank and consorted with prostitutes. It may also have been a commentary on the hypocrisy of the 'unco guid' of Edinburgh.

Within a month he had the book ready for publication and Longmans released it to the market in January, 1886, where it rapidly became a 'best-seller' in Britain and America. He resumed the writing of 'Kidnapped' to appear as a serial in 'Young Folks'.

Then came sad news. His father who had been so good to his son and daughter-in-law, was gravely ill. Louis and Fanny travelled to Edinburgh, but they were too late. Thomas Stevenson died without recognising him, and Louis was too ill to attend the funeral. Three weeks later he and his wife left Edinburgh for the last time. There was now nothing tying him to Britain and so on 22nd August, 1887, with his wife, his mother and his stepson, Stevenson left Britain aboard the S.S. 'Ludgate Hill' for New York. He was never to return.

New York

On arrival Stevenson got a warm welcome from publishers, editors, reporters, old friends and new friends. He and his family were enveloped in luxury. A dramatized version of 'Dr. Jekyll and Mr. Hyde' was produced in New York while he was there, and although he was not fit enough to attend, his mother and his wife went to the first night opening. 'Deacon Brodie' was produced in Philadelphia. Stevenson was the toast of the U.S.A.

But winter was drawing in, and New York was not the best place to be. The family moved out to a sanatorium by the shores of Lake Saranac, high amidst the snows of the Adirondack mountains. While there Mr. McClure, a major publisher, who became a close friend, offered him $10,000 a year for a short weekly essay in the 'New York World', and offered to publish 'The Black Arrow' as a serial in his newspaper syndicate. McClure was later to say that it "brought in more money than any other serial novel we ever syndicated". When Stevenson told McClure that he was planning two more novels - 'Catriona' a sequel to 'Kidnapped', and 'St. Ives' - McClure offered to take either at $8000. Stevenson's eyes were opening to a new scale of publishing values, far removed from the 'Young Folks'.

It was at Saranac that he wrote the first chapters of 'The Master of Ballantrae' a novel conceived in the Highlands of Scotland, to be continued in Tahiti, and to be completed in Honolulu. But he longed for the sea, for only there did he feel well, and when his wife told him that she had sorted out a luxury schooner in San Francisco that they could hire for seven months for $10,000, he jumped at the chance.

South Seas

And so, on the 28th June, 1888, the tall masted, 95 foot 'Casco', manned by Captain Otis and a crew of five, with Stevenson, his mother, his wife and his stepson, glided through the Golden Gate, out into the Pacific Ocean. Although the cruise was meant to last only a few months, he was never to see America again.

Stevenson was wonderfully healthy - happy and sunburned. He was in his element in the South Seas where the climate eased his tortured lungs. Fanny did not take so kindly to sailing but, like the rest of the family, she was willing to endure almost anything for the sake of her husband's health.

In the first week in October they sighted Tahiti where Stevenson was immediately at home. Princess Moe and her husband held a splendid feast of roast pig in his honour and in return he wrote a poem 'To an Island Princess'. He also worked hard on 'The Master of Ballantrae' and he collected songs and legends for his book 'In the South Seas'.

On Christmas Day it was time to say goodbye to their friends, and they sailed for Honolulu where they picked up their mail and called on King Kalakaua. Immediately a rapport was struck, the King drinking five bottles of champagne to welcome him. The Stevenson family were located in small hutted quarters at Waikiki, and here Stevenson finished 'The Master of Ballantrae' the first parts of which were already appearing as a serial in 'Scribners Magazine' in the U.S.A. He welcomed a stream of visitors, including local dignitaries of all ranks, black and white.

But even Honolulu was proving to be too cold for his emaciated body and he arranged a four-months cruise on a hired 'Equator' schooner. His mother had returned to Scotland, and so, five months after landing, he, his wife and Lloyd got an emotional musical send-off from the King and his entourage.

Early in December 1889 they arrived at Samoa, a group of islands of which Upolu, 45 miles long and 11 miles broad, was the most important. Here Stevenson was to spend the last five years of his life building his home, 'Vailima' (Five Waters) on 300 acres of land 600 feet above sea-level, and had his furniture sent out from Scotland. Here he 'held court' having a flow of friends both local and from overseas. But aye he longed for Edinburgh which he would never see again. After her eighteen months sojourn in Scotland, his mother re-joined him.

In October, 1893, he started to write 'St. Ives' but he discontinued it after 12 chapters, for 'Weir of Hermiston'. In this he found his inspiration and skill returning; but he had but two months to live and he described his condition in a letter to his friend, George Meredith:

"For fifteen years I have not had a day's real health. I have wakened sick and gone to bed weary; and I have done my work unflinchingly. I have written in bed and written out of it, written in haemorrhages, written in sickness, written torn by coughs, written when my head swam for weakness; and for so long it seems to me I have won my wager and recovered my glove; I was made for a contest, and the Powers have so willed that my battlefield should be this dingy inglorious one of the bed and the physic bottle. At least I have not failed but I would have preferred a place of trumpetings and the open air over my head".

As he lay reading a chapter of 'Weir' to Fanny, his constant source of inspiration, he raised his hand to his head "Do I look strange?" He went into a coma and died two hours later. He was 45 years of age.

Robert Louis Stevenson was buried on the summit of Mt. Vaea near his home, 'Vailima', his coffin carried there by his beloved Samoans. On his tomb is engraven the 'Requiem' that he had written all these years before in France:

> Under the wide and starry sky,
> Dig the grave and let me lie.
> Glad did I live and gladly die,
> And I laid me down with a will.

> This be the verse that you grave for me
> 'Here he lies where he longed to be:
>   Home is the sailor, home from the sea,
> And the hunter home from the hill.'

REFERENCES AND FURTHER READING

"Life of Robert Louis Stevenson" Graham Balfour (2 vols). Methuen and Co. 1901
"Robert Louis Stevenson". J.A, Steuart. (2 vols). Sampson Low, 1924.
"Robert Louis Stevenson". Lord Guthrie. W. Green and Son, 1924.
"The Life of Robert Louis Stevenson". Rosaline Masson. W. and R. Chambers, 1924.
"Robert Louis Stevenson". G. B. Stern. Longmans Green, 1952.
"Dreams of Exile - Robert Louis Stevenson - a biography". Ian Bell. Mainstream, 1992.
"Robert Louis Stevenson - a biography". Frank McLynn. Pimlico, 1993
"Robert Louis Stevenson". Margaret Moyes Black. 1894 Centenary Year Classic Reissue 1994. Lang Syne.
"Part Seen, Part Imagined". Timothy Neat. Canongate, 1994.
"Pictures of the Mind - the Illustrated Robert Louis Stevenson". John Scally. Canongate Publishers, in association with the National Library of Scotland, 1994.
"BBC Educational R.L.S. Video/Audio Pack" and "BBC Viewers' Guide to R.L.S." BBC Education, White City Building, London W12.

PLACES TO VISIT
Scotland
(1) 17 Heriot Row where Stevenson was born.
(2) National Library of Scotland, Edinburgh where there is an internationally-renowned Stevenson Collection.

U.S.A.
Stevenson House, Monterey State Historic Park, Monterey, California. Formerly the 'French Hotel' where Stevenson and Fanny lived in a back bedroom, it is now a white-washed adobe building full of memorabilia including the massive dining table and sideboard which his mother brought out from Heriot Row.
Robert Louis Stevenson Memorial Cottage, Stevenson Lane, Saranac Lake, N.Y. contains photographs, original letters and articles of Stevenson lore.

South Seas
'Vailima', on Island of Upolu, Western Samoa, where there is his home and his grave.

ARTHUR CONAN DOYLE (1859-1930)

Novelist

"You know my powers my dear Watson"

Sherlock Holmes (Doyle first considered calling him Ormond Sacker and then Sherrinford Holmes) is surely the greatest detective who has ever 'lived'. Victorian, gas-lit, fog-enveloped, Baker Street has engraved itself in the minds of succeeding generations of readers, radio-listeners, and TV - watchers. Every year thousands of people make a pilgrimage in search of the Master's flat in the metropolis and it is said that a well-known Building Society, now occupying 221 Baker Street, gets 20 letters a week addressed to Sherlock Holmes. But he didn't have his origin in London; for this we have to go to Edinburgh.

Inspiration

Conan Doyle was born in Edinburgh in 1859 and in 1876 he returned there to become a medical student in the University, coming under the influence of a Professor Joseph Bell whom he was later to use as a prototype for his famous detective. Bell was a very acute observer and had remarkable powers of deduction. It is said that he could tell which route a particular student had taken to the ward, by a quick glance at the mud or dust on his shoes. Doyle himself relates how Bell, after examining a patient in front of the class deduced that the man had recently been discharged from a Highland regiment where he had served as a non-commissioned officer in Barbados. He explained to the astonished students that the man, although good-mannered, did not remove his hat, when he came in. This of course was mandatory for non-commissioned ranks in the Army, and the man obviously had not yet had time to adjust to civilian ways. He had a Scottish accent (hence probably a Highland regiment) and had an air of authority. As to Barbados he was diagnosed as having elephantiasis, a disease which is West Indian in origin. Holmes could not have done better! After graduating, he 'put up his plate' in Portsmouth and waited for patients. They were slow acoming but one, Mr. Hawkins, was important;

through him Doyle met his sister Louise, and married her in 1885.

The Life and Death of Sherlock Holmes

The lack of patients gave Doyle time to indulge his hobby of writing and within a year of his marriage, his most famous character, Sherlock Holmes, made his appearance in 'A Study in Scarlet'. The story, in which Holmes forms his partnership with Dr. James Watson (who became the teller of his exploits), was not however an immediate hit and he had some difficulty in having it accepted by publishers, before it appeared in 'Beeton's Christmas Annual' of 1887. He got £27 for his effort. This was followed by 'The Sign of Four' in 'Lippincott's Magazine' in 1890, but it was not until he started writing for 'The Strand' that his stories (and their famous detective) really took off. 'A Scandal in Bohemia' had the public clamouring for more, and they were to flow in a steady stream. Ere long Conan Doyle had given up the practice of medicine; soon he was a rich celebrity, a household name, a very famous novelist.

By 1893 Conan Doyle became afraid that Holmes was taking over his life and, after 24 stories, he determined to kill him off. The scene of 'The Final Solution' was Switzerland where at the Reichenbach Falls, Holmes, locked in mortal combat with his arch enemy, the master fiend, the Napoleon of crime, Professor Moriarty, plunged to his death. Watson did not actually witness the scene. He had been walking the mountains with Holmes but had been lured back to their hotel by a false message. He deduced the death from a message left at the spot by Holmes and by signs of the struggle. His 'fans' were inconsolable.

The Boer War

The last year of the century saw the outbreak of the Boer War in South Africa and Conan Doyle, ever the patriot, who had immersed himself in stories of the Napoleonic and Crimean wars, volunteered for active service. He would have liked to have been a fighting soldier, but he was now 40 years of age, and he had to settle for being a Medical Officer.

The outcome of his service was 'The Great Boer War,' a massive account and analysis of that war, written in 1900, and two years later, 'The War in South Africa, Its Cause and Conduct' a book that explained and defended Britain's role. For this, and for his attitude towards the war, he was knighted by King Edward V11 in 1902.

Re-enter Holmes

The end of the war saw the re-emergence of Sherlock Holmes. The public had been clamouring for this since Reichenbach and at last Conan Doyle acquiesced. But he made it clear that the events in 'The Hound of the Baskervilles', considered by some to be the best of all his stories, had taken place years before Holmes's death. So great however was the public response, that Doyle was forced to revive him, ten years after his 'death', by agreeing that Watson's account of Holmes's death "may have been as a result of an hallucination".

In 'The Adventure of the Empty House', much to the delight of readers in Britain, the U.S.A. and in the many countries into whose language his stories had been translated, and to the astonishment of Dr. Watson, Holmes 'came back from the dead' a year after Reichenbach, to tell Watson that he had not really fallen into the chasm but had 'gone underground' to mislead enemies who were intent on his death. Doyle was to continue writing Sherlock Holmes stories for the 'Strand' for the next 22 years until, in 1927, 'The Adventure of Schoscombe Place' closed the book on the famous detective.

Other activities

But all of Doyle's time was not taken up with Holmes. Far from it! He made two unsuccessful bids to enter parliament, one in 1900, and another in 1906. He took up what he perceived to be cases of injustice, his most successful being that of Oscar Slater, a German Jew, who partly because of his unsavoury reputation, had been wrongfully convicted of the murder of a Miss Gilchrist in Glasgow in 1908. Slater served nineteen years in prison before, largely due to Doyle's efforts, a retrial was ordered, and he was pardoned and released.

In 1906 his wife died from tuberculosis, and a year later Doyle married Jean Leckie, a young lady with whom he had had a close platonic friendship for ten years. She bore him three children to add to the family of two by his first wife.

A new Hero

In 1912 he introduced a new hero, Professor Challenger, a fiery scientist, based on yet another Edinburgh professor, William Rutherford, an eccentric physician. In 'The Lost World' Challenger explored the Amazonian jungle and discovered dinosaurs that had been living there for centuries. But although more adventures followed, Challenger failed to grip the public imagination in the way that Holmes had done.

World War

In 1914 Doyle toured the United States and was given a rapturous reception wherever he went. He returned to find Britain at war with Germany and he jumped at the chance to tour the battlefields as a war correspondent. Out of this experience grew his six-volume history 'The British Campaign in France and Flanders' (1916-19).

Historical Fiction

Doyle had a deep desire to be recognised as a 'serious' writer, and throughout his life he wrote many historical novels (all of them chivalrous in tone). But all of them, to Doyle's annoyance, were overshadowed by Sherlock Holmes.

Is there anyone there?

Most of the last fifteen years of Doyle's life were occupied in promoting the cause of spiritualism. It was a subject in which he had long been interested but it came much to the fore after the Great War. Millions of young men had been lost in that terrible slaughter and there was a desperate yearning on the part of so many people to make contact with them; spiritualism became a fertile field. There was an enormous surge of interest and seances, mediums, spirit guides from the other side and ectoplasm, were the order of the day.

Doyle himself had a message from his wife's dead brother in 1916 and from then on he was a complete convert. He lectured on the subject, and even when 'frauds' were exposed he remarked, quite rightly, that this did not invalidate true mediums. But he went further and would not believe his good friend Houdini, a music hall magician, who maintained that he could, by trickery, duplicate the findings of any medium. Despite this, Doyle believed that Houdini had supernatural powers.

Returning from a spiritualist lecture-tour crusade of America in 1923, Doyle began work on his 'History of Spiritualism' that was published as two volumes in 1926. He had already opened a spiritualist bookshop 'The Psychic Bookshop, Library and Museum' in 1925, and in the same year he became President of the International Spiritualist Congress in Paris. He went on spiritualist lecture-tours of Africa and Scandinavia, but his strength was waning, and after resigning from the London Spiritualist Alliance and the Society for Psychic Research, he died, still surrounded by controversy, at his home, Windlesham, on 7th. July 1930.

But the spirit of his most famous creation lives on. Around the world there are hundreds, perhaps thousands, of Sherlock Holmes Societies.

REFERENCES AND FURTHER READING
'The True Conan Doyle'. Adrian Conan Doyle. John Murray, 1945.
'The Life of Sir Arthur Conan Doyle.' John. D. Carr. John Murray, 1949.
'Sir Arthur Conan Doyle, Centenary 1859-1959'. Editors Adrian Conan Doyle and P. Weil-Nordon. John Murray, 1959.
'Conan Doyle'. Ivor Brown. Hamish Hamilton, 1972.
'The Doyle Diary'. Michael Baker. Paddington Press, 1978.
'Arthur Conan Doyle'. Don Richard Cox. Frederick Ungar Publishing, 1985.
The 'Collected Sherlock Holmes'. Ed. Owen Dudley Edwards. Oxford University Press, 1993.

PLACES TO VISIT
Europe
Foundation Conan Doyle, Chateau de Lucens, 1522 Lucens, Switzerland, where there are memorabilia of Doyle and son. Reconstruction of working room and Sherlock Holmes.

JAMES. M. BARRIE (1860 - 1937)
Writer and Playwright

"M'Connachie is the name I give to the unruly half of myself - the writing half. My desire is to be the family solicitor"

Early days

Kirriemuir, where James Matthew Barrie was born on 9th. May 1860, the ninth child and third and youngest son of David Barrie, a handloom weaver, is a little town in Forfarshire, in the north-east of Scotland.

His mother, Margaret Ogilvie (she retained her maiden name, as was the custom in Scotland in those days), daughter of a stone-mason, was a strong-willed woman who focused much of her attention on one of her sons, David, tall, handsome athletic, who, she was sure, was destined to be a minister. But David was killed in a skating accident when barely 14, and his mother never fully recovered from the blow; her one consolation was that he remained eternally young. There are some who would say that David was later to be the inspiration for Peter Pan. Be that as it may, James tried unsuccessfully to fill David's place in his mother's affections; he loved her dearly.

There was quite a wide spread of age in the family and by the time that James was six, his eldest brother, Alexander, had graduated from Aberdeen University with first-class honours in Classics (Latin and Greek). After a spell teaching at Glasgow Academy, he took up a post as Inspector of Schools for Dumfries and District and he arranged for his young brother James, at the age of 13, to leave Forfar Academy and to move to Dumfries. Although he did not shine as a scholar at Dumfries Academy James read widely, developed his writing talents, immersed himself in his beloved cricket, and did enough to gain entrance to Edinburgh University.

Although James Barrie spent but a short part of his life in Kirriemuir he was later to rename it 'Thrums' and to set many of his stories there, based on tales told him by his mother.

Edinburgh

His university days were not happy ones; he was small (only 5ft), round-shouldered, pale, shy and diffident, with a round head that was too large for the rest of his body. He shrank from meeting girls; he admired them, but he was afraid of them. He had no such difficulties with children and he mixed freely with the young families of his associates. One of them, Margaret Henley, aged six, named him as "my Friendly' but as she could not pronounce 'F' properly it came out as 'Wendy'. Barrie used the name later in his most famous play.

His real love however was English Literature and after graduating M.A. in 1882, determined to be an author, he was offered the post of leader-writer on the 'Nottingham Journal', and for the next three years he was writing essays, under the pseudonym 'Hippomenes', on a whole range of subjects.

The Auld Lichts

But he was sending articles to London papers too and some set in Thrums, dealing with the activities of the 'Auld Lichts', an extreme Calvinist religious sect at the beginning of the 19th. century, caught the eye of Frederick Greenwood, a fellow Scot, and editor of 'St. James's Gazette'. Greenwood asked for more Auld Licht tales and Barrie supplied them, dealing in a humorous way with their general intolerance; their abhorrence of the harmonium and hymns; and their love of long services.

London and Literature

On the strength of the success of his articles, but against Greenwood's advice, Barrie gave up his job in Nottingham and set off to freelance in London in 1885, living in a little boarding house in Grenville St., Bloomsbury, where he stayed for four very productive years. He wrote, under the pseudonym 'Gavin Ogilvie', "When a Man's Single - a Tale of Literary Life", in serial form for the 'British Weekly' which was edited by another fellow-Scot and strong supporter, W. Robertson Nicoll. The articles were later to be published in book form, under his own name.

The Kailyard School

He put together as books, his 'Auld Licht Idylls' and 'A Window at Thrums'. He had 'The Little Minister' (which Robert Louis Stevenson described as the work of a genius), accepted for serial publication in 'Good Words' in the same year. These three books, with a chorus of praise from the public, put Barrie into the front rank as an author. His writings were full of fun and humour, though not always appreciated by the good folks of

Kirriemuir who felt that they were being lampooned by 'wee Jimmy Barrie'!

Marriage

Some of his early stage efforts were not particularly well-received and have disappeared without trace, although a minor success was 'Ibsen's Ghost' (a dialogue between Ibsen characters) and the star, Irene Vanbrugh, was again given the leading role in his second play 'Walker, London' in 1892. This play, dealing with an imposter posing as a man of substance, was an enormous success, running for over 500 performances. More importantly however, the second leading lady was a beautiful young actress, Mary Ansell, whom Barrie married (with the approval of his mother) at a private ceremony in Kirriemuir on 9th July 1894. The marriage was not a successful one. Barrie was temperamentally completely unsuited to marriage; it is doubtful if it was ever consummated, and Mary spent 10 unhappy years with him.

America

During a visit to the U.S.A. in 1896 to see the production of his very sentimental, and very successful, play 'The Professor's Love Story', Barrie, who was everwhere feted, carried with him a possible dramatization of 'The Little Minister'. He met the up-and-coming producer, Charles Frohman, who the following year produced it successfully in Washington. It also appeared at the Haymarket Theatre, London, where it ran for a year. The two productions yielded a fortune for Barrie.

The year 1902 was a memorable one, with two big stage successes. 'Quality Street', a sentimental comedy set in a small English town in Napoleonic times, which had been a big success in America, opened on 17th. September at the 'Vaudeville', and 'The Admirable Crichton' illustrating how roles can change with altered circumstances, followed six weeks later at the Duke of York's.

Kensington Gardens

Barrie and his wife had no children, but whereas Mary had to content herself with a large St. Bernard dog - Porthos - Barrie was consoling himself with other people's children, particularly a five-year old boy named George and his brother Peter. The Barries had moved into a flat at Adelphi Terrace, overlooking Kensington Gardens, and it was there that he met and took the two boys for walks every morning. Some have suspected that Barrie was a paedophile, but there is no evidence for that (though his attitude towards the boys was peculiar) and it seems more likely that he was a frustrated father. He was later to write of his relationship with George in 'The Little White Bird'.

The Boys

Barrie was completely infatuated with George and together with Peter and their three brothers, John, Michael and Nico, when they appeared, he enacted scenes in the Park with them, for a play that he had in mind. This eventually, after much secrecy, burst on an excited public in the Duke of York's Theatre as 'Peter Pan' on 27th. December 1904. It was produced by his old friend Charles Frohman and was an enormous success as the audience, transported back to their own childhood, gazed transfixed as boys and girls flew through the air. They cheered Peter and they hissed Captain Hook. Barrie forecast that the play would appear every Christmas for years and years. He was right in that and now there is even a musical version.

Barrie donated all royalties from future performances of the play to Great Ormond St Hospital for Sick Children.

The children, with the possible exception of John, were apparently very happy in Barrie's company. Their parents, especially their father, Arthur Llewelyn Davies, who even moved house to keep them away from Barrie, were a great deal less so at the usurping of their positions, although their mother, Sylvia, later changed her attitude, even to the extent of going on holiday with some of the boys together with Barrie and his wife. Indeed it became clear that Barrie was enamoured of Sylvia, much more so than he was of his poor wife, whom he divorced in 1909, after 10 years of marriage, on the discovery that she was having an affair with another man whom she then married.

When Arthur suffered a long fatal illness, Barrie was extraordinarily attentive to him, and on his death helped to look after the boys. When Sylvia suffered a similar fate Barrie was heartbroken and on her death adopted the five boys rearing them as his own, sending George, Peter, Michael and Nico to Eton and Cambridge, and writing long affectionate letters to them. John went to Osborne Naval College as a cadet. When the play 'Peter Pan' appeared it was clear that Barrie had based the Darling family on the Llewelyn Davies's. He has said: "I suppose that I always knew that I made Peter by rubbing the five of you violently together, as savages with two sticks produce a flame. I am sometimes asked who and what Peter is, but that is all he is, the spark I got from you". The truth is that he is more likely Barrie himself - the man who never grew up.

A Hero

Barrie was a very close friend and admirer of Captain Robert Falcon Scott and was indeed godfather to his son Peter who was named after his most famous stage character. In February 1913 news reached England that Scott and his companions had perished in the icy wastes of Antarctica, and a Mansion House Fund was set up to help their dependants. When it was not going well Barrie sent a letter to the 'Times' pointing out how proud the British people should be of these men. The Mansion House Fund then far exceeded its target.

A month later Scott's widow, Kathleen, passed to Barrie a letter addressed to him, one of the last that Scott had written. In it Scott indicated that death was very near and he asked him to help his widow and his son, continuing. "I never met a man in my life whom I admired and loved more than you". Barrie offered that help but Kathleen declined and carefully evaded it though still remaining a good friend.

Cruel Blows

Barrie suffered many cruel blows during his lifetime. In 1915, during the First World War, his dearly-loved George, aged 22, was killed in action. A few months later his very close friend and colleague, Charles Frohman, the American producer who had absolute faith in Barrie, was drowned when the 'Lusitania' was torpedoed by the Germans on 7th. May 1915. At the time he was travelling to London to try and help Barrie rescue a play which had flopped. His last words, according to one of the survivors, were Peter Pan's, "To die will be an awfully big adventure". On the death of George, Barrie lavished his love on Michael but he was drowned with a friend (in a possible suicide pact) in 1921, a month before his 21st. birthday

Honours

In his lifetime Barrie's worth was recognised. He received Honorary Degrees from St.Andrews University (1898), Edinburgh University (1908), Oxford University (1926), and Cambridge University (1930). He was elected (by the students) Lord Rector of St. Andrew's University (1909) and appointed Chancellor of Edinburgh University (1930). He was knighted (1913) and appointed to the Order of Merit (1922).

The Last Curtain

Towards the end of his life (1933) he took a holiday house near Kirriemuir where he was visited by a number of friends including the then

Prime Minister, Ramsay MacDonald. The Duke and Duchess of York, ere long to be King and Queen, came too on another occasion, with their children, Elizabeth and Margaret; the next day Barrie was invited to Margaret's 3rd birthday party at Glamis. The two hit it off immediately. "He is my greatest friend and I am his greatest friend" the little girl said. For his part Barrie allowed her to contribute two lines to his latest (and last) play ''The Boy David' and he drew up a contract that she would receive one penny royalties for each performance. To Barrie's disappointment the play was not a great success, but he was delighted and amused when he received a message in March 1937 from King George VI (as the Duke had become) reminding him of the contract and informing him that if he did not pay the debt then the King's solicitors would be in touch. Barrie, although gravely ill, gathered together a bag containing the correct number of pennies which he proposed to take to Buckingham Palace in person, but he was not fit enough to do so.

He died in London on 21st. June 1937, aged 72, and was buried in the family grave at Kirriemuir.

REFERENCES AND FURTHER READING

'J.M. Barrie and his Books'. J.A.Hammerton. Horace Marshall and Son, 1900.
'Barrie - The Story of a Genius'. J.A. Hammerton. Sampson Low, Marston and Co. 1929.
'J.M. Barrie'. F.J Harvey Darton. Nisbet and Co. (undated).
'The Barrie Inspiration'. Partick Chalmers. Peter Davies Ltd. 1938.
'Portrait of Barrie'. Cynthia Asquith. James Barrie, 1945.
'J.M. Barrie and the Lost Boys'. Andrew Birkin. Constable, 1979.

PLACES TO VISIT

Barrie's birthplace 9 Brechin Road, Kirriemuir, Angus. Now a museum with much memorabilia.

CHARLES RENNIE MACKINTOSH (1868 - 1928)

Architect

"My pride is in the architecture of our own country, just as much Scotch as we are ourselves" - Charles Rennie Mackintosh

William McIntosh was a Police Superintendent in Glasgow, when his son Charles, one of eleven children, was born on 7th June, 1868. He was rather a frail boy, with a club foot, and the family doctor prescribed plenty of open-air exercise. His father encouraged him in a study of nature and during his boyhood walks Charles, who was a good drawer, would sketch flowers, animals, birds - and buildings!

His surname went through a number of metamorphoses – he changed it to M'Intosh and then MackIntosh before finally settling on Mackintosh.

Art School

After studying at Allan Glen's, he was apprenticed at the age of 15 to John Hutchison, a local architect. Following the usual custom, Charles worked during the day and attended evening classes for ten years at the Glasgow School of Art. He won a range of prizes, including the Queen's Prize, and later the National Gold Medal and in 1891 was awarded a Scholarship tour of Italy, taking in London and Paris. He returned with his notebook full of sketches and drawings which he used as a basis for a number of lectures.

At the age of 24 he completed his time with Hutchison and joined the newly formed firm of architects, Honeyman and Keppie, still continuing with his classes at the Art School.

The Macdonald girls

In the practice there was another young man, Herbert MacNair, who also attended the Art school evening classes. He and Mackintosh became close friends and indeed they were destined to marry sisters, Margaret and Frances Macdonald who also attended the school. Both girls had outstanding ability with their designs of elongated human figures and stylised plants, portrayed in ghostly washes of watercolour, in textiles, in enamel, and in metal. The attenuated figures that they portrayed in ghostly colours led to the sisters being known as 'The Spook School'.

'Toshie', as he was known to his friends, "debonair, tall, dark, and good-looking like a Highlander, with a fine moustache — wearing a tweedy oatmeal-coloured coat with a deep green Liberty of London silk sloppy bow tie", was very attracted to the flamboyant red-haired Margaret. His friend 'Bertie' was equally attracted to Frances.

The Glasgow School of Art

When, in 1896, it was decided by the Governors, prodded by Fra Newbery, Headmaster, that the School of Art needed a new building, an open architectural competition was held. Mackintosh was one of the entrants and from the beginning there was no doubt as to where Newbery's preference lay. He wanted the design put forward by his former pupil, the 28-year-old Charles Rennie Mackintosh. After some persuasion the Governors of the College came round to his view, but they insisted that they wanted a 'plain building'. There was only £15,000 available for the constructing, equipping, and furnishing of the entire building. Well the Governors certainly got their plain building - at least externally. The back of the building, which overlooked one of Glasgow's main thoroughfares, Sauchiehall Street, was a sheer cement wall with incised, rather than projecting, windows. It aroused much comment, one being that "Mackintosh has shown his bare arse to the face of Glasgow". Some of the uninformed thought that it was a gaol; others that it was a workhouse for the poor. Some felt that he should be horsewhipped.

From the start it was obvious that £15,000 was hopelessly inadequate. Only the East wing could be completed in the first stage, and this was ceremoniously opened in December 1899. Mackintosh was not present, the work simply being ascribed to the firm, Honeyman and Keppie, of which he was but a junior member. The second (West) wing had to wait until more money was available and was not begun until 1907 being completed in 1909.

Perhaps the building was rather stark outside but the entrance, which gave the impression of a drawbridge, the arrow-slit windows, and the wrought iron work, combined to give a wonderful baronial effect. And inside there was an astonishing feast of riches and surprises. Among them - the Museum, top-lit by a glazed roof supported on four great timber trusses; the Board Room for the Governors with its tall bow windows and its great fireplace; the Library with its giant mobile of lights in the form of miniature skyscrapers; the Director's room with its deep-set bay window; the Living Animal Room in the basement, where the students sat on a raised platform to view the animals (horses, elephants, and camels) that were brought in from the nearby Hengler's circus. In due course Mackintosh, in his own distinctive style also designed the furniture, light-fittings, clocks, lamps, for the various rooms.

In the years to come The Glasgow School of Art was to be acclaimed as a masterpiece "one of the great buildings of the century" and people were to flock from all over the world to see it. Fra Newbury's faith was vindicated though neither he, nor Mackintosh, were to live long enough to see its full recognition.

The Glasgow style

Although there was a space of ten years beween the completion of the East and West blocks, Mackintosh was not idle in the intervening years. Indeed this was to be his most productive period.

Toshie and Margaret, Bertie and Frances worked their mysterious elongated designs in textiles, embroidery, glass, metal and ceramics, in what came to be known as 'The Glasgow Style'. These designs were not perhaps much appreciated in their day; they were to be later; there is scarcely a jeweller's shop in Glasgow that is not filled with replicas of 'The Glasgow Style'.

The Four, exhibited their work at the Arts and Crafts Exhibition in London in 1896. But alas for their hopes. Almost unanimously the critics turned on them and their work was given harsh, hostile reviews. All that is except one. Gleeson White, editor of the influential magazine 'The Studio' felt that he was witnessing the beginning of a new style in design, and even made the journey north to meet them. His magazine was widely read in Europe. The outcome was an invitation to exhibit in Vienna where progressive forces in architecture - the 'Secessionists' - were at work.

The Exhibition, held in 1900, was an enormous success, including sales and commissions for the Glasgow four; it is said that they were carried shoulder high through the streets of Vienna by adoring students. More exhibitions were to follow - Turin 1902, Moscow 1903, Dresden 1904, Berlin 1905, and again in Vienna in 1909. Charles and Margaret were making their mark on the European scene.

Kate Cranston

This remarkable lady, who gave Mackintosh a commission in the same year that he won the School of Art competition, was responsible for changing the social habits of the Glasgow citizenry by setting Glasgow on the road to becoming 'A Tokio for tea-rooms'. An ardent member of the Temperance Movement, Catherine (Kate) Cranston was appalled at the amount of drunkenness that she saw on the streets of Glasgow. She attributed much of it to the fact that the only 'refreshments' available in the City were beer and whisky; and the only real meeting place was the pub. Furthermore she noted that there were no places where women could meet in the afternoon or evening other than their homes. She determined to do something about both problems. And there was one answer - tea rooms.

She gave Mackintosh a major commission - a free hand in designing and fitting out her 'flagship' the 'Willow Tea Rooms' in Sauchiehall St. It was an interesting friendship - Mackintosh was certainly not a member of the Temperance Movement!

The Hill House

In 1902, Walter Blackie, the well-known publisher, who had been living at Dunblane, Stirlingshire, decided that he needed a home nearer to his Glasgow offices. He selected a site high up in Helensburgh, with wonderful views over the Firth of Clyde, and he asked Mackintosh to be his architect. Mackintosh accepted the commission, and after showing Blackie around some of the other work that he had done, he settled down to his task.

He was determined that this was to be a family home for living in, so first he visited the Blackies to ascertain and assess their needs. Blackie had enough confidence in Mackintosh to give him (within financial limits) more or less a free hand though he had his own views and the two had many discussions together. Mackintosh was delighted to find that they had much in common. Unlike many architects, who are more interested in the 'look' of a building than in its usefulness, he planned the inside of the house first, and then designed the exterior around it. Not surprisingly this exterior, of a light grey 'harle' (a layer of cement mixed with small pebbles) was plain and largely unornamented, though it had very attractive lines and characteristic latticed windows. Inside, the Hall led straight to the Library so that Blackie could interview business clients there without their penetrating into the family home. The large drawing room had pale panels with large pink rose motifs, there was a splendid decorated fireplace, a polished floor, specially designed furniture and lamps, and a wide square, recessed window extending across one wall. Margaret designed and embroidered the curtains. The Main Bedroom was white so that the dark, elongated- backed chairs stood out in splendid relief. There were of course many other rooms and many other features. Mr. Blackie was delighted with his new house.

Difficult Times

The McNairs left for Liverpool when Herbert was appointed instructor in the School of Architecture. Charles and Margaret moved around a few flats in Glasgow imposing their own particular pattern on each, but probably the greatest care and attention was devoted to 78 Southpark Avenue in the West End of Glasgow where Mackintosh and his wife lived from 1906 -1914.

In 1904 he had become a partner in in Honeyman, Keppie and Mackintosh, but by 1909 commissions were beginning to dry up. Drinking heavily, he became ill and was becoming more and more depressed. He was disillusioned and complained about the verbal attacks that were made on him, and at the lack of recognition of his work. Some of his friends from Vienna who had not seen him for some time noticed an enormous difference in him. He had lost his powers of concentration, and self-confidence. At the office, clients complained about his lack of attention. The firm was suffering too and profits were declining.

Farewell to Glasgow

In 1913 he resigned from his firm and by 1914, the year that the First World War broke out, he had had enough. The Mackintoshes left Glasgow never to return and settled for eight months in Walberswick, Suffolk near where the Newberys had a country cottage. Here Charles, looked after by his ever-loving Margaret, painted, in watercolours, the flowers of the countryside. The following year, much refreshed, he moved to Chelsea and resumed architectural practice. He did get a few minor commissions over the next few years but he was largely unknown in London.

They moved to Port Vendres in the south of France where they lived for four years and where Mackintosh produced some beautiful landscapes. Falling ill with cancer of the tongue he returned to London where he died, aged 60, in 1928. He was cremated at Golders Green cemetery, London in a quiet ceremony. The contents of his Chelsea studio, including 31 paintings and four chairs designed by him were valued at £88. Margaret died four years later in her Chelsea studio. They had no family.

There has been much discussion on the influence that Margaret had on

Mackintosh's work, some believing that it was detrimental, others that it was beneficial. One thing is certain - they were devoted to each other and things cannot have been easy for Margaret during his periods of depression and heavy drinking; but always he was her Toshie.

REFERENCES AND FURTHER READING

'Charles Rennie Mackintosh and the Modern Movement'. Thomas Howarth. Routledge and Kegan Paul, 1977.
'Charles Rennie Mackintosh, Architect and Artist'. Robert Macleod. Collins and Son, 1983.
'Charles Rennie Mackintosh' Jocelyn Grigg. Richard Drew Publishing, 1987.
'Remembering Charles Rennie Mackintosh' Alistair Moffat. Colin Baxter, 1989.
'Mackintosh's Masterwork : The Glasgow School of Art'. Ed. William Buchanan. Richard Drew Publishing, 1998.
'Glasgow Girls - Women in Art and Design'. Edited by Jude Burkhauser. Canongate Publishing Company, 1990.
'Charles Rennie Mackintosh' Anthony Jones. Studio Editions Ltd. 1990 (rep. 1994).
'Part Seen, Part Imagined - Meaning and Symbolism in the work of Charles Rennie Mackintosh and Margaret Macdonald'. Timothy Neat. Canongate Press, 1994.

PLACES TO VISIT

Glasgow School of Art. Mackintosh was the architect for this fine building. Inside there is a magnificent collection of Mackintosh furniture, paintings, and designs. (Guided tours only)

Mackintosh House, Hunterian Art Gallery, University of Glasgow. The house in 78 Southpark Avenue where Mackintosh and his wife lived from 1906 -1914 was demolished in 1963, but reconstructed, together with original fittings and furniture (designed by Mackintosh), in a new wing of the Hunterian Gallery.

The Hill House, Helensburgh (1903) Designed and furnished by Mackintosh for Walter Blackie (publisher). Now owned by National Trust for Scotland it contains all the original Mackintosh furniture.

Queens Cross Church, Garscube Road, Glasgow (1897) Since 1977 the headquarters of the Charles Rennie Mackintosh Society.

The Willow Tea Rooms, Sauchiehall St. Glasgow (1903) The only surviving member of Miss Cranston's tea rooms. Designed and furnished by Mackintosh it is now a jeweller's shop but the upper floor is a tea room with reproduction Mackintosh furniture.

Glasgow Art Gallery and Museum, Kelvingrove. Within it is the reconstructed Chinese Room (1911) from Miss Cranston's Ingram St. tea room.

Scotland St. School, Glasgow. A Mackintosh building (1904). Now a museum of Education.

Ruchill Church Hall, Glasgow A Mackintosh building (1898).

'The Art Lover's House'. Designed by Mackintosh in 1901. Built in Bellahouston Park Glasgow in 1988 - 95 due to the vision and determination of Graham Roxburgh.

Author and Statesman

"Don't let them stop you writing a book or two"
James Maxton M.P.

Background

Although John Buchan was born at Perth where his father was a minister of the Free Church of Scotland, his background on both his mother's and his father's side was the Border country. It was to this romantic part of Scotland, redolent of the Douglases, the reivers, and Walter Scott, that John and his brothers and sisters went during school holidays. In Peebles, their paternal grandfather, John Buchan, was lawyer, Town Clerk, magistrate, and manager of the Commercial Bank. Twelve miles away, up the river Tweed, at Broughton Green, their maternal grandfather, John Masterton, was a sheep-farmer. Small wonder that the children felt that they 'belonged' here. Every year they spent two months at the Masterton farm, roaming the glens and fishing the burns of the surrounding countryside.

Gorbals

After a twelve year period in Kirkcaldy, in 1888 Mr. Buchan moved to Glasgow to take over a church in the Gorbals. This was a district that had once housed the prosperous merchants, but which had deteriorated to slum conditions, housing only the very poor. It is interesting to note that the Buchans appreciated the pure air after the linoleum reek of Kirkcaldy! John attended the nearby Hutchesons' Grammar School which had a very high academic reputation and still has today.

Glasgow University

He won a bursary to attend Glasgow University and in October 1892, at the age of 17, he walked the four miles from the Gorbals to Gilmorehill to attend the classes that began at 8a.m. This was to be his morning walk for the next three years as he studied Latin, Greek, Mathematics, Logic, History, Moral Philosophy and Natural Philosophy, for the splendid

Scottish general Master of Arts degree. He came under the influence of Gilbert Murray, who had been appointed Professor of Greek at the age of 23, and Henry Jones of Moral Philosophy. He wrote for the University magazine and for other periodicals and magazines. The elegance of his writing- style was being noted and commented on. And he was reading voraciously.

Oxford University

In 1895, at the age of 19, he won a scholarship to Oxford and after a slow start, in which he thought that it compared very unfavourably with Glasgow both in the quality of its professors and in the attitude of its students, he began to enter into college life.

He was short of money which curtailed his social activities, but, determined not to be a burden on his father, he turned to journalism writing articles for the 'Glasgow Herald', 'The Academy', and 'Blackwoods'. His first novel 'Sir Quixote of the Moors' had been published just before he came to Oxford and a number of publishing companies were now angling for his second, 'John Burnet of Barns'. It came as a very pleasant surprise to him when Lane, the company who had published a series of his essays under the title 'Scholar-Gipsies', appointed him their literary adviser. This kept him busy for he had many manuscripts to read, but it eased the financial situation, enabling his social life to expand and he made many friends.

He made his mark in the University too. In his second year he was invited to write the history of his College, Brasenose; in his fourth and final year he was elected President of the Union and also gained his First in Greats, Classics plus Philosophy and Ancient History.

Buchan was disappointed, however, not to win a Fellowship of All Souls which was one of his listed aims. Instead, he moved to London, apprenticing himself to a solicitor, studying for the Bar, supporting himself financially by writing for the 'Spectator' and having stories serialized in other journals. But greater things lay ahead.

South Africa

In 1901 the Boer War was drawing to a close and Lord Milner, High Commissioner for South Africa, was in London on the look-out for young men who would help him in the re-organization of the Transvaal and the Orange Free State which were now British colonies. Buchan was offered and accepted a post, though only after persuading his mother that he would be safe and that he would return after two years.

The so-called 'concentration camps' where civilian Boers, mainly women whose husbands had gone off to war, were housed by the British Army under frightful conditions, became Buchan's responsibility. He was appalled at what he found there, with more than 118,000 whites and 43,000 coloured people huddled together under the most insanitary conditions. The water supply was contaminated and they were tormented by insects. Ravaged by measles, typhoid, whooping cough, scarlet fever, the children were dying like flies and the total death rate was a monstrous 344 per thousand. In all, 20,000 women and children died in the camps compared with the 3,700 Boers who died in battle. "The refugee camps have made my hair turn grey", wrote Buchan. Oxford 'Greats' had not prepared him for this and yet within a short period this young man had revolutionized the whole system and restored the camps to civilized living.

His next task was to re-settle the two colonies. Milner's aim was to improve the land by irrigation and modern farming methods and to introduce as many settlers as possible from Britain, Canada and Australia. With this in view Buchan bought up farms. The scheme was not as successful as Milner had hoped. In the end only 12,000 people 'settled'.

After two years, when his contract was completed, Buchan left South Africa with real regret. He loved the country and liked the Boers ('we were only just in the right') though they "lacked imagination"; also he admired Milner.

London and marriage

He returned to London with 'colonialism' in his blood, hoping to get a post as an under-secretary to Lord Cromer in Egypt, but this went to another. As well as continuing his legal work Buchan wrote for the 'Spectator', and he joined the publishing firm Nelson as 'literary adviser' with the pleasant task of supervising their new venture 'The Best Literature'.

He was now having a busy social life wining and dining with the powerful of the land and at one dinner-party he met his future wife. Susan Grosvenor was related to the Duke of Westminster and counted the Duke of Wellington among her ancestors. Buchan, given the the chance to join Nelson's as literary editor in London at £1500 a year, thereafter asked for Susan's hand in marriage. Susan's mother, who liked the young man, was delighted. Not so Mrs. Buchan - his prospective wife was English, out of his class, and couldn't even sew - and before being accepted Susan had to be 'given the once over' by Buchan's many relatives at Peebles. She survived this ordeal and the two were married by a fellow Scot, Cosmo Lang, later to be Archbishop of Canterbury, on 15th July 1907 in London. The Free Presbyterian Mrs Buchan glowered through the ceremony - Lang wore a scarlet cassock, and her own husband, in those non-ecumenical days, was not allowed to take part in the ceremony.

Now Buchan had time to indulge his literary tastes. Out of his African tour there emerged three books, the best known being 'Prester John', an adventure yarn for boys in which the action starts in Fife, moves to the Transvaal, and ends at Edinburgh University. He also attempted 'straight' history but his 'Marquis of Montrose', published in 1913, was ill-received by some critics.

There was also a busy social whirl and he and his wife were mixing with the most powerful in the land. They had many holidays abroad and in the Highlands of Scotland, but there was always time for holidays in Peebles and, when their children arrived in due course, they joined the happy band of relatives in the Borders too.

Allied to the loss of his father, his mother's depression, and his daughter's requiring a mastoid operation, a tremendous strain was put on Buchan's health. His stomach pains became increasingly worse. .

The Great War

The outbreak of war found Buchan abed with his now diagnosed duodenal ulcer 'playing up', but his time was not wasted. At a fairly early stage he began writing his 'History of the War', which was issued in February 1915 by Nelson the publishers in fortnightly parts. It eventually grew into a 24 volume work. He also completed a novel that he had begun some time before. This was the immensely successful 'The Thirty Nine Steps', a spy story set in the hills of Galloway, introducing the South African engineer Richard Hannay who was to re-appear in a number of future novels.

When Buchan had recovered his health sufficiently 'The Times' appointed him as their special correspondent and sent him off to the Western Front in 1915 where his realistic reports brought the war home to the civilians. He was in touch with the British High Command and the War Office recruited him as a lieutenant in the Intelligence Corps, appointing him to the staff of the Commander in Chief of the British Forces, General Haig, a fellow-Scot and friend of his South African days.

He came home in 1917 to have surgery for his ulcer, but ere long he was back in full harness, persuading Prime Minister Lloyd George to set up a

Ministry of Information with himself as executive head.

The war yielded a trilogy of adventure stories - 'The Thirty-Nine Steps' was followed by 'Greenmantle' in 1916 and 'Mr. Standfast' in 1918. There were poems too. In the conflict Buchan lost his young brother Alastair and many of his close friends, including Tommy Nelson. "There are far more dead than living now".

A Country Squire

In 1920 the Buchans moved out of London to Elsfield Manor, a country house near Oxford. He accepted the post of full-time Deputy Chairman of the Reuters news agency but this did not put a brake on his writing. He condensed his massive 'History of the Great War' into four volumes. Here in the peace and quiet of the English countryside he wrote 'Huntingtower' in which he introduced the Glaswegian middle-class Dickson McCunn and his allies the 'Gorbals Diehards' in their adventures. These Glesca keelies, based on the boys that Buchan had taught in his father's Sunday School, sang hymn tunes, but the words were altered:

"Class-conscious we are, and class-conscious wull be
Till our fit's on the neck o' the Boorjoyzee"

McCunn saw great promise in these boys who had never had a chance in life, and ended up adopting the lot of them. Buchan followed up with 'Castle Gay' in which one member of the 'Gorbals Diehards' was now a journalist and another an undergraduate at Cambridge.

Member of Parliament

Buchan was keen to become an M.P. and in 1927 came the ideal opportunity. The graduates of the four Scottish Universities had for long been allowed to elect three members to the House of Commons. Buchan was asked to allow his name to go forward as a candidate and in due course he was duly elected with a massive majority over his Labour opponent and he remained a Member until 1935. Although he made few speeches in the House, when he did do so, as in his speech against the reform of the House of Lords, and in his plea to allow the Church of England to manage its own affairs, he was impressive.

Taking note of the criticisms that had been made of his earlier version he revised 'Montrose' in 1928. This was to be the first of many great biographies - 'Sir Walter Scott'(1932): 'Julius Caesar' (1932): 'Oliver

Cromwell'(1934): and 'Augustus'(1937) - were others that he wrote in the following ten years.

Order of Merit and Lord High Commissioner

In 1932 Buchan was appointed to the Order of Merit. This was a signal distinction. The Order had been instituted by King Edward V11 in 1902. It is awarded by the Monarch to distinguished people in all fields of endeavour and there cannot be more than 24 members at any one time.

A further honour awaited him the following year when the Prime Minister, Ramsay Macdonald, appointed him Lord High Commissioner to the General Assembly of the Church of Scotland. The Assembly is a gathering of churchmen - ministers and lay - who meet for ten days in Edinburgh to discuss church matters. As Commissioner, Buchan was the King's representative, called 'Your Grace', lived in the Palace of Holyroodhouse with a military guard of honour, and was given a 21-gun salute from the guns of the castle. With his Church background, dressed in the uniform of a Deputy Lieutenant of Peebleshire and Oxfordshire, with his latent love of the gallant side of militarism, the pageantry, the pomp, the robes and uniforms, the ceremonial, the combination of religion and the sense of history, Buchan was in his element. He was given the keys of the city by the Lord Provost. He enjoyed every minute of it and his mother was proud of him too! At last her son was on the right path - if he could not be Moderator then Lord High Commissioner was the next best thing!

She, and many members of the family from Peebles and his mother-in-law from England, stayed at Holyrood. So successful was his tenure that he was appointed for a second term in 1934.

Governor General

But a greater honour was in store. In March 1935 he was summoned to the Palace and offered the Governor-Generalship of Canada. He had been the unanimous choice of both the outgoing and the incoming Prime Ministers of Canada, Bennet and Mackenzie King, though they both belonged to different political parties. When Buchan drew up the pros and cons, as he always did before coming to any decision, among the cons was that "I shall be a week further away from mother" and among the pros, "An immediate peerage might revive mother".

After discussions with the Prime Minister, Ramsay Macdonald, and with Stanley Baldwin, leader of the Conservative party, who both strongly urged him to go, he resigned from the Commons, accepted the post and took the title Lord Tweedsmuir of Elsford, the first a little village on the Tweed and the second his home in Oxfordshire. His mother wrote "I am sure that the King is fortunate to get you". Among the letters of congratulation was one from Clement Attlee, the leader of the Labour Party "you will leave a gap" and one from the red Clydesider Jimmy Maxton "don't let them stop you writing a book or two". He was given the Freedom of Edinburgh, and on 2nd November he and Lady Tweedsmuir disembarked at Quebec to take up residence at Rideau Hall, a few miles from Ottawa.

Buchan's Governorship was immensely successful. He travelled widely to north and east Ontario, eastern Quebec, through the prairies to the Rockies and British Columbia, and down the Mackenzie River to the Arctic. Everywhere he went Buchan established contact with the people.

The Tweedsmuirs entertained a string of visitors from Britain and the U.S.A. He realized how important it was to maintain good relationships with America, and Canada and Britain were delighted when the President, Franklin. D. Roosevelt, visited him in 1936.

A Royal visit to Canada took place in 1938 and although it was immensely successful, Tweedsmuir felt the strain of it all. In September of the following year he had the sad task, with three sons in uniform, of signing Canada's Declaration of War on Germany. Six months later he suffered a cerebral thrombosis and died a week later without re-gaining consciousness. He was brought home to Elsfield to be buried in the churchyard there.

REFERENCES AND FURTHER READING

'Memory Hold-the-Door' An autobiography by John Buchan.
'Unforgettable, Unforgotten' Anna Buchan (O. Douglas).
'John Buchan' by his Wife and Friends. Hodder and Stoughton, 1947.
'Mr. Buchan, writer' Arthur C. Turner. S.C.M. Press, 1949.
'John Buchan' Janet Adam Smith. Rupert Hart-Davis, 1965.
'The Interpreter's House - A Critical Assessment of John Buchan' David Daniell. Nelson, 1975.
'John Buchan and his World' Janet Adam Smith. Thames and Hudson, 1979.
'John Buchan - A Memoir' William Buchan. Buchan and Enright, 1982.

PLACES TO VISIT

John Buchan Centre Broughton Tweeddale.

ALEXANDER FLEMING (1881-1955)

Penicillin

The most important discovery of the 20th. century"
(Peter Medawar)

When Alexander Fleming was born in 1881, every wound was a potential amputation, every infection a potentially fatal septicaemia, every pneumonia a possible death knell. The 'septic wards' of our great hospitals had to be seen to be believed. They were crowded with patients for whom little or nothing could be done. Simpson had taken the terror out of operations. Lister and Macewan had ensured that, as far as possible, surgical wounds did not become infected, but neither could do much with an infection once it had gained a grip. The doctors were virtually powerless, and had no weapons in their bags.

By 1928, the year in which Fleming began investigating the properties of a mould, the picture had altered not one whit.

Less than 30 years later, by the time he died in 1955, medicine and surgery had been revolutionized. Operations were being performed that could not have been dreamed of before, the septic wards were no more, the bacterial diseases were all but conquered, the venereal diseases were in retreat, and a few jabs in the arm cured the most intractable septicaemia. And the change was brought about by that mould producing a yellow juice ... Fleming had discovered penicillin.

Early days in Ayrshire

Alexander (or Alec, as he was known to his family and friends) was born on 6th August 1881 at Lochfield Farm, Darvel, which stands on the borders of Ayrshire adjoining the neighbouring counties of Lanark and Renfrew. His father, Hugh Fleming, was a tenant farmer who leased his farm (a holding of about 800 acres on which he grew oats and root crops, and grazed his sheep and cattle) from the Earl of Loudon.

Alec grew up a sturdy boy who spent his spare time working on the farm or wandering the moors of Ayrshire, fishing for trout in the burns, chasing hares and rabbits in the glens. At the age of five he went to the little Loudon Moor School which was about a mile from Lochfield. He was very happy there. "That wee school up on the hill, that's where they really taught you something. There were 14 or 15 of us. The teachers that I remember best were Marion Stirling and Martha Aird, and they taught us to read, write, spell, and count".

He moved to the village school at Darvel when he was ten and he and brother John walked the eight-mile round trip every day. At the age of 12 he moved on to the Academy at Kilmarnock, sixteen miles away, which meant boarding-out, and going home only at week-ends.

London

A year and a half later, at the age of 14 he was on his way to London to join his brothers - Tom, who was a doctor (having graduated at Glasgow University), and John who was training to be an optician.

Alec attended the Polytechnic School in Regent Street, and then found a job as a clerk with the American Line Shipping Company where he was paid tuppence halfpenny an hour. When the Boer War broke out in 1900, he enlisted as a private in the London Scottish Territorial Regiment. He was not required for overseas service but joining the London Scottish was to have far-reaching consequences for Alec (and the world!).

A windfall and St. Mary's

When Alec was 20 his Uncle John, an old bachelor who farmed in Ayrshire, died, leaving his considerable fortune to his brothers and sisters and their decendants. Alec's share was an eighth part of an eighth part, but this still amounted to £250. His brother Tom persuaded him to use his legacy to study medicine. He took a few classes, sat the entrance examinations of the Senior College of Perceptors, and came out top of the United Kingdom candidates. With this certificate he had the pick of twelve medical schools, and chose St. Mary's "because I had once (when in the London Scottish) played water-polo against them".

It should be noted that he had not entered the University of London, for although the medical schools were part of the University and offered its MB ChB degree, they also retained the right to accept students, to study for a special diploma known as the 'Conjoint', which enabled the holders, who did not meet the university entry requirements, to become general practitioners. The 'Conjoint' is no longer available and it is a sobering thought that nowadays Alexander Fleming would not be accepted for the study of medicine.

He entered St. Mary's in October 1901 and while studying medicine he also studied for the entrance requirements of London University which he passed a year later. He transferred to the MB.ChB. degree and once on course he began winning all the distinctions and medals that were available. He had the rare ability to flip through text-books and memorize all the salient features at a glance. In 1906 on his 25th birthday Fleming gained his medical qualification, and a day later he joined Almoth Wright's Inoculation Department at St. Mary's.

Almoth Wright

Wright carried out experiments in the development of vaccines against typhoid fever, and he resigned his post when the War Office refused to make immunization compulsory in the Armed Forces. He was a man ahead of his time, and later the War Office saw the error of its ways, but Wright had moved on to St. Mary's. Here he reigned supreme for 45 years inspiring all who came into contact with him, quoting the Bible, Shakespeare, Milton, and Goethe, to anyone who would listen. He encouraged a flow of distinguished poets and writers to visit his laboratories to talk to his staff. One of them was Bernard Shaw and Wright became the model for the leading character in Shaw's play 'The Doctor's Dilemma'.

This was the atmosphere into which Fleming moved. Within two years he was awarded the Gold Medal in Medicine of the University of London. He also wrote a thesis on 'Acute Bacterial Infections' and this subject was to dominate his researches for the rest of his life.

War

On the outbreak of war with Germany in 1914, Almoth Wright was given the rank of Colonel and sent to France to establish a pathology laboratory, with Fleming, as a Captain. There Fleming's eyes were opened to the full horror of war wounds and it was brought home to him how pitifully inadequate were the medicines that they had to deal with infections.

Peace

In January 1919 he was demobilized and he joined his wife Sarah McElroy, a nurse whom he had married whilst on leave in 1915, at their home in Chelsea. Their son, Robert, was born in 1924.

Lyzozyme

Fleming returned to St. Mary's on demobilization and in 1921 was made Assistant Director of the Laboratories. It was around this time that he made one of his great discoveries. He added a little of his own nasal mucus to a dish on which he was growing bacteria, and some weeks later noted that where the mucus was, no bacteria grew. He concluded that there was some substance in the mucus that dissolved the bacteria. He named this substance 'lyzozyme' and found it not only in mucus but also in tears, nail-parings, skin, saliva, hairs, sperm, women's milk; in tulips, buttercups, nettles, and turnips; in white of egg and in eathworm slime. It was indeed universal in living things.

Papers that he published on the subject had a cool reception from fellow medicals. He was unable to purify lyzozyme; he did not have the chemical know-how, and he was unable to persuade others to undertake the work. But he always said "we shall hear more about lyzozyme one day". And he could well be right. In 1937 a Dr. Roberts and a Dr. Abraham, working for Professor Howard Florey (see below) succeeded in extracting pure lyzozyme, and Dr. Ernest Chain (see below) showed how it worked. It is still the subject of much interest.

Growing bacteria

Bacteriologists customarily grow bacteria in petri-dishes. These are circular, flat, glass containers about 4 inches in diameter and an inch deep. Each dish is overlaid with a fairly close-fitting glass lid. Within the dish is a sterile jelly-like material (agar) containing the sugars, proteins, and mineral salts, that the bacteria require for their growth. A little loopful of the pus from, say, a boil, is spread over the surface of the agar, and the plate is covered with its glass lid. In a few days time little 'colonies' of the bacteria, responsible for the boil, will appear on the agar. Some are then picked off, stained, and examined under the microscope for identification. More detailed identification can be obtained by putting others through certain biochemical tests. In order to pick off the colonies it is necessary to lift the lid of the petri-dish. This may inadvertently allow bacteria and moulds from the air, 'contaminants', to enter and grow there, although every possible care is taken to prevent this. The longer that the plates are kept, the more likely they are to become contaminated.

Fleming was not a 'tidy' worker. Whereas most bacteriologists dispose of their cultures of bacteria after they have examined them, Fleming was inclined to leave them lying about in his laboratory, sometimes for weeks. And it is fortunate for mankind that he did.

Penicillin

In the summer of 1928 Fleming was examining old plates on which were growing colonies of 'staphylococci' - the very virulent bacteria responsible for causing boils, abcesses, and some forms of blood-poisoning. He noticed that one of the plates had become contaminated with a greenish mould, and that where the mould was growing, and for some area around it, there were no staphylococci bacteria growing. The mould was later found to be 'Penicillium notatum' and the juice that it exuded and which prevented the growth of the staphylococci, Fleming named 'penicillin'. It was active against a whole range of pathogenic bacteria.

He grew the mould in various liquids and made many vain attempts to isolate the active ingredient. He was not a chemist and the expertise to do the work was not available in his laboratory. Nor did he get much encouragement from his chief, Almoth Wright, who was no believer in 'antiseptics'.

Fleming himself had great faith in penicillin and he published numerous scientific papers on the subject. But he could not stimulate the necessary chemical work. He found that after a day or two the liquid lost its potency and was completely inactive against bacteria.

And so for a number of years penicillin became little more than a laboratory curiosity.

Florey and Chain

In 1939 Howard Florey, an Australian Professor of Pathology at Oxford University, and Dr. Ernest Chain, a German Jew who had come to Britain to escape the Nazi terror, were experimenting with lyzozyme which, as we have noted earlier, was discovered by Fleming. They were looking up references to Fleming's work on this substance, when they came across his account of penicillin. Their interest was aroused and they, with the aid of a team of research workers, crystallized penicillin as a brown powder. Test cases were tried out on animals and humans and the results were astounding. Seemingly hopeless cases of septicaemia were completely cured a few days after being given penicillin.

These tests were carried out in 1940/41. Britain was at war with Germany and although the tremendous potential of the drug was realized, resources in Britain were fully stretched and unable to deal with it. Florey turned to the United States of America and the big chemical companies there combined to produce penicillin. A new word – 'antibiotic' (a substance produced by a micro-organism that is active against pathogenic microrganisms) – entered our everyday language.

One of the sad notes is that Britain had thereafter to pay royalties on the production and marketing of penicillin. Neither Fleming nor Florey had patented their discoveries.

A search was on to develop strains of Penicillium that would produce more penicillin. One of the most active was found growing on a rotten apple purchased in a market in Peoria, Illinois, by Mrs. Coghill, the wife of a researcher! Geneticists were hard at work too, subjecting the mould to X-rays so that it would produce mutants. All of this resulted in a stepping-up of penicillin production, so that today there is mould yielding 55 times more penicillin than Fleming's original strain. The chemical structure of penicillin has been determined and it is now possible to manufacture penicillins 'tailor-made' in the laboratory to deal with almost every disease-producing bacterium.

Honours

The prime workers in this story were awarded high honours. Fleming, Florey and Chain were knighted. All three were elected to Fellowship of the Royal Society, and they shared the Nobel Prize for Medicine in 1945. Their work, as well as saving millions of lives, gave tremendous impetus to the search for new antibiotics, leading to the discovery of streptomycin, aureomycin, and others.

All over the world Fleming was feted and given honorary degrees. He was elected Rector of Edinburgh University by the students. He was made a Freeman of his native Darvel. But the honour that he prized most was a letter from Durban, South Africa:

"Dear little Alex,
Please forgive me - but you were about 8 or 9 years of age at most when I knew you, a dear little boy with dreamy blue eyes —. This letter is just to congratulate my dear little friend of many moons ago and to tell him that I have been following his career and rejoicing in all his wonderful successes. I have just been reading the marvellous story of penicillin - and feel almost proprietor. By the way, your wonderful injections cured a very delicate little grand-niece of mine - by name Hazel Stirling.
Kindest regards to you and just go on as you are doing.
Marion Stirling."

Marion Stirling was one of his teachers from the little school on Loudon Moor.

Fleming's first wife died in 1949 leaving him 'broken' but in 1953 he married Dr. Amalia Voreka, a Greek lady who had been a research worker with him. They had but little time together. Fleming died of a coronary thrombosis on Friday 11th March 1955. He was buried in the crypt of St. Pauls, close to the tombs of Wellington and Nelson.

REFERENCES AND FURTHER READING

'Miracle Drug'. D. Masters. Eyre and Spottiswood, 1946.
'Fleming - Discoverer of Penicillin'. L.J. Ludovici. A. Dakers Ltd., 1952.
'The Life of Sir Alexander Fleming'. A. Maurois, Jonathan Cape, 1959.
'Alexander Fleming - Man and the Myth'. Gwyn Macfarlane. Chatto and Windus, 1984.

PLACES TO VISIT

Scotland
Darvel, Ayrshire. Lochfield Farm is still there where Fleming was born, and lived as a boy. It is privately owned and permission would be required before visiting it. So too is the building that was Loudon Moor School, which Fleming attended. In the village there is a small Memorial Garden with a bust of Fleming in it.

England
St. Mary's Hospital, London.

JOHN LOGIE BAIRD (1888 - 1946)

Television

"Well, sir, you will be pleased to hear that I have invented a means of seeing by wireless"

John's father was a graduate in Arts and Divinity of Glasgow University and had moved to Helensburgh, a little town on the Firth of Clyde, to become minister in a small parish church. It was in his church that he met and married Jessie Inglis, the daughter of a wealthy shipbuilder who took his family to Helensburgh each year for their summer holidays, and it was there that their son John was born.

As was not uncommon in Victorian times, the boy respected his father and adored his mother - "the only experience that I have had of pure unselfish devotion. Her whole life was taken up in looking after others, particularly after myself, with very little reward unless one can except the whole-hearted love of one small boy".

College Days

After schooling in Helensburgh he was accepted to study for an Associateship in Electrical Engineering at the Royal Technical College in Glasgow, from where he graduated in 1914.

With further six months study at Glasgow University John was awarded the degree of B.Sc. In the middle of his course, war was declared on Germany and he volunteered for the Army, but after a medical examination was declared unfit.

After graduation he got a job as Assistant Mains Engineer with the Clyde Valley Electrical Company. But his inventive spirit was beginning to blossom.

All his life Baird suffered from cold feet so it is perhaps not surprising that his thoughts turned to a way of alleviating this misery. From a wholesaler in Leicestershire he bought six dozen pairs of unbleached half-hose. He sprinkled them with borax and put each pair in a large envelope bearing the printed legend 'The Baird Undersock - medicated, soft, absorbent, worn under the ordinary sock, it keeps the feet warm in winter and cool in summer. Ninepence per pair, post free.' For good measure he also enclosed a number of carefully prepared 'home-made' testimonials. He advertised his socks in the 'Glasgow Herald', visited chemists and drapers, sold the first two dozen, and got orders for six dozen more. He employed 'travellers' to sell his socks throughout Scotland and England - the famous London store, 'Selfridges', bought six dozen - and for further advertising he sent squads of women round Glasgow streets with sandwich boards. Business was booming. "My whole stock was sold out at once and I booked further substantial orders," he wrote.

But ill-health robbed him of success; he fell ill and the one-man business foundered. Baird decided to go abroad where the climate might be kinder to his troubled chest.

Ventures in the West Indies

With the £1600 profit that he made from the undersocks, he sailed for Port of Spain.

Baird noticed that the island abounded with fresh fruits of all kinds - guavas, oranges, lemons, mangoes - and sugar-cane. Why not make jams, preserves, and chutney? Why not indeed! A quick visit to a scrap-merchant produced a large copper pan capable of holding one hundredweight of jam. A brick fireplace and chimney inside a hut was hurriedly put together and the cauldron, filled with sugar and oranges was soon boiling merrily. Great clouds of scented vapour rose in the air and dissipated into the surrounding jungle where they stimulated the antennae of the billions of insects abounding there, who homed in on this nectar. Soon the hut was thick with insects of all kinds; an entomological paradise - and Hell! They flew into the steam above the cauldron where they fell into the boiling jam. Baird, clad only in his trousers, fled the scene but his two assistants, Ram Roop, a Hindu youth, and Tony, a simple youth of mixed races, were made of sterner stuff and continued to stir the jam and pour it into pots.

Unfortunately the inhabitants of Port of Spain were no more interested in Baird's jam than they were in his cotton goods. He packed his preserves into crates and sailed for England, setting himself up in a small shop in Lupus St. in London. Perhaps not surprisingly, Londoners didn't take to his jams and chutneys so he gave up business and sold the lot to a sausage-maker for £15.

Soap

His entrepreneurial spirit was still alive, and he moved into soap. But it too came to an end when a lady washed her child's bottom with 'Baird's Speedy Cleaner' and angrily invited him to inspect the results. Baird was forced to admit that it looked like boiled lobster and in vain protested that his soap was for cleaning floors, not babies' bottoms.

Hastings

He was now near the end of his tether. Tired, worn, thin, and dispirited, with only £200 in his pocket, he retired to Hastings hoping that the climate would suit his health. It did more than that. This was to be the most exciting and productive period of his life; but it did not have an auspicious start. He invented a glass razor-blade with which he almost severed his jugular vein; he was equally unsuccessful with pneumatic-soled shoes which depended for their buoyancy on two balloons inside each. When he tried out the shoes, they almost catapulted him over the cliffs of Hastings.

Television

Then came his major breakthrough. Baird himself has said that while walking on the cliffs thoughts came back to him about the possibility of television. There is some circumstantial evidence that he was already tinkering and experimenting with T.V. while in Port of Spain. Although Baird was always more than willing to laugh at himself and to talk and write about his escapades, he was remarkably secretive when it came to his television work. And rightly so! Industrial espionage was just as rife then as it is now. There were many investigators in the field including August Karolus, in the Physical Institute, Leipzig; Denes von Mihaley in Budapest; Vladimir Zworykin, a Russian who had moved to the United States; C.F. Jenkins who had started his working life as a stenographer's clerk and had developed into one of America's most prolific inventors; Colonel Green (son of Hetty Green, financier) in his laboratories at Buzzard Bay, Massachusetts; and the remarkable Philo Farnsworth, a 17 year-old Mormon boy in Utah who was later to shake the major companies of the U.S.A. with his patents, and ally himself with Baird.

It does not really matter now where Baird developed his idea. The important thing is that he did so and was the first man in the world to produce working sets.

Soon he was translating his thoughts into action and his room at 8 Queens Arcade was overflowing with hat boxes, tea chests, darning needles, sealing wax, glue, batteries, valves and transformers. He transmitted a shadow of a cardboard box across the room. It was a simple beginning, but it was a beginning! He needed more apparatus and apparatus cost money - and he had little of that. £50 from a 'well-wisher' helped; so too did £200 (in return for a 1/3rd share in the invention) from a Mr. Day (a successful wireless and cinema proprietor).

London and success

Baird was elated and with his health much improved he left Hastings in 1925 to live in an attic in 23 Frith St. London. His methods improved to such an extent that he was able to put on a three-weeks demonstration in Harrod's stores. In return he got £60! He tried to involve the giant Marconi radio company in television but they weren't interested.

On 27th. January 1926 he demonstrated his invention before an audience of scientists at the Royal Institution in London. In the same year with the help of the B.B.C. he carried out transmissions from Frith St. to the B.B.C. studios and back again. In addition, using infra-red light, he was able to transmit pictures of people sitting in total darkness. He named it 'Noctavision'. He moved his experiments to more spacious rooms in Motograph House, near Leicester Square and with two friends he formed 'Television Ltd.' with a capital of £500.

In 1928, using a disc with three spirals of holes, each covered with a red, blue, or green, filter, he demonstrated colour television in Glasgow. He was also experimenting with, and demonstrating, stereoscopic television.

In the same year, using a short-wave transmitter, he sent a television picture to the U.S.A. and to a ship, the 'Berengaria' in mid-Atlantic. He launched 'Baird International Television' with a capital of £1 million to exploit television commercially. Baird himself got 400,000 one shilling shares and was made Managing Director. An important Company later offered him £125,000 for his shares and the post of Managing Director, with an annual salary of £10,000 in the new Company. He refused.

Following a number of 'secret' tests in 1928 the B.B.C. carried out its first experimental transmission in 1928. It was seen by about 30 people in the U.K. who had bought receivers from Baird International. At this time it was difficult to get vision and sound in phase, but this was achieved in 1930 when Gracie Fields, the film actress and singer, took part in the first synchronized transmission.

Meanwhile Baird had been experimenting with 'big screen' T.V. and the first show was put on in the London Coliseum picture house, using a screen some 5ft. by 2ft. made up of 2,100 ordinary filament electric bulbs, fronted by a sheet of ground glass. It was a great success. In 1932, Baird televised the Derby.

Feted in the U.S.A.

Baird was now at the height of his fame. He sailed aboard the 'Aquitania' for New York to launch his T.V. system, with additional plans for Canada and Mexico. Earlier, in Britain, he had met and fallen in love with a concert pianist, Margaret Albu, daughter of a Johannesburg diamond merchant. Now he sent a wire to her inviting her to come out to the U.S.A. and marry him. Margaret accepted. But his plan to set up his system in the U.S.A. came to nought. T.V had started there in 1928 but by 1933 it had closed down due to the limits of its range, and its consequent inability to attract enough advertising.

Life - and Death - with the B.B.C.

In Britain the B.B.C. had a monopoly on broadcasting and at its head was John Reith, Bairds' erstwhile fellow student at the Royal Technical College, Glasgow. Reith's great love was radio and he took a lot of persuading that television had a future. In addition, even if that hurdle were overcome, the danger signals were beginning to ring for Baird. Although in 1932 the Gaumont British Company with its vast resources acquired a controlling interest in Baird's company, there were competitors in the field, particularly Marconi-EMI. They had developed a 405 cathode ray scanning system that was said to be superior to Baird's 204 line mechanical scanning system.

In January 1934 the British Parliament set up a Television Committee to look into the various systems that were available. After long deliberation the committee, unable to decide, proposed that the Baird and Marconi systems should be tried by the BBC for two years, after which one should be adopted at the B.B.C.'s discretion. Over the period the two systems were transmitted in alternate weeks and the public received both systems on the same receivers. In 1937, the year in which Baird was awarded the Gold Medal of the International Faculty of Science, and was elected an Honorary Fellow of the Royal Society of Edinburgh, the B.B.C. opted for the Marconi system.

The end of a dream?

It was a bitter blow but Baird came bouncing back. He persuaded Isadore Ostrev who was head of British Gaumont Cinemas, to form a new company called 'Cinema Television' which would incorporate 'Baird Television'. Big screens were erected in several cinemas, and the company had a monopoly on colour television (very difficult to achieve with the Marconi system). Also, home receivers made by the Baird Company were selling well, and Baird was convinced that the Company was on its way to success. In February, 1938, he transmitted colour pictures from a small studio at Crystal Palace, London, to a large screen in the Dominion Theatre 8 miles away. The pictures were viewed by an audience of 3000 people.

Then, in September 1939, war was declared on Germany, and television in Britain, though interestingly enough not in Europe, was closed down for the duration. It could have been the end of Baird's dream.

The war years

There is a mystery about what Baird did during the war. According to his own account the British Government made no use of him and, despite tempting offers from the U.S.A., he continued his television researches in his little private laboratory at Sydenham, Kent.

Some maintain however that he was secretly involved in radar work for the Government and that is why he resisted the American offers. We shall never know for sure.

But one thing is certain. Baird decided to go it alone and by the end of 1940 he had designed a high definition colour television receiver that could project a picture on to a 2.5 ft. by 2.0 ft. screen and the following year he produced stereoscpic colour. There was one snag. His system of producing colour was by means of rotating colour filters. He was determined to achieve a fully electronic colour television receiver. And he did. Using a two colour (blue-green, orange red) cathode ray system he demonstrated, on 16th August 1944, the television picture of his favourite tailor's dummy, dressed in a pink jacket and blue trousers, to a group of journalists in his workshop near his home at Sydenham London.

Baird died in his sleep at Bexhill, Sussex, aged 58, on the 14th. June 1946, before he could complete his work. No place in Westminster Abbey for this genius, no lavish praise from the B.B.C., no honours from his country. John Logie Baird was buried in the little churchyard at Helensburgh, the place of his birth. He left behind his wife Margaret who now lives in Hamilton, Scotland, with their daughter Diana and her family; and a son, Malcolm, who is professor of chemical engineering at McMaster University, Canada.

REFERENCES AND FURTHER READING

'John Baird, the Romance and the Tragedy of the Pioneer of Television'. Sydney Moseley. Odhams, 1952.
'Baird of Television'.R.F.Tiltman. Seeley Service, 1933.
'Television Baird'. Margaret Baird. HAUM (Cape Town), 1973.
'The Secret Life of John Logie Baird'. Tom McArthur and Peter Waddell. Hutchison, 1986.
'Sermons, Soap, and Television' John Logie Baird. Royal Television Society, 1988.

PLACES TO VISIT

Scotland
Baird is buried in Helensburgh.
There is a very good collection of books etc. on Baird in Helensburgh Public Library.
There is a display of his television sets in the foyer of Baird Hall (A University of Strathclyde hall of residence), Sauchiehall St. Glasgow. Make enquiries before visiting.

England
There is a collection of Baird's apparatus in the Science Museum, South Kensington, London.